EMPLOYMENT AND WORK RELATIONS IN CONTEXT SERIES

Series Editors

Tony Elger and Peter Fairbrother

Centre for Comparative Labour Studies,

Department of Sociology,

University of Warwick

The aim of the Employment and Work Relations in Context series is to address questions relating to the evolving patterns of work, employment and industrial relations in specific workplaces, localities and regions. This focus arises primarily from a concern to trace out the ways in which wider policy making, especially by national governments and transnational corporations, impinges upon specific workplaces, labour markets and localities in distinctive ways. A particular feature of the series is the consideration of forms of worker and citizen organization and mobilization in these circumstances. Thus the studies will address major analytical and policy issues through case-study and comparative research.

GLOBALIZATION, SOCIAL MOVEMENTS AND THE NEW INTERNATIONALISMS

Peter Waterman

MANSELL

London and Washington

First published 1998 by
Mansell Publishing Limited, *A Cassell imprint*
Wellington House, 125 Strand, London WC2R 0BB, England
PO Box 605, Herndon, Virginia 20172–0605, USA

© Peter Waterman 1998

British Library Cataloguing in Publication Data
A catalogue record for this book is available from the British Library.
ISBN 0–7201–2351–8

Library of Congress Cataloging-in-Publication Data
Waterman, Peter.
    Globalization, social movements, and the new internationalisms /
Peter Waterman
        p.   cm. — (Employment and work relations in context)
    Includes bibliographical references and index.
    ISBN 0–7201–2351–8 (hardcover)
    1. International labor activities.   2. Internationalism.   3. Labor
movement.   4. Social movements.   I. Title.   II. Series.
HD6475.A1W38 1998
331.8—dc21
                                                                    97–40769
                                                                    CIP

Typeset by York House Typographic, London
Printed and bound in Great Britain by Biddles Ltd, Guildford and King's Lynn

CONTENTS

Figures and Tables

Figures

Tables

Acknowledgements

First, I would like to thank Robin Cohen, of Warwick University, a former teacher and old friend, who recommended this manuscript to Peter Fairbrother and Tony Elger, co-editors of this series. Second, my thanks to Peter Fairbrother in particular, since without his eagle eye and dogged persistence, this book would not only lack such consistency as it might have but would not even have been published. Further thanks go to tens of colleagues, friends, *companeros* and *companeras*, whose political activities, books, articles, information and ideas have been incorporated into this work. Their various contributions are often, but not always, mentioned in chapter endnotes. Amongst them are, in no particular order, the following: Joaquin Arriola (Spain and Central America), Marcel van der Linden (Netherlands), Nigel Haworth (UK and New Zealand), Denis Sulmont (France and Peru), Jeremy Brecher and Tim Costello (USA), Bill Ridgers (UK), Marieme Helie-Lucas (Algeria and France), Ken Post (UK and Netherlands), Denis MacShane (UK), Kirill Buketov (Russia), Juan Madrid, Carlos Garcia, Javier Lozano, Enrique Gonzalez Arana (Spain), Mike Carden (Liverpool, UK), Ib Lund (Arhus, Denmark), Kim Scipes (USA), Roger Southall (UK and South Africa), John Witeck (USA), Dave Spooner (UK), Rob Lambert (South Africa and Australia), Linda Yanz (Mexico and Canada), Ewa Charkiewicz (Poland and the Netherlands), Allen Hunter (USA). My thanks also go to a number of book editors and journals who or which provided space or feedback for papers that have fed into this book: Annabelle Sreberny-Mohammadi (UK), *Transnational Associations* (Brussels), *Nueva Sociedad* (Caracas), Immanuel Wallerstein and *Review* (New York); to some NGOs that provided support or encouragement along the way: Flora Tristan (Lima),

Agencia Latinoamericana de Informacion (Quito), Instituto Latino-americano de Servicios Legales Alternativas (Bogota); to the Institute of Social Studies (The Hague), for tolerating, for 25 years, someone who never believed in 'development' anyway; more specifically to John Steenwinkel, Head of the Computer Department, who spent hours finding or inventing solutions to my computerized database problems; and finally to Gina Vargas (Peru), who opened my eyes, mind and heart to many more things than feminist internationalism.

Much of the material in this book has previously appeared, in other form, elsewhere. Thanks are hereby expressed for permission to use this material in the following chapters: Chapters 1 and Postscript (*History Workshop*), Chapter 2 (*Alternatives*), Chapter 3 (*Review*), Chapter 6 (*Economic and Political Weekly*), Chapter 7 (Hampton Press, *Transnational Associations*). Most of the material in the book originally appeared in the *Working Paper* series of the Institute of Social Studies, a serious, useful, speedy and effective form of pre-publication, made widely available, on exchange or free, in the Third World and elsewhere, and for which I would like to express my particular appreciation.

ABBREVIATIONS

AATUF	All African Trade Union Federation
AFL–CIO	American Federation of Labor–Congress of Industrial Organizations
AMRC	Asia Monitor Resource Centre
ANC	African National Congress
APC	Association for Progressive Communication
ASM	alternative social movement
BBC	British Broadcasting Corporation
BUKO	Bundeskongress Entwicklungspolitischer Aktiongruppen
CCOO	Comisiones Obreras/Workers' Commissions
CCP	Chinese Communist Party
CEBEMO	Catholic Organization for Development Co-operation
CEEP	Coordinadora Estatal de los Estibadores Portuarios/State Co-ordination of Port Dockworkers
CGIL	Confederazione Generale Italiana del Lavoro/General Italian Confederation of Labour
CGT	Confederation Generale du Travail
CI	Consumers International
CIA	Central Intelligence Agency
CMC	computer-mediated communication
CNN	Cable News Network
CNT	Confederacion Nacional del Trabajo/National Labour Confederation
Comintern	Communist International
COSATU	Congress of South African Trade Unions
CPGB	Communist Party of Great Britain
CPP	Communist Party of the Philippines

CSCE	Conference on Security and Co-operation in Europe
CUT	Central Unica de Trabalhadores/United Workers' Centre
DFA	development funding agency
ECT	European Container Terminals
EEC	European Economic Community
END	European Nuclear Disarmament
FAC	Federacion Autonoma de Colectivos/Federation of Autonomous Collectives
FAO	Food and Agriculture Organization
FES	Friedrich Ebert Stiftung/Friedrich Ebert Foundation
FGN	Filipijnen Groep Nederland/Netherlands Philippines Group
FMC	Federacion de Mujeres Cubanas/Federation of Cuban Women
FNV	Federatie Nederlandse Vakbeweging/Netherlands Trade Union Confederation
ICATU	International Confederation of Arab Trade Unions
ICCO	Inter-Church Co-ordination Committee for Development Projects
ICFTU	International Confederation of Free Trade Unions
ILO	International Labour Organization
ILR	*International Labour Reports*
ILRIG	International Labour Research and Information Group
ILWU	International Longshoremen's and Warehousemen's Union
IMF	International Metalworkers' Federation
IMF	International Monetary Fund
IMO	International Mineworkers' Organization
INGO	international non-governmental organization
IOCU	International Organization of Consumer Unions
ITF	International Transportworkers' Federation
ITS	International Trade Secretariat
IUF	International Union of Food and Allied Workers' Associations
IWY	International Women's Year
JAW	Confederation of Japanese Autoworkers' Unions
JILAF	Japanese International Labour Federation
KMU	Kilusang Mayo Uno/May First Movement

KOR	Committee for Workers' Defence
LAC	Latin America and the Caribbean
LMLC	Lakas Manggagawa Labour Centre
MaM	Mujer a Mujer/Woman to Woman
MEMCH	Movimiento de Emancipacion de Mujeres Chilenas/ Movement for the Emancipation of Chilean Women
MIF	Mineworkers' International Federation
MRTA	Movimiento Revolucionario Tupac Amaru
NAFTA	North American Free Trade Agreement
NGO	non-governmental organization
NILS	*Newsletter of International Labour Studies*
NLI	new labour internationalism
NOVIB	Nederlandse Organisatie van Internationale Ontwikkelingssamenwerking/Netherlands Organization for International Development Co-operation
NPSSC	National Ports Shop Stewards' Committee
NSM	new social movement
OATUU	Organization of African Trade Union Unity
OEPB	Organizacion de Estibadores del Puerto de Barcelona/ Barcelona Port Dockworkers' Organization
PWSC	Philippine Workers' Support Committee
SACP	South African Communist Party
SACTU	South African Congress of Trade Unions
SALB	*South African Labour Bulletin*
SC	solidarity committee
SLMM	Sindicato Libre de Marineros Mercantiles/Free Union of Merchant Seamen
SVZ	Samenwerkende Vervoersen Zeehavenondernemingen/ Co-operating Transport and Seaport Companies
T&GWU	Transport and General Workers' Union
TEU	twenty-foot equivalent units
TIE	Transnationals' Information Exchange
TNC	transnational corporation
TUCP	Trade Union Congress of the Philippines
UGT	Union General de Trabajadores/General Workers' Union
UK	United Kingdom
UN	United Nations

UNCED	United Nations Conference on the Environment and Development
UNDP	United Nations Development Programme
UNICEF	United Nations Children's Fund
UNIFEM	United Nations Development Fund for Women
USA	United States of America
USSR	Union of Soviet Socialist Republics
VB	Vervoersbond/Transportworkers' Union
WCL	World Confederation of Labour
WFTU	World Federation of Trade Unions
4WCW	Fourth World Conference on Women

SERIALS
(NON-ACADEMIC)

Asia Labour Monitor (Hong Kong)
Asian Labour Update (Hong Kong)
Beehive (London, UK)
Correspondencia (Toronto, Canada)
Cotidiano Mujer (Montevideo, Uruguay)
Debate Feminista (Mexico City, Mexico)
Die Gleichheit (Equality, founded Stuttgart, 1892)
El Pais (Madrid, Spain)
Forum '95 (Beijing, China)
Free Labour World (Brussels, Belgium)
International Labour Reports (Manchester, UK)
International Trade Union Rights (London, UK)
ITF News (London, UK)
IZ Bulletin (Amsterdam, Netherlands)
La Correa Feminista (Mexico City, Mexico)
La Estiba (Barcelona, Spain)
Mujer/Fempress (Santiago, Chile)
Newsletter of International Labour Studies (The Hague, Netherlands)
Philippine Labor Alert (Honolulu, USA)
Socialist Affairs (London, UK)
South African Labour Bulletin (Johannesburg, South Africa)
Southern Echo (Southampton, UK)
The Other Side of Mexico (Mexico City, Mexico)
Transnationals Information Exchange Bulletin (Amsterdam,
   Netherlands)
Transnationals Information Exchange Reports (Amsterdam, Netherlands)
Workers' World (Cape Town, South Africa)
World Marxist Review (Prague, Czech Republic)

DEDICATION

To the memory of: Maria Elena Moyano (1961–92), feminist leader of
the Women's Federation and Deputy Mayor, Villa El Salvador, Lima,
Peru; Chico Mendes (1944–88), leader of labour and ecological movements, Amazonia, Brazil; Shankar Guha Niyogi (1943–91), leader of
Chhatisgarh Mineworkers Union, of the community and tribals, Dalli-
Rajhara, Madhya Pradesh, India (1943–91), Ken Saro-Wiwa (1941–95),
a community and even communalist leader in the oilfields of Southern
Nigeria, who became a spokesperson for ecological and ethnic minority
rights. All murdered. They died in the hiatus between the old internationalism and the new. This work is intended to help keep such local
heroines and heroes alive, so that more of us can hear of and learn from
them, and so that they can find their own ways of being in solidarity with
us.

1 INTRODUCTION: BEYOND LABOUR INTERNATIONALISM AND A SOCIALIST UTOPIA

General Argument

In the nineteenth century, Marxists presented labour and socialist internationalism *as* internationalism, or at least as the *primary* internationalism, with all others subordinate to it. Anti-capitalist internationalism was understood as the negation of nationalism (a concept, structure and practice on which it therefore was, and remains, dependent). The aim of such an internationalism was the creation of a world socialist community, understood as the desirable and necessary future society, one which would replace hostile relations between nation-states with peaceful co-operation. It was understood that there was one bearer of such internationalism, the industrial proletariat. This privileged internationalist and revolutionary subject would, however, first of all have to take power nationally. Labour and socialist internationalism – complex and contradictory as they might have been in practice – provided a new sense of community for workers without such and an inspiring utopia for marginalized and persecuted socialist activists and intellectuals.

In the twentieth century, strategies based on this understanding led to the creation of societies marked by an extreme statism in both national and international policy. This process occurred not only after both world wars, but also – in analogous manner – following the collapse of colonialism. The states coming out of these transformations, which were always supported by internationalist movements, in no way *surpassed* capitalism, nationally or internationally, but merely remained on its periphery, to eventually achieve full or partial reinstatement, or to have this thrust upon them.

For the twenty-first century, it seems to me, it is both possible and necessary to have an alternative concept, drawing on the nineteenth- and twentieth-century values of liberty, equality and solidarity, but

1   recognizing the increasing limits on the autonomy, authority and legitimacy of the state in the contemporary world;
2   relating to the transformation of global space rather than – or as well as – the national place;
3   allowing for a multiplicity of global contradictions, subjects and movements;
4   adding to the lay trinity the values of diversity, peace and ecological care; and
5   insisting on the interrelation of a) global utopias, in the sense of imaginable humane global communities, and b) the immediate necessity of civilizing a capitalist world order that threatens not so much that order itself as the existence of the human species.

Let us expand this argument a little.

Nineteenth- and Twentieth-Century Values

Liberty, equality and – as it was then called – fraternity were the lay trinity of the French Revolution. That they were or became figleaves for capitalist, industrialist, nationalist, imperial, eurocentric, racist, patri- archal, militarist and even consumerist projects and ideologies does not mean that they should be identified with or abandoned to such. Liberty, equality and solidarity had and have a popular and democratic reso- nance, and an emancipatory potential. They also have a worldwide appeal that socialism, for example, has lost. The trinity can and needs to be rearticulated for the conditions of an increasingly post-industrial or late capitalism.

Recognizing the Increasing Limits on the State

For one hundred years or more the state has been understood as almost synonymous with both 'society' and 'politics', in both academic and popular discourse. Today the nation-state, or state-nation, is being increasingly challenged not only from above and outside, by a dynamic, capital-driven, globalization, but also from 'below' from sub- or cross- national places (sub-national regions, cross-frontier ethnicities), and from or by spaces that are super-territorial (the International Court of Justice) or non-territorial (in the sense, for example, of a growing community of environmentalists, or women).

The Transformation of Global Space

Space has been previously understood largely in terms of territorial place, particularly in the development of the state-nation, of imperialism or 'spheres of influence', and for the operation of nationally based and nationally dependent capitalists. Place matters, but capitalism, in its electronic and computerized forms, increasingly operates in a *cyberspace* that crosses, surrounds and penetrates territorial places that are increasingly unable to defend themselves by Chinese or Berlin Walls, by bans and censorship, or by appeals to 'national sovereignty' (the last resort of authoritarians?). Progressive and humanistic forces and voices are increasingly recognizing that defence of national or ethnic variety, or of threatened places, requires activity in global spaces, including cyberspace.

Allowing for a Multiplicity of Contradictions, Subjects, Movements

In the nineteenth and twentieth centuries both liberalism and socialism have been simplifying, serializing and reductive, whether in terms of a standardized voting citizen or a class-conscious proletarian. Contemporary globalized capitalism is capable of simultaneous standardization (the 'world car') and of at least consumptive variation ('niche products', 'glocalization', local or ethnic advertising). Progressive forces are learning that it is variety and variation that provides for survival capacity in times of rapid and continuing global change, and that this kind of variety relates not to 'consumer choice' but to human and ecological creativity and adaptability. Freedom is increasingly being understood less as 'the recognition of necessity' than as the possibility of questioning, challenging and even changing 'necessity'.

Values of Diversity and Care

These follow from the above, with care suggesting responsibilities not only in the present but respect for the past and responsibility for the future.

3

The Interrelationship of Immediate Survival and Eventual Utopia

Strategies for immediate survival can no longer be successful if they ignore or threaten social or geographical others (increasingly informed of such threats or dangers by mainstream television or alternative email). Utopias can no longer represent 'the world turned upside down', since too many people have paid the price of such apocalyptical reversals, whether in Russia, Ghana or the squatter settlements of Lima. Increasingly needed are local/global survival strategies informed by utopian thinking, and utopian alternatives based on or informed by survival struggles.

The purpose of this book is to provide a general introduction to, and understanding of, the wave of international solidarity activity associated with the new alternative social movements (ASMs). This varied activity, which I initially characterize as 'the new internationalisms', has a growing political presence and impact as the twentieth century draws to a close, but has been subject to little strategic reflection and has as yet little or no theoretical status.

Attempts to understand the new activity in terms of 'socialist internationalism', or 'non-governmental international relations', are limited by their inability to recognize the autonomy and novelty of the phenomenon and the subsequent necessity for a new language. I attempt to offer such a language and therefore make it possible to talk about the new internationalisms in critical and even technical terms. In so far as it does this, the book is a policy-relevant one, with the policy relevance being for such movements themselves and for civil society more generally.

The work relates to studies of

1 international relations,
2 the alternative social movements,
3 the 'old' social movements of industrial capitalism (including trade unions, nationalist and socialist parties),
4 globalization and its implications for emancipation,
5 postmodern critique of Eurocentrism, utopianism, universalization and Enlightenment rationalism more generally.

It is, however, critical of many of these.

The discipline of *international relations*, for example, is state-fixated, and could better be called 'interstate relations'. The same is true for its radical or socialist variants. Although radical international relations specialists go beyond the state, they tend to be capital- or imperialism-fixated. There is a growing literature on 'alternative' international relations, or alternatives to international relations, which questions the orientation of that discipline to dominant power structures/processes, and which seeks out emancipatory forces internationally. But this literature tends to either celebrate or generalize about the new movements (as, for example, 'globalization from below'). In so far as it does either of these, it lacks critical force or political effectivity.

There is original literature on *new or alternative social movements*, generally sharing their emancipatory orientation. Most of this work assumes a local/national/regional framework, or deals with relations in comparative terms. This is true of the now-classical – but Eurocentric – work of Alberto Melucci (1989) as well as of the influential – and internationally oriented – essay of Andre Gunder Frank and Marta Fuentes (Frank and Fuentes, 1990). It is also true of more-recent literature on social movements in, for example, Latin America (Escobar and Alvarez, 1992), itself critical of such earlier writings. These literatures customarily fail to problematize the global and the range of relationships *between* the forces or movements internationally. Much of this literature, moreover, either ignores or writes off labour as an issue – and workers as a potentially progressive force – nationally or internationally. Things are changing (Waterman, 1996c). But it is still possible for a prominent international relations specialist of the socialist tradition to mention labour in such restricted terms that it can be covered in his index by *'international labour movement, decay of'* (Shaw, 1994: 181).

Such work as there is on *international labour* or *labour internationalism* has tended to be narrowly focused (particularly on union, or multinational-worker, internationalism), concerned with single issues or cases, and/or non-theoretical. It does not relate union internationalism to the traditional aim of the 'abolition of wage slavery', nor to contemporary emancipatory movements (Waterman, 1996b). Thus, in the spirit of Shaw, a work on globalization and Third World unionism notes the disappearance of the old kind of labour internationalism and offers, as 'silver lining', the following: 'the international labour movement may have to take on the heavy responsibility of co-designing new [Third World] strategies and even participating in their implementation' (Thomas, 1995: 237). From the context it is clear, however, that for 'international labour movement' we have to read 'state-dependent

Western union development projects', and for 'heavy responsibility', 'the white man's burden'. Even works sympathetic to labour internationalism and grassroots activism seem to have adapted themselves to 1990s 'realism'; so much so that a major work on the paternalistic (at best) international operations of the Japanese unions allows only 11 of its 300 or more pages to the, admittedly marginal, unions and labour support groups that suggest a way forward from national or international strategies self-subordinated to the logic of either national or international capital (Williamson, 1994).

There has recently been a dramatic growth in the critical or radical literature on *globalization*. Some of this specifically rejects the international-relations or political-economy perspectives, seeing globalization in much more general terms, and developing new theoretical perspectives or conceptual tools – which themselves have implications for the interpretation of society in general and for emancipatory movements in particular. Most of this literature again, however, gives limited attention to alternative international movements or strategies. One of the best and most thought-provoking is the work of Boaventura de Sousa Santos. He identifies himself quite clearly with what he calls the transnational non-governmental organizations (NGOs). He argues, with some qualification, that these represent the global alternative to what is being offered by transnational corporations (Sousa Santos, 1995: 268). Such recognition of international NGOs, in a major work of social theory, is welcome but it does not really tell us much about how such NGOs do and do not, can and cannot, relate to social movements.

Much 'postmodernist' writing (liberal-reformist as well as radical-democratic) is targeted precisely at the kind of Western or Eurocentric universalism to which socialist internationalism clearly belongs. It provides powerful tools for deconstructing traditional universalistic discourses, as well as for sensitizing us to the multiplicity and plasticity of, for example, worker identities. Postmodernists, however, would tend to be either suspicious of or hostile to any such attempt at rethinking internationalism as it is represented by this work. I see such literature as expressing, rather than comprehending, current experiences or feelings of fragmentation, insecure or multiple identity, suspicion of grand ideological discourses and apocalyptical strategies. Here I would go along with Fred Pfeil who, talking of international solidarity (in admittedly postmodernist style), none the less indicates a way out of its cul-de-sac:

there is surely something wrong with summarily dismissing the language and politics of rights, equality and collective solidarity with the poison-skull labels of Eurocentrism and masculinism and leaving it (and them) with that. For insofar as they are also, and, indeed, preeminently concepts formed out of the long experience of *capitalism* – or, if you will, industrial culture – itself, precisely as the always contested, uncertain terrain of countercultural resistance to the exploitation and degradation intrinsic to that culture's workings and effects, then regardless of its geographical point of origin or initial exclusions, some transliterated version of them [i.e. rights, equality, solidarity] will become necessary in any place or situation in which capitalism is found at its deterritorialising/reterritorialising work – which is to say, very nearly everywhere on the planet, and not least in Central America or . . . Nigeria. (Pfeil, 1994: 225)

The present book is meant to make good on some, if not all, of these literatures. Its general, introductory and innovatory nature has implications for the form. It represents a historical, theoretical, political and personal itinerary. The historical itinerary moves us from the old labour and socialist internationalism to the new multiclass and democratic movements for global solidarity. The theoretical itinerary is one that moves from the critique of 'labour and socialist internationalism', via 'the new labour internationalism' to the specification of 'global solidarity'. The political itinerary is represented by its explicit or implicit engagement with contemporary Marxist, Populist, Social Democratic or Developmentalist internationals or internationalisms. The personal itinerary is that of someone with a lifetime involvement in international solidarity activity, as will be suggested below.

In so far as the work moves beyond labour and socialist internationalism to a new global solidarity, the reader might question why I continue to bother with labour, and why feminist internationalism is the only new one to which I give detailed attention.

The answer to the first question is that I still believe wage labour central to a world I consider still to be capitalist, and that I therefore consider the limitations on labour internationalism a major challenge to the movement for global solidarity. Perhaps I should reformulate this slightly, to allow for the increase in non-wage forms of surplus-extraction, and for a broader understanding of human labour. Perhaps one should say that we need a *global social movement on labour issues*, with an understanding extended from traditional wage labour forms to the multiple forms recognized by Andre Gorz (1989). Gorz adds to the traditional wage labour form those of homeworking, working for one-self (primarily the additional task of women), and autonomous activity (artistic work, relational work, educational work, the work of mutual-aid, etc.). He argues for a social development from the first type to the third, and for the second form to be increasingly articulated with the third rather than subordinated to the first. The creation of *such* a labour movement would be a challenge not only to new social movements (that sometimes talk as if no one worked for a living any more), but also to unions that consider that work is only what is done for wages.

The answer to the second question is that whilst I could have contrasted labour with ecological or human rights internationalisms, these are 'issue' rather than 'subject' internationalisms, directed to 'life' rather than 'emancipation' issues. The women's movement is a subject internationalism and belongs to the tradition of emancipation internationalisms (such as those concerned with slavery, national independence and, of course, wage slavery). Feminism has shown itself particularly sensitive to the forms and relations of movements, both old and new. Moreover, the women's movement, its related ideologies and its internationalism go back at least as far as the labour movement. The similarities/differences between the labour and women's movements internationally make for intellectually suggestive and politically potent comparison.

Analytically (in Chapters 2, 4, 5 and 6), I consider historical and contemporary cases, the former from the nineteenth and early twentieth centuries, the latter from the late twentieth century. The historical study of classical labour and socialist internationalism was unavoidable. The late twentieth-century cases are chosen from many I have studied during the last ten to fifteen years, because of the new information they provide and because of the difficult questions they raise. It has been these case studies that have driven my research for more adequate and more general theory.

Theoretically, I attempt to synthesize elements from Marxist, 'alternative social movement' and 'critical globalization' theories. Such a selective and critical synthesis would seem relevant to a work that attempts to recognize the contribution to the new global solidarity of the traditional labour/socialist movements, the new ASMs, and of the politically or socially engaged intellectuals developing critical globalization theories. The theoretical development within the work takes place in two phases. In the first stage (particularly in Chapter 3) I theorize trade union and labour internationalism in the light of emancipatory elements within Marxism and ASM theory, developing the concept of 'the new labour internationalism'. Further case studies make necessary a more general theorization. This leads me to consider (particularly in Chapter 7) the possible meaning of 'globalization', of 'global solidarity' and 'global civil society'.

Readers, therefore, are being invited to accompany me in my own voyage of discovery, a voyage simultaneously professional, political and personal.

The Professional, the Political and the Personal

The first reason for talking of myself here is one of theoretical or methodological principle. It comes from feminism – as might already have been suggested by reference to the 'personal and political'. It is true that feminism got this notion from the Civil Rights movement in the USA, when Black militants insisted that it was necessary not only to 'talk the talk but also to walk the walk'. But it is the feminists who turned this potent political slogan into a matter of both theoretical and methodological principle. Feminist writing implicitly adds the professional to the personal and the political:

> The best ... analysis ... insists that the inquirer ... be placed in the same critical plane as the overt subject matter, thereby recovering the entire research process for scrutiny in the results of research. That is, the class, race, culture, and gender assumptions, beliefs, and behaviours of the researcher ... must be placed within the frame of the picture that ... she/he attempts to paint. This does not mean that the first half of a research report should engage in soul searching (though a little soul searching by researchers now and then can't be all bad!). Instead, as we will see, we are often explicitly told by the researcher what ... her/his gender, race, class, culture is, and sometimes how ... she/he suspects this has shaped the research project – though of course we are free to arrive at a contrary hypothesis about the influence of the researcher's presence on ... her/his analysis. Thus the researcher appears to us not as an invisible, anonymous voice of authority, but as a real, historical individual with concrete, specific desires and interests. (Harding, 1987: 9)

In the process of developing this work, I became increasingly conscious that what I was writing about was not just a theoretical or historical movement but also a personal one. I come from a Jewish Communist family, was involved even as a child in a cosmopolitan culture and solidarity activities, and joined the Young Communist League in London, in 1951, at the age of 15. I worked twice in Prague, in the mid-1950s and mid-1960s for international Communist organizations. After leaving the Communist movement, in the aftermath of the Soviet invasion of Czechoslovakia in 1968, I joined in the new wave of non-sectarian and democratic international solidarity activities. From the late 1970s till 1990 I edited the *Newsletter of International Labour Studies*, and was involved in various other international labour solidarity networks. Since 1984 I have turned increasing attention to the new internationalisms in communication terms, being here engaged in dialogue with 'alternative international communicators' from San Francisco to Hong Kong and Manchester to Moscow. I have thus traced part of the route from the old internationalism to the new in my political and professional life (Waterman, 1993a) and, as we will see, I have been politically involved in some of the processes I analyse.

A more direct stimulus to the production of this work has been the world transformation which began in 1989 and is still continuing as I write. This transformation is well captured in the title of a book by Alain Lipietz, *Berlin, Baghdad, Rio: The 21st Century Has Already Begun* (Lipietz, 1992). Berlin represents the end of the 'Second World', Baghdad and the Gulf War represents the end of the 'Third World' (at least as an emancipatory force or myth, or an explanatory concept), and the global environmental conference in Rio represents the dramatic announcement of a global society, global problems and the necessity for global solutions.

The events of 1989 meant the collapse of Communism. For twenty years I had waited and worked for this day. I noted wryly, of course, that as the walls came tumbling down, the trumpets were playing Beethoven's 'Ode to Joy' (anthem of the bourgeois-liberal European Community) rather than Potier's 'Internationale' (song of the revolutionary socialist proletariat). I could well understand that the patient, sophisticated and courageous East European dissidents were largely replaced by the sellers of second-hand Opels and third-hand Thatcherism. These things I had been prepared for since living in East Europe and breaking with Communism. But miners beating student demonstrators in Romania? A nineteenth-century inter-ethnic war with twentieth-century technology in Yugoslavia? East German Nazis?

The Gulf War in 1991 was something for which I had been in no way prepared, never reflected on nor, therefore, taken any action to prevent. I was unwilling to cast this obscene war in terms of any of the rent-a-slogan categories of right or left (World Civilization versus the Arab Hitler; Western imperialism versus Third World nationalism). I concluded (along with a movement at my institute) that it was a crisis of a whole world capitalist, statist, patriarchal and militarist civilization – the right's demonized Saddam Hussein sharing fundamental Western values with the left's demonized Bush.

The year 1992 saw the United Nations Conference on Ecology and Development (UNCED) in Rio. I had been involved in the setting up and development of the first ecology course at my institute. I followed the conference preparatory work of the NGOs. I saw the TV performance of the heads of states and United Nations (UN) representatives. This international event demonstrated to the world what I had long been feeling:

1 that the international statesmen of North and South stood up to their necks, in a swamp of their own waste, blaming each other for the stink;
2 that the moral (if not yet the political) high ground internationally was occupied by the new global solidarity movements and organizations; and
3 that these new movements were problematic and contradictory phenomena.

We have, since 1989, it seems to me, been in one of those periods in which the intellectual Horatio may learn that there are more things in heaven and earth than are dreamed of in his (or, as we will see, even her) philosophy. This has required me, as a would-be internationalist, to reflect on my own responsibility or non-responsibility for what has happened or was happening in the former Communist world and in the former Third World (now Second?). It is not a matter of wanting to have been some kind of internationalist Superman, nor to be in the future some kind of internationalist Superperson. It is simply a matter of wanting to be both responsible and effective in a new but so far undefined world order full of both dangers and opportunities.

Structure of the Work

Chapter 2 is actually theoretical as well as historical. It considers the political development and theory of labour and socialist internationalism, concentrating on Europe, the nineteenth century, and on Marx and Engels. Examination of the history of socialist and proletarian internationalism shows it to have been a more complex and varied phenomenon than socialist myth or contemporary analysis suggests. It also reveals that its decline was due not to prematurity, mistakes or betrayals, but to the nature of the working class and socialist doctrine themselves. There is, none the less, much to be learned from both the strengths and the shortcomings of traditional proletarian and socialist internationalism. Examination of the classical international theory, of Marx and Engels, reveals its part in the failure, saddling working classes of flesh and blood with a Promethean role in international emancipation. What they, however, described, predicted and implied about the overcoming of alienation on a world scale also speaks relevantly to both the old labour and socialist movement and the ASMs.

Chapter 3 represents my initial attempt to reconceptualize internationalism. It presents a set of concepts that would seem both necessary and adequate for understanding and advancing labour organization and protest activity in contemporary international space. It does this in both a general and a more technical manner. This first theoretical approximation requires:

1 defining such terms as internationalization, internationalism and solidarity;
2 identifying the mass subjects and political purposes of internationalism;
3 specifying the space or field occupied, the strategy, geographical direction and scope;
4 considering forms of organization and communication, the role of organizers and intellectuals.

The potential value of the 'new internationalisms' concept for the understanding of labour is suggested in a brief case study. The meaning of a 'new labour internationalism' is defined and the possible meaning of a contemporary socialist internationalism is considered.

Chapter 4 represents a narrow, in-depth, case study. It considers the Spain-based European dockers' network of the 1980s, showing both the possibilities and difficulties of creating a new kind of labour internationalism within the old labour tradition alone. The case reveals the history of traditional dockworker internationalism, from the 1890s to the present day. It considers the attempt to create a non-bureaucratic and non-ideological 'waterfront' network in the 1970s and 1980s. It also examines the particular role of the Coordinadora of Spanish dockers which was the linchpin of the project. It evaluates, finally, the internationalism of the Coordinadora in the light of the earlier conceptualization.

Chapter 5 is another case study, but one which takes a much broader view. It also represents an explicit intervention into a labour movement debate about the then new Third World labour internationalisms – just as the Third World was disappearing. This chapter also makes it possible to look at the complex relationship between such new Southern/Eastern labour internationalisms, and the multiple social subjects, organizations and orientations they have to relate to in the North/West.

Chapter 6 is the only one on a 'non-labour', or 'new alternative social movement', internationalism. It is a study of the international solidarity thought and activity of what is often considered to be the exemplary alternative international social movement. This overview not only brings the earlier developed understanding to bear on the women's movement. It also enables us to garner relevant theoretical, methodological and strategic insights. Paradoxically, it is the focus of this theoretically underdeveloped internationalism on 'global' rather than 'international' issues that suggests the necessity for moving our theoretical focus from the latter to the former.

Chapter 7 makes use of the new wave of critical and radical writings on globalization to develop the concepts of 'globalization', 'global civil society' and 'global solidarity'. The new problematic, it is argued, is not primarily that of relations between nations or states, but of global processes and structures that reduce the centrality these have previously been accorded in emancipatory thought and action. The women's, ecological and other new social movements have made us aware of the 'global interdependency' of both reform and emancipatory struggles (as well as helping overcome the binary opposition customarily posed between them). The new wave of radical-democratic movements and thinking raises the question of the implications of globalization for democracy and for democratic control over global processes. The alternative global order, or process, is conceived of in terms of 'global civil society'; the new movement and ethic in terms of 'global solidarity'.

The Postscript allows for a final personal reflection, or reflection on the personal, in trying to develop this new kind of internationalism.

Before proceeding, it is necessary to specify on some recurring terms. These are not the focus of the study and are therefore not theorized, but they can raise questions in readers' minds. The first might be why I talk of 'alternative' rather than 'new' social movements. There are two problems with 'new': it sets up a binary opposition with 'old' when I wish to suggest both difference and continuity; and there are other new international social movements than those I am concerned with and that have pro-capitalist, statist, authoritarian or fundamentalist characteristics. 'Alternative' would seem to be empty of content or value. But ever since Rudolf Bahro's *The Alternative in Eastern Europe* (1978), it has come to mean a rejection of both capitalism and statism, and a new democratic and emancipatory project. It will, hopefully, be given more specific meaning during the course of this work. The second set of problematic terms are socio-geographic ones such as Third World, South, and their related others. These are here used as familiar shorthand descriptors. In so far as globalization undermines such reality as these have captured, and as a critical and committed globalization theory provides a more empowering model, these terms have for me no theoretical weight. With these preliminaries disposed of, our journey may commence.

2

HISTORY: WHATEVER HAPPENED TO SOCIALIST AND PROLETARIAN INTERNATIONALISM?

Introduction: A Complex, Ambiguous and Contested Tradition

It is not my task here to either praise or bury the nineteenth-century tradition of proletarian and socialist internationalism: it is to reconsider it in the light of contemporary social developments, social movements, and of thinking related to these. The general purpose of the chapter is to reveal the complexity and ambiguity of the nineteenth-century tradition. This has been overlaid by decades of simplification, mythologizing and tendentious analysis. Worst of all, it has been forgotten. Yet, as I hope to show, it has much to teach us in our present predicament. My strategy here will be to consider nineteenth-century internationalism first as political activity and then as social theory or ideology.

In the first part I will try to show how quite particular social conditions gave rise to labour internationalism, and that these conditions gave rise to quite particular forms of labour internationalism. I will try to show how change in each of these social conditions later undermined this. We will see that it was, above all, the parallel growth of the nation-state along with the working class, of nationalism along with socialism, that confounded the internationalist hopes of the early socialists.

In the second part of the chapter I will consider the theory or ideology of such early socialists. Here I will critique just two texts of Marx and Engels. I will deal with these because of the influence of one of them, the *Communist Manifesto* of 1848, and the pertinence of the other, taken from the *German Ideology* of 1845–6. I will limit myself to these two because, if the internationalist theory of Marx and Engels was

– as we will see – limited, later internationalist theory was poverty stricken. The argument will conclude on the necessity of liberating internationalist theory and politics from the parameters of an early, industrial, state-nationalist and imperial capitalism.

The fact that the history of classical labour internationalism has been either forgotten or overlaid by myth requires that I provide at least a thumbnail sketch of its first 100–200 years. Since this will inevitably simplify and distort, it can be well expressed in terms of one of the ideological discourses current 50 years ago. Like other such discourses of internationalism, and much historical myth-making about the recent and recorded past, this discourse reveals as much as it conceals, conceals as much as it reveals. It runs as follows.

The widening and deepening of capitalist industrialization in the nineteenth century led to successive waves of labour protest, union and party organization and of internationalism. They were marked by the creation of the First International (1864–72/6), the Second International (1889) and the Third International (1919). Each of these waves expressed a closer approximation to the international theory and internationalist strategy expressed with such prescience by Marx and Engels in 1848. The development of monopoly capitalism and imperialism at the end of the nineteenth century, however, allowed for the development of a labour aristocracy (of certain national working classes; within each national working class; amongst union and party officers), subordinated to national or imperial capital and to chauvinistic, militaristic and imperialist states. It was their betrayal of the working-class interest and of internationalist principles at the beginning of World War I that required the creation of the Third International in its aftermath. The tradition of the increasingly reformist and nationalist Second International was continued by Labour or Social-Democratic parties, unions and ineffective 'letter-box' internationals. It was the Communist International, based on the increasing number of socialist states, that continued the Marxist tradition, demonstrating this in its consistent support to working-class protest and organization worldwide, to the Republic during the Spanish Civil War, to the Resistance in World War II, and to national-liberation struggles in the following period. Despite Communist efforts and compromises, at the end of World War II, to create all-embracing internationals for workers, peace-lovers, women and other democratic forces, the labour aristocracies in the West were again largely subordinated to the national and international strategies of the imperialist West, particularly in its wars – cold or hot – against the socialist and (post-)colonial world. Despite divisions and contradictions, the worldwide size, spread and density of the working class, its movements and organizations, continues and, despite setbacks, the internationalist tradition of Marxism will inevitably win, given that it expresses the long-term and general interest of the international working class and, consequently, of all democratic and peace-loving forces worldwide.[1] Against this brightly coloured backcloth, let us reconsider the history and theory of labour and socialist internationalism.

Action: The Dramatic Rise and Strange Decline of Proletarian Internationalism[2]

From Proletariat to Internationalism
There was in the industrializing world of the nineteenth and early twentieth centuries an intimate relationship between, on the one hand, proletarian status, working-class struggle, the labour movement and socialist ideology and, on the other, internationalist identity, organization and action. This intimate relationship lay, however, in a unique combination of circumstances. The first was the creation of national and international labour markets, with truly massive national and international labour migrations, the labourers experiencing capital as disruptive, destructive and foreign – if not specifically international. The second was that the formation of working-class communities often preceded the consolidation or enforcement of national languages or cultures, with workers thus commonly unidentified with the state of their rulers. The third was the denial to workers of citizen rights, thus excluding them from the polity. A fourth was the non- or anti-communalism essential for labour if, in the absence of state regulation, workers were to establish any defence against labour-market competition. A fifth was the existence of a stratum of largely self-educated and skilled artisans, with their own culture and intellectuals, open to democratic and socialist ideas of local or foreign origin. Two final points. Unlike the typical political organizations and aims of the industrial or petty-bourgeoisie, the labour movement was *originally conceived of* as international in structure and internationalist in aim. And whilst the industrial and petty-bourgeoisie was primarily occupied with nation- or

state-building, the labour movement was more concerned with social transformation (Billington, 1980; Guerena, 1988; Hobsbawm, 1988; Johnson, 1979; Logue, 1980).

A notable expression of this artisan experience, situation and consciousness can be found in an 1863 letter by a group of British trade unionists to their French opposite numbers in the labour paper, *Beehive*, of 5 December 1863.[3] This document is all the more significant for having been produced by a group of *non-socialist* and *non-industrial* worker unionists, including a painter, joiner, bookbinder, carpenter and shoemaker, and for *preceding* the creation of the International Working Men's Association, later known as the First International. The letter followed an international conference which had supported the Polish uprising against Russian rule and was itself followed by a massive worker turnout when the Red Republican Italian, Garibaldi, visited London (Collins and Abramsky, 1965: chs 2–3).

The force for such internationalism represented a quite specific combination. First we should mention the skilled urban artisans who had behind them a tradition of *compagnonage* – this including the practice of foreign travel and work – as part of craft apprenticeship. Whilst the British artisans, such as those responsible for the letter above, may not have had this experience, they may have been more acutely conscious than their continental brethren (sisters were disregarded) of the onslaught of industrial capital and the internationalization of the labour market. It was this stratum of the working class that provided the base for local, national and international labour organizations. Second, we must mention the labour organizers, many of whom were involved in continental migration or re-migration. Consider two leaders of the late nineteenth-century New Unionism of unskilled and semi-skilled labour in Britain, Tom Mann and Ben Tillet. The first migrated temporarily to the United States, South Africa and Australia. The second seems to have considered the organization of transport workers in Antwerp or Rotterdam a simple extension of his work in London. As for the socialist politicians/theoreticians, it is possible to identify both those like Rosa Luxemburg, simultaneously or consecutively involved in the Polish, Russian and German movements, and those who became leaders of a foreign movement, like Anna Kuliscioff in Italy (Hobsbawm, 1988: 12). The most famous cases are, of course, Marx and Engels, *the* theorists of socialist internationalism. It seems possible that it was their shared experience of international capitalism and state repression that enabled people with such different backgrounds or places within the labour and socialist movement to produce together classical labour internationalism. If we consider the itinerary of the anarchist Emma Goldman, we will see not only her successive exiles or migrations but her combined or successive movement roles as worker, organizer, political strategist and literary figure. This combination, in one person or one lifetime, of geographical mobility and multiple social roles was not unique in the nineteenth-century socialist movement and facilitated the articulation of proletarian and socialist internationalism (Billington, 1980: ch. 17; Colas, 1994; Golding, 1964; Goldman, 1977; Hobsbawm, 1988; Linden, 1988a, b, c; Logue, 1980; Torr, 1956).

Types of Labour and Socialist Internationalism

Even if we can for some purposes assume that labour internationalism involves one actor with one purpose, a closer examination identifies the variety of both. The multiple aspects of labour existence, its multiple needs and aspirations under the above mentioned conditions, were increasingly given institutional form at international as well as local or national level. The First International (1864–72/6) was an all-purpose organization of varied membership. It dealt with both industrial and political issues. It played an important role in the strike wave of that period – possibly at the cost of its other activities and aspirations.

Later, the working class *as wage labour* was separately organized internationally, with separate trades or industries being separately institutionalized internationally. In the decades following 1890 there was an astounding growth of international *trade union* organizations and activities.[4] The campaign for the eight-hour day was launched by the first conference of what is now called the Second International. The first May Days were truly mass international and internationalist events. The period saw widespread victories in the struggle for limitations in working hours, the right to organize and to strike, and these victories went way beyond the industrialized capitalist countries (Dutt, 1964; Foner, 1986; Knudsen, 1988; Sulmont, 1988a).

Labour as a *political* force was increasingly organized by internationally inspired or co-ordinated parties (Claudin, 1970; Devreese, 1988; Dutt, 1964; Frank, 1979a, b). Workers as *consumers*, and sometimes as producers, were independently organized in the International

Co-operative Alliance. Co-operative internationalism was in the late nineteenth century more highly and intensively developed than that of the unions, and it involved working-class women and children as well as men. It not only attempted to set up international co-operative trading institutions but was prepared to discuss questions of peace and war and to support the Russian Revolution (Gurney, 1988).

Socialist *women* were brought together in international conferences initiated by Clara Zetkin. Her paper, *Die Gleichheit* (Equality), was its organ. That such activities had their own independent base and autonomy is suggested by the efforts of the German Social-Democratic Party to abolish them (Mies, 1983: 144). In a commentary on the role of women revolutionaries in the nineteenth century it has, indeed, been argued that '[r]evolutionary movements tended to become more internationalist and visionary whenever women played a leading role; more parochial and pragmatic whenever workers were in command' (Billington, 1980: 5).

We can even see the creation of a specific international working-class *culture*, beginning with songs and the celebration of May Day and reaching its most structured forms within the Socialist and Communist Internationals of the inter-war period. There were international worker organizations for sport, theatre, youth, students, film, photography, nature-lovers, tourism and even Esperanto (Bouvier, 1988; Guercna, 1988; Jones, 1988; Kramer, 1988; Mattelart and Siegelaub, 1983: 153–64, 176–82; Samuel, MacColl and Cosgrove, 1985; Steinberg, 1988).

Finally, there were the international links of the *thinkers, journalists and theoreticians*. As Billington (1980: ch. 11) vividly demonstrates, newspapers and journals were the 'magic medium' of nineteenth- and early twentieth-century revolutionaries. They represented not simply an instrument for political ends (creating 'party spirit' and thus prefiguring the party). Printing shops also represented a microcosm of the future society, with artisans and intellectuals (or artisan intellectuals) using modern machinery, and combining hand and brain in the production of information and ideas that would liberate the minds and organize the bodies of the previously ignorant and powerless masses (see also Waterman, 1992a). But, as Billington also reveals, these publications often travelled, they were often produced in exile, or were produced for exiles – who were themselves often key forces in the introduction of internationalist ideas. A new and more sophisticated publication, the international theoretical journal, was represented in the late nineteenth century by the German Marxist journal *Die Neue Zeit* (New Times). Despite its limitation to the German language, this was intended to be an international Marxist journal and it attracted contributions from leading Marxists in France, Britain and elsewhere (Haupt, 1986; Institut fur Marxismus-Leninismus, 1986: 86).

The Different Levels of Internationalist Activity

In understanding classical internationalism it is necessary to distinguish at least between the internationalism of the class, the national organizers and the theorists. Some idea of the range of attitudes between levels within the labour movement can be gained from consideration of European mineworkers. It is a far from 'senseless question' (Hobsbawm, 1988: 13) to inquire into the internationalism of, for example, the Welsh miners 'who both followed revolutionary syndicalist leaders and also poured into the army as volunteers in 1914 [and then] brought their coalfield out in a solid strike in 1915, deaf to the accusation that they were being unpatriotic in doing so' (ibid., 11). In the first place, it might have been *different* miners who did these things. But even if we assume it was not, it is important to understand the social base on which there arose mineworker union internationalism and the socialist internationalism of the ex-miner Member of Parliament, Kier Hardie. Workers in an industry early involved in the international commodity and labour markets, miners were also commonly isolated in communities which kept them not only from the factory working class and urban centres of national and international politics, but even from each other. If not a 'corporatist internationalism' (Michel, 1988), theirs was certainly a sectional one, that combined a comparatively high level of international organization and action with low levels of integration into national miners' and general labour movements. The British socialist leader Keir Hardie was nearly lynched in his Welsh mining constituency for his opposition to World War I. This can be better understood if we note 1) the hostility of Lanarkshire miners to Irish and Polish labourers, and 2) Hardie's own characterization of immigrant Polish miners in Scotland as 'beastly, filthy foreigners' (Michel, 1988: 444, fn 13), than if we note the peaceful absorption of English-speakers into Welsh pits (Hobsbawm, 1988: 9). It would seem possible that, in traditional labour and socialist internationalism, attachment to the principle increases as we move away from the class basis. Internationalism would seem to have been most firmly adhered to by certain socialist organizers and theorists, attempting to graft the universalism, cosmopolitanism and democratic internationalism of European radical tradition on to the more locally rooted discontents of the working class (Herrmann, 1988; Hobsbawm, 1988; Michel, 1988; Nairn, 1980; Peterson, 1988).

Relationship to Non-Labour Internationalism

Classical proletarian and socialist internationalism relates to religious universalism, bourgeois cosmopolitanism and democratic internationalism (for which see Chapter 3) in complex ways. The ancient desire for *universal peace and community*, made religious doctrine and moral imperative by Christianity, finds significant echoes within labour internationalism. That the British Independent Labour Party resisted the war hysteria of 1914, whilst most of the more Marxist continental parties did not, is largely explained by such influences (Young, 1986: 194–7).

Bourgeois cosmopolitanism is closely linked with classical political-economic doctrines on the mutual dependence, the civilizing and homogenizing effects, of the international division of labour, industrialization and trade. This tradition can be clearly identified within proletarian and socialist internationalism, including the Marxist version. Bourgeois cosmopolitanism, at least in its liberal free trade version, was itself, however, an ambiguous doctrine. Given its own articulation with republican-democratic internationalism and Christian universalism, it was capable of winning the support of British textile workers for a self-sacrificing boycott of slave-produced cotton during the American Civil War (evidently *easier* for workers when they have little to lose but their chains). But the Eurocentric, evolutionist and technological-determinist elements of bourgeois cosmopolitanism also influenced socialist internationalism, and certainly undermined anti-war and anti-colonial activity within the labour movements (Claeys, 1988; Harrison, 1957, 1965; Kaarsholm, 1988; Mergner, 1988; Saville, 1988; Tichelman, 1988).

Republican or democratic internationalism, aimed at oppression rather than exploitation and based on national rather than class movements, finds its expression within the worker declaration cited in Note 3 at the end of this chapter, as well as in such major labour-based protests as the 1850 London brewery workers' attacks on the 'Butcher of Budapest' and the 1864 welcome for Garibaldi. In this declaration of the significantly named (and short-lived) Democratic Friends of all Nations in 1844, the address is clearly to the oppressed, not to the exploited:

The Democratic Friends of all Nations being deeply impressed with the importance of cultivating a brotherly feeling among the people of all countries, and of advancing their social and political rights, conceive that those desirable objects would be promoted if a few democratic friends belonging to different nations could be brought together monthly, for the purpose of friendly conversation; for reading such newspapers of different countries as may be desirable; for affording some assistance to such political offenders as may be driven from their country for advancing the cause of human liberty: as well as for calling public meetings, from time to time, for hearing the democratic opinions of different countries; and for adopting all legal means to create a public opinion in favour of the great principle of human brotherhood. (cited in Lattek, 1988: 271)

This organization consisted primarily of socialists and it was clearly a forerunner of later labour, socialist and Marxist internationalism. It could also be seen as a forerunner of what today is called the human rights movement. (Claeys, 1988; Dutt, 1964: 42, Kramer, 1988).

Relationship to Proletarian Nationalism

We must here concentrate on the relationship between the internationalism and nationalism of *proletarians*, rather than that of their unions, parties and theoreticians (for which see Jenkins and Minnerup, 1984; Munck, 1986; Nairn, 1975, 1979, 1980; Vogler, 1985). We have already earlier noted that mineworkers could move between, or combine, contradictory identifications. The problem is that working-class and national identity were developing simultaneously in the nineteenth century, that workers could choose these (or other ethnic and religious) identities according to circumstances, and that: 'working-class consciousness, however inevitable and essential, is probably politically secondary to other kinds of consciousness. As we know, where it has come into conflict in our century with national, or religious, or racial consciousness, it has usually yielded and retreated' (Hobsbawm, 1984: 59). In so far as this is so, and in so far as labour organizers and socialist theorists did not recognize the fact, this itself helps us to understand the failure of traditional internationalism.

The Limitations and Decline of Proletarian Internationalism

In so far as we are able to specify the situation, forces and features of traditional labour internationalism, it should also be possible to specify on its decline. Some suggestions may have already been made but these need to be spelled out. One way of doing this is to reconsider some of the previously mentioned conditions, types and relations of proletarian internationalism.

First, the *conditions*. The widening and deepening of capitalist internationalization increased competition between, and consequent insecurity amongst, proletarians from a European or industrialized-world scale to a truly global scale. It simultaneously increased 'statification' – the national and international formalization, hierarchization and legalization of social relationships – also those amongst and between workers. This was accompanied by the consolidation of state-national cultures (compulsory education in a dominant language, dialect or accent) and the inclusion of the masses within the polity (Social Democratic *labour* parties, Communist *vanguard proletarian* parties, populist *people's* parties). The popular press, once the magic bullet with which the masses would slay their national and international oppressors and exploiters, became the privileged means for the spread amongst them of disinformation, for trivialization, the creation of national chauvinism, militarism and racist imperialism. As inter-state and inter-bloc relations were militarized on an ever more apocalyptic scale, the nature of modern warfare (both military and ideological) required increasing mass involvement with military-patriotic symbols and rituals. It also required concession of political rights and social welfare to the working classes. The nation-state, which even before industrialization had been appealed to for protection against the market, was increasingly appealed to by labour movements for protection against international capital – now customarily perceived in terms of the capital of 'foreign' nation-states, nationals or, even, nationalities. Ethnic or religious differences between workers nationally and internationally were now codified and enforced by the law, police and army. Labour movements, whether in their Social Democratic, Communist or populist emanations, were increasingly involved in nation- and state-building (Billington, 1980; Connell, 1984; Hobsbawm, 1984, 1988; Johnson, 1979; Mann, 1987; Vogler, 1985).

Second, the *forces*. The class or functional differences and levels that we have already identified within the labour movement became formalized, with institutional status, employment situation, income level and life chances differentiating intellectuals (increasingly professionals and academics), organizers (increasingly full-time union or party officials) and the rank and file. This process also increasingly formalized the different interests in internationalism. The socialist intellectuals gained unprecedented international access and contact, the interested labour organizers could satisfy themselves with both the institutionalized internationalism of parties and unions, and with those multifarious inter-state organizations – like the International Labour Organization (ILO) or the European Parliament – through which they could, and still evidently can, pursue their own interests. At the international level we can see the transformation of leaders with a popular national and international following into anonymous functionaries of international bureaucracies. The changing nature of the labour process (destruction of crafts, craftsmen and their culture), the consequently changing composition and education of the working class (mass- rather than self-educated), and the domination of the labour movement by unions of semi-skilled or unskilled factory and public-sector workers, was also of significance in the decline of classical proletarian internationalism (Haupt, 1986).

Third, the *types* of internationalism. These need to be dealt with in some detail. *Party internationalism* increasingly reproduced the model of diplomatic inter-state relations, with struggles for domination between parties and conflicts over national representation and sovereignty, reaching its apotheosis in a Comintern (Communist International) subordinated to Soviet state interests. The ideological split, principally between the Communist and Socialist Internationals, not only anathemized (as 'reformist' or 'totalitarian') major mass organizations and their followers within certain countries. It also increasingly coincided with inter-state and inter-bloc conflict, the internationals being largely identified with either of two ideological entities – the 'socialist world' or the 'free world'. Particular international organizations, distanced as they already were from the members *of* their members, were now isolated from the experiences of actually existing proletarians in whole quarters, thirds or halves of the world.

Trade union internationalism had always combined elements of national protectionism with those of international solidarity. And union internationalism must be seen historically as an instrument for the establishment of both national union movements and national union demands. Nineteenth-century internationalism was, thus, largely a 'nationalist internationalism'. Just as it led to incorporation within the nation-state, so did the international demands eventually lead to incorporation within such inter-state organizations as the ILO. The desire of the Mineworkers' International Federation (MIF) for an internationally planned coal market led it, shortly after its foundation, to support the project of a Belgian mineowner for an International Ministry of Mining. When the British miners went on strike in 1925, the members of the MIF donated considerable sums of money, but industrial solidarity action foundered on the rocks of bureaucracy, nationalism and ideological division (Herrmann, 1988; Michel, 1988). As for international solidarity with the British miners' strike 60 years later, in 1984–5, this revealed the same complex articulation of the old and the new as the strike itself (Howells, 1986; Saunders, 1989). Support, nationally and internationally, was largely organized by traditional left and socialist organizations, from anarcho-syndicalist *groupuscules* to the Communist-based and state-socialist International Miners' Organization (IMO). The response, however, came from the left-liberal and humanitarian middle classes, as well as from such new socialist movements (NSMs) as those of women and gays. Neither of these impacted more than marginally on the institutionalized internationalism of the unions or the institutionalized union internationals.

The *co-operative* strategy of gradually extending consumer power nationally and internationally was one which was not integrated with other forms of labour organization and struggle. The movement was also incapable of confronting an increasingly monopolized world trading system, or the forces of revolution, counter-revolution and war (Gurney, 1988).

As for the *cultural* internationalism of the labour movement (sport, nature, literature, tourism, youth, etc.), whilst it might be true that it was both wider in implication and deeper in impact than the political variety, it could not escape the politicalization and statification process. The remarkable worker cultural movement of the inter-war years was largely a Communist cultural movement and by that token simultaneously sectarian, workerist, elitist and statist. What in the Netherlands had been an allegedly internationalist Association for Popular Culture had by 1931 transformed itself into an unambiguous Association of Friends of the Soviet Union (Jones, 1988; Kramer, 1988; Mattelart and Siegelaub, 1983: 153–64, 176–82; Shiach, 1989: ch. 5; Waterman, 1990a).

The final type is the internationalist '*theoretical practice*' of socialist parties. Here it would be necessary to trace the line of descent (in more senses than one) from the *Neue Zeit* at the beginning to the more recent Social Democratic *Socialist Affairs* and the Communist *World Marxist Review*. Suffice it to say that the latter are the last places that a theoretically minded socialist would look for any original thought or important debate, indeed for anything other than official declarations and partisan analyses. The one contemporary exception to the decline might seem to have been *Socialism in the World*, published in Yugoslavia from 1977, but, despite its apparently non-sectarian contributions and the importance of its themes, this journal related to no movement and was little known even amongst independent Marxists internationally. Moreover, it was in fact a state/party-subsidized substitute for the internationally reputed Marxist-Humanist journal *Praxis*, which the Yugoslav state was attempting to destroy at that time. The decline of the state/party in Yugoslavia also meant an end to this magazine.[5]

Fourth, the *relationship to nationalism*. The failure of the labour and socialist movement to understand the specificity and autonomy of the national and popular, and its tendency to reduce national to class interest, has been sufficiently demonstrated and criticized. The left, like the liberals, also failed to understand modern militarism and its mass appeals, dealing with it simply as primitive and irrational rather than examining its contemporary bases and effects. It is these failures that led to the combination of high internationalist principle with low nationalist action, to either sectarian or opportunist policy swings as particular nationalisms and militarisms were judged to serve the class struggle of the national or international proletariat. It is one of history's more bitter ironies that the most ambitious attempt to systematize and even codify a principled internationalism, in the Comintern, led to the most extreme and far-reaching subordination to nation-statism in the history of the labour movement (Claudin, 1970; Jenkins and Minnerup, 1984; Mann, 1983, 1987: 40; Munck, 1986).

Fifth, *relationship to non-proletarian internationalism*. Given the Promethean characteristics accorded the proletariat either by the proletarian activists or by their socialist leaders/theorists and given the combination of scientific vanguard role and prophetic power that the socialists granted themselves, it is evident that they could allow religious universalism, bourgeois cosmopolitanism and radical-democratic internationalism only a historical place as predecessors, or an ideological existence as, perhaps, opiates of the peoples. The result, on the Communist side, was the creation of that complete set of party controlled international organizations mentioned above. Whilst these movements sometimes played a pioneering role (Young, 1986: 198), their relationship to the other tendencies was at best diplomatic and at worst crudely instrumental. On the Social Democratic side, whilst there was some attempt at matching the Communists one for one, the problem was rather that of a merging with or subordination to bourgeois cosmopolitanism. At the apogee here is surely the proposal of Karl Renner, previously a leading Austro-Marxist, later President of Austria, to conceive the new United Nations in 1946 as the Fourth International (Friedemann and Holscher, 1982). Although unsuccessful in this specific case (Trotskyists still struggle between themselves over the copyright), the project has had some success with regard to intent; 'internationalism' in the West today is far more associated in the public mind with the UN and associated activities than with any labour or socialist organization. Social-Democrats have actually made the running in North–South 'internationalism', but it is noteworthy that their various reform projects are subordinate to liberal theories, structures, values and practices, particularly in their acceptance of an inter-state frame of action and in their reference to First World self-interest, usually conceived of in national terms (Brandt and Manley, 1985; Court, 1990; Elson, 1983; Evers, 1982; Evert Vermeer Stichting, 1985; Institut Socialiste d'Etudes et de Recherches, 1983; Michanek, 1985; Seddon, 1986; Waterman, 1996a).

There are two possible ways of coming to terms with the process sketched above. One is to refer to the underdevelopment of capitalism, of the working class, of the labour movement and of Marxism, and therefore to predict a Second Coming of proletarian and socialist internationalism. The other is to suggest that the problem is rather one of a misunderstanding of the nature of proletarian internationalism, of a misinterpretation of its activities, of erroneous strategy, with the consequent necessity for a fundamental rethinking. Whilst the two types of response do not necessarily exclude each other, it is evident that they have radically different political implications. It will be clear that this analysis is leaning heavily towards the second type of explanation, so it is now necessary to discuss why.

Reflection: The Social Theory and Utopian Ideology of Internationalism

Here, as earlier stated, we will concentrate simply on two documents of Marx and Engels, a virtually unknown passage from the *German Ideology* (Arthur, 1970) and the famous *Communist Manifesto* (Marx and Engels, 1935). This is, in the first place, because of their richness in content and, in the second place, because – unlike nationalism – there was little if any major development in either the theory or strategy of internationalism after these early statements. What we seem to get instead is – as we have seen – either up-dated reproduction, pragmatic adjustment or successive attenuation.

The two documents are complementary in a number of ways: the first is philosophical, the second political; the first deals with the global level, the second with that of the nation-state; the first deals with communism primarily as historical transformation and social movement, the latter with it as programme and organization. The first could be seen as reflective and theoretical, the latter as persuasive and utopian. Although I am already 'comparing and contrasting', this is not with the intention of praising the 'theoretical' over the 'utopian'. Both combine rational-analytical and utopian-prophetic elements – a combination essential to any emancipatory social theory. Whilst Marx and Marxism have an ambiguous attitude towards utopianism (Geoghegan, 1987), contemporary libertarian socialism, feminism and ecological movements have refamiliarized socialists with the necessity of an appeal to emotion, desire and imagination in challenging the myriad inhumanities, indignities and banalities to which we are accustomed. I find these documents amazing and moving, dated in significant ways, yet none the less capable of throwing light 150 years forward and therefore worthy of the critical attention not simply of contemporary socialists but all democratically minded people. Before consigning this doctrine to some garbage bin of early industrial history or totalitarian discourse, we should consider the possible connection between Marxist internationalism and the new alternative social movements. In the words of Pieterse (1990: 67):

Emancipatory projects of our time – the new social movements, feminism, the movements of oppressed peoples and minorities throughout the world – are generally not cast in the framework of rationalist ideology. Usually they oppose policies which are conceived and presented as utterly rational, that is, given certain values and priorities. In an environment that advertises itself as utterly rational, where official rhetoric tends to conform to the standard of rational discourse, appeals to rationality per se need not be particularly liberating. This is not to say that the arguments of contemporary emancipatory movements are irrational, quite the contrary, but the discourse has shifted from rationality to values, and direct appeals are made to values: to equality, solidarity, democracy, human dignity, quality of life, peace.

I will interrogate the texts both for their main themes and their contemporary resonances and lacunae.

Communism as International Social Movement

Let us examine first the passage from the *German Ideology* of 1845–6:

This 'alienation' (to use a term which will be comprehensible to the philosophers) can, of course, only be abolished given two *practical* premises. For it to become an 'intolerable' power, i.e. a power against which men make a revolution, it must necessarily have rendered the great mass of humanity 'propertyless', and produced, at the same time, the contradiction of an existing world of wealth and culture, both of which conditions presuppose a great increase in productive power, a high degree of its development. And, on the other hand, this development of productive forces (which itself implies the actual empirical existence of men in their *world-historical*, instead of local, being) is an absolutely necessary practical premise because without it *want* is merely made general, and with *destitution* the struggle for necessities and all the old filthy business would necessarily be reproduced; and furthermore, because with this universal development of productive forces is a *universal* intercourse between men established, which produces in all nations simultaneously the phenomenon of the 'propertyless' mass (universal competition), makes each nation dependent on the revolutions of the others, and finally has put *world-historical*, empirically universal individuals in place of local ones. Without this, 1) communism could only exist as a local event; 2) the *forces* of intercourse themselves could not have developed as *universal*, hence intolerable powers: they would have remained home-bred conditions surrounded by superstition; and 3) each extension of intercourse would abolish local communism. Empirically, communism is only possible as the act of the dominant peoples 'all at once' and simultaneously, which presupposes the universal development of productive forces and the world intercourse bound up with communism. Moreover, the mass of *propertyless* workers – the utterly precarious position of labour-power on a mass scale cut off from capital or from even a limited satisfaction and, therefore, no longer merely temporarily deprived of work itself as a secure source of life – presupposes the *world market* through competition. The proletariat can thus only exist *world-historically*, just as communism, its activity, can only have a 'world-historical' existence. World-historical existence of individuals means, existence of individuals which is directly linked up with world history.

Communism is for us not a *state of affairs* which is to be established, an *ideal* to which reality [will] have to adjust itself. We call communism the *real* movement which abolishes the present state of things. The conditions of this movement result from the premises now in existence. (Arthur, 1970: 56–7, original emphases)

I identify six main elements within this passage, and intend to rearrange them for purposes of analysis, which I think can be done without violence to the argument.

The International Nature of the Conditions for Overcoming Alienation

The contradiction between the propertylessness of the 'great mass of humanity' and an 'existing world of wealth and culture' has been increasing since Marx's time. However, this has been not only, and certainly not simply, in the form of a contradiction between capital and proletariat. We are witness to processes of mass proletarianization (deprival of means of production) without creation of a majority proletariat, of situations in which it is a privileged minority of the proletarianized that becomes – or remains – a permanent proletariat. We are witness to deepening contradictions between worlds of wealth and culture, and those denied these, both between and within 'creditor' and 'debtor' states (Burbach and Nunez, 1987a; Sklair, 1991). We are cognizant of a continuing or even increasing coincidence of propertylessness with female or minority (ethnic, religious) status. So this truly international contradiction has been accompanied not with a growing homogenization of the propertyless but a continuing heterogenization that is repeatedly restructured.

For Marx, the development of these international contradictions required such an increase in productive power and wealth that their resolution would permit a surpassing of want, destitution and a struggle for necessities. The computer-based technical revolution now advancing in the industrialized capitalist world is capable of ensuring rising productivity and full employment with a decrease in labour time, in these countries, from an average 1,600 to 1,000 hours per year in the next fifteen to twenty years (according to Gorz, 1989: 228). Although this development opens up the potentiality for overcoming the 'old filthy business', we know, of course, that it is currently being used to further fragment (industrially/occupationally), segment (by nationality, gender, ethnicity, religion) and stratify the propertyless.

For Marx, it was the above process that would ensure two crucial conditions, the 'empirical existence of men in their *world-historical,* instead of local being' and the making of 'each nation dependent upon the revolutions of the others'. On the one hand, the absence of the earlier mentioned requirements explains why the latter conditions have not yet come about. On the other hand, we can empirically identify the growth of these two processes. Increasing numbers of movements demonstrate mass awareness of global community, and we cannot but note the increasing demonstration effect of national revolutions or uprisings, student protest movements or, even, social reform waves.

The Proletariat and Communism as Only Existing Internationally

What we have witnessed so far, increasingly national proletariats and increasingly national communisms, is accepted by more and more Marxists. There is, however, the temptation to escape from this leaden empirical contingency to the nebulous freedom of theory: the proletariat and communism do not *yet* fully exist because they have forgotten or never learned what Marx pronounced: but one day they will. Since neither historical nor contemporary social analysis reveals much evidence for such an assertion, we are left dependent on faith in an existing doctrine and ultimate authority – something orthodox Marxists reject in all other cases. I propose a radical solution: that we take Marx's position here as figurative rather than literal. It is clear why he attached his aspiration for the end of human alienation to the proletariat – the new, modern, mass, international class of the exploited and oppressed. I propose we should here take 'proletariat' as a metaphor for all the alienated, all those denied their past rights, their present capacities, their future potential (this does not, of course, mean we should or could do this wherever Marx refers to the proletariat). There is increasing evidence and argumentation for the increasing internationalism of those alienated in many different ways. That the overcoming of alienation ('communism' in Marx's language) is inconceivable nationally is surely demonstrated by the collapse of 'socialism' not only in one country but also in one bloc. Increasing 'interdependence', moreover, seems to imply that you cannot today build, or preserve, even a capitalist welfare state in just one country. My interpretation further implies neither writing off the proletariat as an autonomous contributor to internationalism, nor abandoning appeals from outside or above (or below) that it consider the advantages and even the necessities of a global identity. It means only abandonment of any assumption that its internationalism is structurally determined and/or exemplary. On this understanding, the proletariat would also have to go to school, and not so much with Marx (or me) as with the other alienated categories. It would also have to opt for the untrodden but exhilarating world of internationalism rather than the familiar, well-trodden but imprisoning parish of nation-statism. The proletariat may still have a world to win, but it also has more than its chains to lose.

Communism as the Real Social Movement

Here I feel we have the most valuable kind of theoretical formulation since it invites us to question its own formulator and its social forms. Communism has *long been* for the world primarily a 'state of affairs' – an affair of Communist states. It has also *always been* largely an 'ideal to which reality [will] have to adjust itself', increasingly an ideal in the heads only of socialist intellectuals (who could thus be fairly named 'idealist socialist intellectuals'). If communism is meant in the first instance to be 'the real movement which abolishes the present state of things', then this requires us to address ourselves to such real movements (movements in the sense both of societal transformation and mass feelings, ideas, organization and action). The real movements that are presently transforming the *international* order are the new alternative social movements. These do not have to be understood as replacing or in opposition to the labour movement. Amongst the real movements could also be counted the 'social movement unions' or 'new social unionism' that have explicitly or implicitly, to a greater or lesser extent, for a longer or shorter period, surpassed the 'economism' and 'politicism', or the reformist or insurrectionary workerism, of their predecessors (Aronowitz, 1988, Brecher and Costello, 1990a; Waterman, 1993b, forthcoming).

The Necessity for Simultaneous Revolution by the Dominant Nations

The importance of this assertion is what it reveals to us of Marx's apocalypticism and Eurocentrism. The latter was not so much *sur*passed as *by*passed by Lenin's notion of the weak link, and by Trotsky's notion of uneven and combined development. What they understood, because Russia experienced it, is that the international spread of capitalist social relations is multifaceted and uneven in essence. But this does not imply, as it did in part for Lenin and increasingly for some of his followers, that we can shift revolutionary *primacy* from 'advanced' to 'backward' nations, or revolutionary *agency* from the anti-capitalist proletariat of the industrialized centre to the anti-imperialist masses of the agricultural periphery. It rather requires us to abandon any idea of countries or blocs or parties that are either industrial/cultural models or revolutionary vanguards. Recognizing the differential implications and experience of capitalist internationalization requires us to:

1   identify the similar structures, processes and experiences in different countries that lend themselves to common internationalist action;
2   recognize that differential position and experience within an increasingly capitalist world order implies different movement priorities, discoveries, inventions and achievements; and
3   work out principles and forms of solidarity amongst and between the different significant movements of particular countries or blocs (e.g. both peace movement with peace movement and labour movement with women's movement).

Finally, we need to ask ourselves why Marx had an apocalyptical vision of emancipation. I here suggest that apocalypticism is a requirement of a mass emancipatory ideology or movement in a situation in which masses of people are capable of rebelling against existing conditions but not of fully conceiving or controlling a desired alternative. I will further suggest that the masses today are potentially capable of doing the latter, which is why apocalyptical visions and strategies are associated with early, undeveloped or (self-)isolated socialist movements (Sendero Luminoso in Peru, the Communist Party of the Philippines, both inspired by Maoism). Visions of sudden and complete transformation to a land of milk and honey, where 'the people will rule' (as in the original African National Congress Charter), are declining in the more sophisticated socialist movements of the Third World, such as those of South Korea, South Africa and Brazil. This does not, of course, mean that apocalyptical visions are absent amongst large parts of the masses locally.[6] Contemporary political apocalypticism, for the rest, appears increasingly a characteristic of reactionary, militaristic and obscurantist forces (religious fundamentalists, chauvinist nationalists, racists, global militarists).

The Existence of the Premises for Communism
The reason why, almost 150 years later, these premises have not yet translated themselves into either empirical international reality, or even mass internationalist aspiration, has been sufficiently argued above.

What Will Happen in the Absence of the Necessary Conditions
The value of this passage lies not only in its quite remarkable prescience but also in reminding us that such prescience is the outcome of a new theoretical approach linked with new emancipatory struggles (compare contemporary feminist or ecological theory). Marx says that if the conditions are not ripe, capitalism and the market will continue to appear 'home-bred conditions surrounded by superstition'. He also says that the further extension of the world market will 'abolish local communism'. What we have, of course, witnessed over the last century and a half is working-class advances within capitalist states (by nationally self-defined workers, without or against others), and of anti-capitalist revolutions being repeatedly penetrated, de-radicalized and restricted by the dynamic growth of international capital. What we have so far witnessed internationally have, in other words, been working-class

movements *within*, or national revolutions *against*, capitalism. Surpassing capitalism is another matter entirely.

Communism as International Political Movement

We turn now to the *Communist Manifesto* of 1848 (Marx and Engels, 1935). Certainly the best remembered part of this are the closing words, 'Workers of all countries, unite!'. But the Manifesto does not give so much place to internationalization and internationalism as memory might suggest. What it does have to say is, of course, determinant for the Manifesto as a whole. Within it I identify three main elements, once again rearranged for purposes of analysis and discussion.[7]

Bourgeois Internationalization as Progressive

Whilst it is evident that Marx and Engels by no means identify themselves with the bourgeoisie, they clearly consider its international role as progressive, as modernizing, developing, homogenizing and unifying the world. The violent 'pain of extinction' with which the bourgeoisie threatens 'barbarian and semi-barbarian' nations is presented as civilizing. The bourgeoisie is even credited with undermining 'national one-sidedness and narrow-mindedness' and of creating a 'world literature'. It is hardly necessary, in the face of the last century and a half, to criticize this picture. Nor is it necessary to argue the linkage between the attitudes here expressed and those of European bourgeois racism, evolutionism, modernism and cosmopolitanism. This has been done extensively and convincingly elsewhere (Berman, 1983; Horne, 1986). What is necessary is to stress what is missing, since this helps us to understand why internationalization has not led to internationalism: why industrialism is not merely disruptive but destructive, why the bourgeoisie is chauvinist and imperialist, why capitalist statism is essentially militaristic, why world capitalist civilization is essentially individualizing and divisive. Far from creating its own international and internationalist grave-digger in the industrial proletariat, for example, capitalism has divided the labour process of grave-digging technically, socially and geographically, assigning different parts of the task to the differentially proletarianized, of various gender, ethnic or religious categories, under diverse political and labour regimes. In addition to a world literature, it has created a commercialized transnational culture which simultaneously provides immense profits, homogenizes audiences as consumers, spreads dehumanized bourgeois values, erodes local popular cultures containing elements of resistance or opposition and, finally, obstructs any such communication between these as would be necessary for the creation of an internationalist culture (Schiller, 1990).

To add all the above is to qualify, not reverse, the evaluation. It is, for example, equally evident that the development of railways and other technical channels of communication *were* determinant in the rapid organization of labour nationally and internationally (Marx and Engels, 1935b: 215). An interesting and important question follows. If the railways thus *allowed* labour organization, did they not, perhaps, also *restrict its shape?* Railways are physically fixed, monopolistically or state-owned, hierarchically managed, centripetal channels. Their international connections mechanically connect the separate nationally owned and controlled systems. Did not national and international labour organizations unconsciously reproduce the pattern, structure and management of such industries? Capitalist industrialization and internationalization is, in any case, a highly contradictory phenomenon, simultaneously denying, provoking and even stimulating possibilities for self-organization and liberation. The effective use of computers in both individualistic sabotage of the computer society, or in collective struggle against it, would be one example (for the latter, see Downing, 1989; Lee, 1996; Waterman, 1992a). Another would be the radical recycling of the white, North American individualist Superman myth by the apparition in Mexico of *Superbarrio*, the protector of urban squatters, who – tongue firmly in cheek – states that he draws his power only from the collective (Alcocer, 1990; The Other Side of Mexico, 1987). Superbarrio (significantly for our subject) operates amongst *Latinos/as* in both Mexico and the USA, declaring 'We didn't make the border, we don't want the border' (Hernandez, 1989).

The Proletariat as a Liberated, Liberating and Internationalist Subject

The proletariat is endowed with positive and universalistic qualities. It is free of 'every trace of national character' and 'bourgeois prejudices'. The workers 'have no country', they 'have nothing to lose but their chains'. They have to complete the task begun by the bourgeoisie. By ending class antagonisms within countries they will end them between countries. They must end them first within nations, become the leading class within the nation, become the nation. Although these phrases come from different parts of the Manifesto, they none the less amount to a clear argument: since the proletariat is free of bourgeois and nationalist prejudices, since it is free of any stake in existing society, it can therefore put an end to conflicts between nations, this requiring that it first take over the nation-state from the old ruling classes that are responsible for international conflicts.

In considering this view, it is necessary to make a number of points:

1   The positive, progressive and Promethean characteristics the working class is here accorded have little or no correspondence with the early nineteenth-century British proletariat as described by Engels (1953) four years earlier. In later political dealings with, and writings on, the British working class, its leaders and organizations, Marx and Engels identified national and stratum privilege, narrow self-interest, subordination to bourgeois ideas and institutions, and chauvinism (Marx and Engels, 1953).

2   The argument is class-reductionist in assuming that state and nation are forms of existence, or expressions, of classes, or of secondary import to classes in determining social liberation. It would seem superfluous today to have to argue for the continuing, indeed *growing*, weight of state and nationality/ethnicity in determining relations between people and peoples. The commonly tense and sometimes violent relations between and within even culturally close Communist states – and the long-standing state discrimination against ethnic or religious minorities within them – was evidently due to these forces. In the late 1970s, Banas (1979) even characterized one of these regimes as 'Ethno-Communist'. As the Communism has disappeared, it is often only ethnicity that seems to remain.

3   The argument is evolutionist in suggesting that the proletariat has to complete a task begun by the bourgeoisie rather than to criticize and transform all bourgeois relations and processes.

4   The argument is 'stageist' in so far as it suggests that national struggle somehow proceeds the international struggle, or that international conflicts cannot be ended without proletarian rule nationally. This implies a priority of struggles, or an order of

separate levels, at odds with the 1847 document and with a dialectical understanding of inter-penetrating and mutually determining national and international spheres (Brecher, 1987).

5 The argument is, of course, sexist. At a time when a large part of factory labour was carried out by women and children, the proletariat is assumed to consist of adult males – who presumably neither beat, rape, nor more subtly oppress, their family members.

Given, in sum, the complex nature of both the nineteenth- and twentieth-century proletariat, given the complexity of social structures within which it existed and exists, the portrayal of the proletariat as a liberated, liberating and vanguard internationalist subject is precisely an 'ideal to which reality [will] have to adjust itself' (see Lovell, 1988, on Marx's proletariat).

The Communist Role

The only thing that distinguishes communists from other working-class parties is that within national struggles they press the common interests of the proletariat internationally, and that at any stage they press the interests of the movement generally. The conclusion to the last section applies here with equal force. We are today confronted with the situation satirized by Tom Nairn (1980): the metropolitan internationalism of those socialists with power and the spiritual internationalism of those without. The aspiration represented by the Marx–Engels assertion has evidently been disappointed by the nationalization and statification of socialists and socialism. Once again, however, we have to abandon dependence on a Second Coming, a Last Really International. We cannot today see, even in such internationalist traditions as those of the Trotskyists (Frank, 1979a) or Anarcho-Syndicalists (Longmore, 1985; Thorpe, 1990), the embryo of a body which is not only internationalist but also possessed of the other characteristics required by the Manifesto – that it be not opposed to other working-class parties, that it be not separate from the proletariat, that it have no sectarian principles.

In their concept of the role of Communists, Marx and Engels combined traditional religious notions of salvation (an Elect, possessing the Word, leading the Chosen People, via an Apocalypse, to a Promised Land[8]) with the quintessentially bourgeois form of political organization, the party! The power – or limitations – of this highly specific combination of forms (in relation to their ideal of a global movement to end human alienation) is witnessed by the way socialist parties have not so much failed to embody or further the project but have actually negated it. The two utopias socialist parties can offer us today are represented, I suppose, on the one hand by the West European 'social market' society and, on the other, by the 'society of great harmony' which the terroristic *Sendero Luminoso* (Shining Path) was trying to 'drive home' into the minds of Peru's miserable but resilient masses (Degregori, 1991). But these were or are either national or bloc projects. The Sendero type is one that is so inhuman, and implies such isolation from the world, that it has been abandoned by rulers or rejected by their subjects almost everywhere. And the social market society, whilst still exercising attraction for people in the East and the South, is one that cannot be reproduced internationally without despoiling the planet itself.

It is curious, finally, that the Manifesto, the more concrete and political of the two documents, should seem more dated or less relevant than the earlier, more abstract and philosophical one. This once again suggests that we have to liberate the project of internationalism from the politics of a nineteenth-century world dominated by the market, industrialization, worker–capitalist conflict, nation- and empire-building, deification of the masculine and struggle for the control of the machinery of the state.

Conclusion: From an International of the Imagination to the Imagination of an Internationalism

We may end by considering the response of two British socialist labour historians to the decline and fall of classical internationalism. Both observe that the flag of nineteenth-century internationalism is somewhat tattered, but they seem to have rather different attitudes towards the tatters.

The first historian is Eric Hobsbawm (1988), who remained a Communist even as communism was being rejected by massive labour and democratic movements wherever it still had power. Although Hobsbawm evidently has many brilliant and suggestive insights into the nature of classical internationalism, he has no real explanation for its decline, except in terms of the rise of nationalism and the decline of internationalist parties (Hobsbawm, 1988: 14–15). This is an almost tautological position, and one that begs many questions about these parties and their doctrines. He shows little or no awareness of contemporary internationalism, and he offers even less perspective for the future. What he has to say about traditional internationalism today is that it has been undermined by racism nationally and that it is difficult for nationally organized trade unions to fight internationally organized multinationals (ibid.: 8). This is again a question-begging statement, and one that shows no knowledge of what workers and unions *have* recently been doing to confront transnational corporations (TNCs) internationally. For the future, Hobsbawm offers no perspective other than raising again the flag of internationalism 'even today when the storms of history threaten to tear it to tatters' (ibid.: 12). The sole example Hobsbawm can offer for a reviving labour internationalism is the African National Congress (ANC) of South Africa. The passage from which the above quotation is taken runs more fully as follows:

[T]he flag of internationalism in labour movements must be held high, even today when the storms of history threaten to tear it to tatters. That is why movements like the African National Congress in South Africa deserve our admiration as well as our support: for against racist white rulers and racist or tribalist black rebels, it has won the leadership of the oppressed African people on the basis of a platform of non-racialism: of equality of African and Indian, coloured and white in a free South Africa. In this internationalism there lies the only hope, small and faint through it is, for the future. (Ibid.: 16)

It is significant that Hobsbawm rested his small faint hope for the future of *labour internationalism* on the ANC, which was, of course, a *nationalist movement*, aimed (like past Communist ones) at the capture of state power. It is equally significant that Hobsbawm considered neither the problematic internationalism of the (then) pro-Soviet ANC nor the rich and complex history of relations between workers and unions inside and outside South Africa (South African Labour Bulletin, 1991a, b). One therefore remains with historical storms, tattered flags and small faint hopes in Third World nationalist movements.

Edward Thompson broke with communism in 1957, became a founder of the New Left and a leading figure in the democratic rights movement in the UK and the peace movement in Europe. He was also involved in international debates around the new peace and democracy internationalisms (Thompson, 1988, 1990). Writing in 1978, in the hiatus between the democratic international waves of 1968 and 1989, Thompson identified himself as a socialist internationalist, traced his personal itinerary, and felt obliged to say the following:

> The 'banner' of socialist internationalism has become tattered indeed in the last decades, and on every side. It has not been one to carry proudly aloft. At the most one has carried a few sheets of paper, and often one has been reduced to muttering to oneself. The commitment has been to an 'International' of the imagination, which has had only fleeting embodiment in real movements, detached unequivocally from both Stalinism and from complicity with the reasons of capitalist power. To maintain that commitment has been to be an 'alien' not only within this country but within great sections of the purported socialist and Marxist movement itself. (Thompson, 1978: iv)

Sharing the determined orientation – and the political experience – of Thompson it is now necessary for me to move from an international of the imagination to the imagination of an internationalism.

Notes

1 This was the Communist myth with which I grew up in Britain in the 1950s. It received official form in the book of Raji Palme Dutt (1964). For a more scholarly social democratic account, see Braunthal (1980). For a brief account of the historiography of the three successive internationals, see Linden (1988b). For accounts of two marginal socialist internationalist traditions see the Trotskyist one of Frank (1979a) and the anarcho-syndicalist one of Longmore (1985).

2 My debt to the work of Holthoon and Linden (1988) will be apparent to anyone checking the Bibliography for the following account. Indeed, it was a conference on the history of internationalism (up to 1940), organized at the International Institute of Social History, that gave rise to this collection and inspired me to work on the history of internationalism. It also provoked me to consider the post-1940 period.

3 As a means to check the existing *abuse of power*, we echo your call for a *fraternity of peoples*. let there be a gathering together of representatives from . . . all countries, where there exists a will, to cooperate for the good of mankind. Let us . . . discuss the great questions, on which the *peace of nations* depends . . . This would clear the way for honourable men with comprehensive minds to come forth and legislate for *the rights of the many*, and not the privileges of the few.

A fraternity of peoples is highly necessary *for the cause of labour*, for we find that when ever we attempt to better our social conditions by reducing the hours of toil, or by raising the price of labour, *our employers threaten us with bringing over French-men, Germans, Belgians and other* [sic] *to do our work* at a reduced rate of wages; and we are sorry to say that this has been done not from any desire of our continental brethren to injure us, but through a *want of regular and systematic communication* between the industrious classes of all countries, which we hope to see speedily effected, as our principle is *to bring up the wages of the ill-paid* to as near a level as possible with that of those who are better remunerated, and *not allow our employers to play us off* one against the other, and so drag us down to the lowest possible condition, suitable to their avaricious bargaining.

To do these things is the *work of the peoples*. The few liberties held by the masses were *won by themselves*, and recent experience has shown that, the more we trust to princes and potentates, the surer we are of being betrayed and sneered at. (cited in Rjazanov, 1928; 171–3, emphases added)

4   These are rather well documented but very little studied. Transport workers may be the exception. See the archive of the International Transport-workers' Federation described in Aubry and Vermote (1983), Baldwin (1985), and the studies of Golding (1964), Koch-Baumgarten (1988), Northrop and Rowan (1983), Purtill (1980), Simon (1983) and Waterman (1980, 1990b), many based on the archive.

5   Conversation with Mihailo Markovic, October 1990.

6   A thought I owe to the Brazilian socialist scholar, Maria Helena Moreira Alves, at the Conference on The Future of Socialism, New York, October 1990.

7   However brief the international elements in the Manifesto, they are too substantial to be reproduced here. They can be found in Waterman (1989a) as well, of course, as in the Manifesto itself – which everyone should read or reread every ten years.

8   This is a familiar and – at first glance – banal criticism, often directed at the revolutionary left by its secular opponents. James Billington (1980) spells out the case in a way that shows both the intimate connection with religious tradition and the historical specificity of the secular apocalyptical revolutionary project – socialist or not. In so far as contemporary socialist internationalists project into the future the nineteenth-century vision of world revolution (e.g. Lowy, 1988), it might be well to reflect on Billington's view:

Revolutionaries were generally sustained . . . by secularised nineteenth-century versions of the old Judaeo-Christian belief in deliverance-through-history. At a deep and often subconscious level, the revolutionary faith was shaped by the Christian faith it attempted to replace. Most revolutionaries viewed history prophetically as a kind of unfolding morality play. The present was hell, and revolution a collective purgatory leading to a future earthly paradise. The French Revolution was the Incarnation of hope, but was betrayed by Judases within the revolutionary camp and crucified by the Pilates in power. The future revolution would be a kind of Second Coming in which the Just would be vindicated. History itself would provide the final judgment; and a new community beyond all kingdoms would come on earth as it never could in heaven. (Billington, 1980: 8)

3 RECONCEPTUALIZATION: THE NEW LABOUR INTERNATIONALISM

Introduction: The Value of a Reconceptualization

Having examined classical internationalist action and reflection, it is time to come up with a positive alternative understanding. Even an initial restatement can provide us with a radically different perspective and suggest a radically different strategy for labour. I speak here of a 'reconceptualization', not of a 'theory'. I think it will be demonstrated that a collection of appropriate tools can do much that the old blunt instruments could not.

The respecification below is largely inspired by the internationalist activity of the alternative social movements (ASMs), and by writings on or from them. This could, hypothetically, mean that it is incapable of specifically addressing labour movements or trade union organizations, that it is incapable of analysing them, or – at the very least – that it is incapable of appealing to workers. I think it will be shown that even an initial and general reconceptualization *can* address, analyse and appeal to labour movements. Indeed, my thinking also draws in part from new experiences of labour internationalism, and I recognize that it is necessary to specify the meaning of a new internationalism in a way that directly addresses this potentially internationalist subject. In the rest of this chapter I deal in turn with: some essential definitions, the subjects and purposes of internationalism, its forms, its problems of organization and leadership. I then apply the new understanding to both a new labour and a new socialist internationalism.

In later chapters I will demonstrate the value of the new understanding in greater detail, and in Chapter 7 I will carry out a more ambitious theoretical exercise, addressed not simply to labour internationalism but to the nature of the dominant global order, of solidarity movements more generally, and of an alternative world order.

Definitions

Here are some initial understandings and distinctions between key terms necessary to understanding and developing a new kind of internationalism.

Internationalization

By internationalization I mean the global spread of modernization in a capitalist dominated world, in terms of the following:

1 industrialization, commoditization, proletarianization and capital concentration;
2 bureaucratization and statification, nationally and internationally;
3 particular gender, sexual and family patterns;
4 cultural centralization and standardization (Connell, 1984).

The most dynamic process is that of capital accumulation, with, as its most dynamic institutions, the multinational production, trading and – increasingly – financial concerns (Arrighi, 1990; Cox, 1981; Elson, 1986; Resnick, Sinisi and Wolf, 1985). The processes of industrialization, commoditization, proletarianization and capital concentration are – given the world of nation-states that capitalism itself creates – uneven and incomplete. We thus get proletarianization (loss of means of production) without the creation of a classical proletariat, de-industrialization and de-proletarianization, peasantization and repeasantization, etc. Growing numbers of working people find themselves in temporary, part-time, individualized, subcontracted labour relations. The rapid changes and movements of capitalist internationalization create and re-create intra- and inter-state differentiation, insecurity, competition.

Bureaucratization, allied with specialization and technocratization, removes power from or denies it to the masses, separates and then professionalizes knowledge. It centralizes these both nationally and internationally. Whatever the power of inter-state agencies to limit nation-state sovereignty and regulate disputes between states, they simultaneously reproduce bureaucratization, remove decision-making even further and reinforce the system of nation-states (*pace* Brecher, 1987). They also obstruct the creation of genuinely supranational organizations (Vogler, 1985: 30).

The bourgeois family model (nuclear household, waged male bread-winner, housewife, school-socialized children) is propagated alongside competitive, commoditized and dehumanized sexuality. This propaga-tion continues in the face of the breakdown of the nuclear family norm in the more industrialized countries and its virtual unrealizability in the less industrialized countries. Whilst, evidently, the subordination of women did not begin with capitalism, contemporary international capitalism has created the international pornography and sex-tourism markets (for the latter see Truong, 1991, 1996). It also universalizes fashionable standards of feminine shape and beauty that are unrelated to women even in their countries of origin, never mind those of obviously differing skin colouring and build (Chapkis, 1987).

Cultural industrialization (Horne, 1986) means the global spread of North Atlantic norms and forms, including the cult of possessive indi-vidualism and an instrumental attitude towards both humanity and nature ('human resources', 'natural resources'). The repeated commo-ditization of local and popular cultural products, which are then industrialized and centrally distributed for mass consumption, not only prevents the direct cultural dialogue of equals but can also burn up and destroy the original creative impulse. The new information technologies, electronic mass media and industrialized/commercialized/statified sport and recreation increasingly colonize the intellect, body and 'free time', obstructing physical and mental creativity.

Given the intimate relationship between the most powerful multi-nationals and the most powerful states or groupings of such (which may change over time), it is misleading to talk of an 'international capitalist class'. For analogous reasons it is misleading to talk of an 'international ruling class' (for these or related terms, see Arrighi, Hopkins and Wallerstein, 1989, Cox, 1981). What keeps capitalism going is, as Connell (1984) argues, less the coherence of the exploiters/oppressors than division amongst the exploited/oppressed. This is not to deny the existence and increase of organs of capital and state that are to a considerable extent beyond the control of the individual nation-state. These inter-state or transnational organs are also increasingly able to influence and control nation-states. As immensely powerful, wealthy and undemocratic concentrations of wealth and power they and their agents represent an increasingly important enemy and target for popular movements. Their existence also indicates a new terrain of struggle – one that popular movements enter, but armed with their own democratic, pluralist and collectivist alternatives – as at the United Nations Conference on the Environment and Development (UNCED) in Rio, 1992 (Lipietz, 1992).

Given that the spread of capitalism requires the nation-state, that national-community formation appeals to and reflects popular aspirations, and that nation-state development has been commonly accompanied by liberalization and democratization, the internationalization of capital has witnessed the simultaneous, interpenetrating and mutually determining development of class and national identities (Vogler, 1985). Internationalization does not, therefore, 'give rise to' internationalism. Internationalism cannot complete an internationalization that capitalism is unable to fulfil (cf. Bauer, 1978). Internationalization does not create an internationalist subject in the global proletariat (for a classical statement that it does see Mariategui, 1986). Internationalization 'leads to' internationalism only through the self-creation of popular non-territorial identities and their combination into self-conscious, democratic and self-activating internationalist subjects.

Universalism

Universalism has a bad name amongst contemporary critics of 'grand narratives' in general, or Westernizing universalisms in particular (for the latter see Meszaros, 1989: 156–60), but without such a notion it becomes impossible to think about, or develop, a democratic community (Alexander, 1991). That special or particularistic interests customarily appeal to political or moral universals testifies to the significance of the latter. When I use the term here, however, I refer more specifically to a belief in the oneness of humanity, traditionally religious in nature (Nairn, 1980). This universal communion is conceived of in terms of an unchanging universe, and counterposed to an unchanging sin and evil. Like other influential religious or spiritual doctrines, this one expresses human experience of division, competition and conflict, and a desire for a peaceful, all-inclusive, friendly community. The traditional religious universalisms – coming out of local and specific situations at different historical moments – were customarily posed against one another: each tended to claim authority for itself and to offer community within a specific faith. Such universalisms also lived in uneasy combination with the state ('render unto Caesar ...'), whether this was theocratic or not.

Growing ecumenicism amongst Christian churches, combined with the increasing relative weight of Third World Christianity, the 'option for the poor' and liberation theologies, have led certain churches or religious instances to make practical contributions to a non-sectarian internationalism, amongst which is that of labour. At a time when most labour and socialist organizations are state oriented and dominated by 'economic' and 'political' concerns, the Christian address to moral principles and human relationships can allow it to respond to, and even sponsor, a grass roots internationalism. Like other spiritualistic or humanist beliefs of pre-capitalist origin, such universalisms lack an understanding of political and economic processes, or of specific strategies in the face of them (and therefore often depend on a simplistic Marxism).

Cosmopolitanism

By cosmopolitanism I mean a political or cultural universalism, giving priority to world order over that of a specific state or nation. Although apparently of Greek origin, it was actually the expression of a pre-industrial European intellectual elite, responding to the mercantile phase of internationalization, and considering states as obstacles to the advance of civilization (Bergh, 1986). Cosmopolitanism thus implied the domination of the world by European bourgeois liberal values and structures. We could apply the word to any elite internationalism that ignores popular national feelings and attempts to impose on them 'universal' values and structures that represent its own self-interest or world view. It might be useful to conceive of nineteenth-century liberal internationalism under this head. The American doctrine of 'interdependence' is an outstanding contemporary example. So is the slick Japanese neologism 'glocalization'. It might also be useful to talk of 'socialist cosmopolitanism' in the case of socialists who see themselves as possessing the most advanced internationalist ideology/organization/strategy and wish to remake the world in this particular image. Such a 'socialist cosmopolitanism' is distinct from the concealed but crudely statist internationalism of the Soviet Union (Kubalkova and Cruickshank, 1980, 1989), which always inveighed against 'bourgeois', 'Zionist' or 'rootless' cosmopolitanism.

Cosmopolitanism, in its original sense, clearly overlaps with religious universalism and an anti-capitalist internationalism (Claeys, 1988). This is most evidently the case with the bearers or articulators of all three doctrines – European or Westernized intellectuals sharing both the old and modern values of the cultured, linguistically skilled and travelled elite. The world order of cosmopolitanism is as much one of culture and learning as of politics, expressing both an existing reality and a future aspiration. Official intellectual anti-cosmopolitanism (whether in Hitler's Germany, the Soviet Union, China, or the Argentina of the generals) has repeatedly been defeated or collapsed.

The other face of cosmopolitanism is most evident in the case of those outstanding nineteenth-century internationalists who were them-selves cosmopolitans. These were the revolutionaries who changed their countries more often than they changed their shoes. They were educated (Neruda, 1977) or self-educated (Goldman, 1977), often emigrants or exiles, bi- or multi-lingual. They belonged to an inter-national community of European or Westernized socialist intellectuals and activists (Mariategui, 1986), with which they often felt as much identity as with 'their' nation-state.

Internationalism

This was classically a critique of the nation-state and of capitalism; a recognition that the capitalist nation-state was too limited to deal with social problems and human needs. Positively, it implied and implies cross-national, global or non-territorial solidarities, communities and organizations of an egalitarian and democratic nature. Internation-alism emerged out of the experience of capitalist industrialization and the construction of centralized, modern, elitist states. These were destroying old loyalties and communities without providing the masses with any satisfactory new one. Internationalism developed particularly out of the relationship between cosmopolitan socialist intellectuals and the new artisan-based labour movements (Nairn, 1980; Hobsbawm, 1988; Holthoon and Linden, 1988). The influence of liberal cosmopol-itanism and religious universalism is usually ignored but should be allowed for.

Given that workers experienced class and national consciousness as complementary rather than contradictory (or drew on each selectively), and that socialists did not understand this, socialist and proletarian internationalism have declined – with the partial exception of areas or moments in which the nineteenth-century European conditions exist or appear. Even at its peak, the internationalism of socialists and proletarians may have been more on national and democratic issues than on specifically proletarian ones. The twentieth-century increase in the internationalization of capital, the increasing rapidity of capital and labour transfers internationally, may have increased as much as decreased working-class appeal to and dependence on the nation-state in industrialized capitalist societies (Vogler, 1985). The effect appears also in peripheral capitalist societies (Waterman, 1992b; Waterman and Arellano, 1986), although the causes may be somewhat different.

The generalization of commoditization, bureaucratization, militarization and other modernization processes, nationally and internationally, have meanwhile created numerous social categories (teachers, housewives, students, ethnic and regional minorities) aware of their transnational or global existence, and increasing social problems of an increasingly global nature (arms proliferation, Aids, nuclear waste, refugees, debt crisis, global warming). Increasingly, also, these problems are being dealt with in international as well as inter-state fora, and the interests are expressing themselves in internationalist terms.

A contemporary internationalism – based on recognition of the interconnections between capitalism, racism, sexism, statism, etc. – would need to be at least implicitly critical of all of these. It would also – recognizing the distinction between nationality and statism – need to positively favour national and other cultural identities. Such national, cultural and even religious identities would, however, have to be understood in a non-essentialist, non-exclusive and non-hierarchical manner. The reason for the respecification of the meaning of internationalism will become clearer when discussing solidarity below.

The most active agents in the new wave of internationalism are in the intermediate wage-earning or wage-dependent strata. These are categories that are historically descended from the nineteenth-century educated middle class, and that are intermediate – and mediate – between the masses (workers, peasants, petty-producers, women, 'ethnics') on the one hand and the ruling/owning elites on the other. It is thus not too misleading or contradictory to call this a middle-class and democratic internationalism.

Given that internationalization processes operate within, and create, different national or bloc conditions, the particular local syndrome will differ, as will the priority of problems and the nature of the internationalist forces (Arrighi, Hopkins and Wallerstein, 1989; Frank and Fuentes, 1987). The nineteenth-century socialist model of worker–worker solidarity, based on 'immediate economic' self-interest of the class and the common 'long-term political' interest of society, is not the typical one today. Contemporary internationalism is highly complex and differentiated in nature. It is commonly *from* the industrialist capitalist West, or *by* the intermediate strata here *for* the masses there, or *between* different sorts of movements (in the 1980s between the Western peace movement and the Eastern human rights movement). Whilst the absence of mass (worker, women, peasant, ethnic minority) internationalism remains a problem, the multiplicity and diversity of internationalism represents a considerable potential. It is, indeed, essential today, even if it was possible to deny this previously, to talk of internationalism*s* in the plural and to recognize the pluralism as essential to the meaning of a contemporary internationalism.

Solidarity

By solidarity I mean a community of interests, feelings and actions. This is the more general ethical value and human relationship underlying internationalism. International solidarity (cf. Vos, 1976) should be taken to mean not only an expression or striving for human *identity*, but also *reciprocity* (mutual advantage), *affinity* (shared feelings), *complementarity* (differential contribution) and *substitutionism* (taking the part or place of the other).[1] Solidarity has customarily been understood in terms of identity, principally that of an oppressed and divided class or category in opposition to a united oppressing force. The connection with universalism is evident, so also with the third term in the French Revolution's lay trinity – liberty, equality, fraternity (the sexist nature of which is significant). If the bourgeoisie and liberalism prioritized political liberty, the proletariat and socialism have prioritized economic equality, for the first solidarity was understood primarily in national terms, and the second in class terms. In the first case, in other words, solidarity referred to that of the nation, in the second to that of the class. In both cases solidarity was subordinated to the other term and was exclusionary in practice.

It is, of course, the term 'solidarity' that provides us with a positive, democratic and humanistic linkage between internationalism, nationalism and local or specific communitarianisms. The five-point specification does not include competition, hierarchy, authoritarianism or coercion. It is, implicitly, in opposition, or an alternative, to these. A Cuban, Jewish, lesbian, or Ford worker solidarity that expressed the five values in its internal practices and external relations would either itself be, or be consistent with, internationalism. This argument is further developed in Chapter 7.

Subjects and Purposes

Whilst the proletariat, or industrial/geographical sections of such, does provide one possible base and force for a certain kind of internationalism, it was not the unique one in the past and is not the primary one today. Where capitalism was once industrial and national, it is now social and global. This implies that questions of solidarity practice, subverting or pointing beyond capitalism/state-nationalism, can arise in and from contradictions within market, state, civil and cultural/identity relations. My choice below of consumer/co-operative, migrant and human rights movements is in one sense quite arbitrary (where are peace, ecology and women?). In another sense it is pertinent, since each of these had early expression within the labour movement, and today they both lie close to it, could transform it, and open out toward civil society more generally.

Mass Subjects of Internationalism

There are no natural, spontaneous, economically determined subjects or vanguards of internationalism. Proletarians may have been, may be now and might be again. But whilst internationalization processes show the growing significance of the international sphere, and suggest or provoke internationalist responses, they evidently do not encourage or force them. In the face of internationalization processes, options other than internationalism are clearly available. For labour today these options include the continuation of traditional reformist strategies . . .

and a conservative and isolating protectionism, chauvinism, racism, fundamentalism or local sectionalism (Gordon and Reilly, 1986; Peij-nenburg and Ridgers, 1987; Picciotto, 1984). Could it not be that it is precisely because of their central role within the internationalization of capital that multinational workers could be both those most aware of the necessity for internationalism and those who have most difficulty in realizing it? Let us move away from production and consider the social practice of consumption, the capitalist shaping and reshaping of this, its social definition as a problem, and organized national and inter-national responses to this problem over time.

The first consumer movement was the co-operative movement of the industrial working class, taking collective action against the adultera-tion of foodstuffs and the bad quality of other necessities. This was a class option, with co-operatives linked organically to the rest of the labour movement. Already in the late nineteenth century there was formed a co-operative international (Gurney, 1988). But this move-ment, nationally and internationally, was increasingly affected by the 'divisions of labour', with unions, parties and co-operatives separated and separately institutionalized and incorporated. Co-operative inter-nationalism took increasingly liberal and bourgeois forms, whilst remaining linked to a 'labour culture' (Horne, 1986: 166–74) of a subordinate nature. The consumer movement of the 1950s was of middle-class origin and liberal-democratic inspiration but addressed the problems of a developed capitalist society. It was initially concerned with overcoming 'abuses' and it took a pressure-group form nationally and internationally. In so far, however, as whole populations and the whole world have been subjected to industrialized and multination-alized mass-consumption goods, the new phenomenon has taken on certain mass movement characteristics, with connections being made to international strategies of multinational companies, to worker health and safety, to environmental issues, and to the special position of women. To what extent this is or could be an internationalist (anti-capitalist, anti-statist) movement, a mass movement, and one that moved from defence or amelioration toward the offering of alternative consumption models, is a matter for investigation and engagement.

Whilst, evidently, socialists and the labour movement were deeply involved with the traditional co-operative movement, one is not aware of their specific presence within – or even in alliance with – the contemporary consumer movement. It is a feminist who has reminded

us of consumption as an international problem requiring an internationalist response (Mies, 1986), although without consideration of
existing consumer movements, national or international. Self-
recognition as a consumer, the nature of that self-recognition, the
manner in which this self-perception is expressed nationally and internationally, the connections between the self as consumer and the self as
worker or woman, the alliances made with the Third World or union
movement, are all matters to be settled by those engaged. So is the
question of whether the movement seeks solutions within or amongst
existing nation-state and social models or proposes an alternative one.

The notion of migrants as an international*ist* force (Galtung, 1980) is
one of the most startling propositions and one that cannot be fully
explored here. Migration is thought of primarily as an important effect
or process of internationaliz*ation*. International labour migration is a
typically capitalist process which, like so many others, was uncritically
adopted – if in typically statist form – within the 'world socialist market'.
The bearers of this process, the immigrants, are customarily seen as
noble but tragic victims (Berger and Mohr, 1975) or defined as a social
problem. Thus, in typical nation-statist discourse, we have not a 'racist
problem' but an 'immigrant problem'. Traditional labour movements,
whether of Marxist or Social Democratic inspiration, consider that
these foreign, semi-proletarianized workers have to be naturalized and
then absorbed into the existing national labour movement (Castells,
1979). That the decision to migrate is a *choice* (even if a forced and
painful one), that immigrants successfully struggle, individually and
collectively, to survive and that they are in certain countries and at
certain times more radical than local labourers does not usually lead
socialists or labour movements to recognize their potential to liberate
the native labour force from its nativism. It would seem worthwhile
exploring the potential of immigrant workers as internationalist subjects, given that they combine within their persons, positions and life
trajectories the Third World labourer (often rural), the First World
worker, the discriminated ethnic and the trans-state national. The
multiple identities and interests of migrants would then be seen as
being of positive value to the kind of polyvalent labour internationalism
necessary to an increasingly internationalized world of labour.

Let us consider another case, that of the international human-rights
movement (Eide, 1986). This is one of the most powerful and influential internationalist movements today, capable of forcing concessions

from the world's most powerful and most repressive regimes. The Soviet Union's release of dissidents in the 1980s must be understood as a concession to this movement, albeit as mediated by the United States government. What, or who, is the subject of this movement? I propose that it be conceived as the citizen (cf. Alexander, 1991; Nerfin, 1986). Self-definition as a (would-be) citizen means a demand for the 'priority of free and public political activity over other types of human action', to borrow from Feher and Heller (1987: 3) on republicanism. Although the citizen is originally the literal subject of the city-state and later that of the nation-state, this is a universal subject with a universalizable demand (something we return to in Chapter 7). Self-definition as a citizen seems to me potentially different from self-definition as a national, with its inbuilt particularism or exclusionism. I have earlier suggested that labour internationalism might have been most effective when it was least proletarian. What this recognition leads to is the idea that citizen consciousness was highly developed amongst workers or, more likely, that a combination of a worker- with a citizen-subjectivity gave the latter a sharper cutting edge, a popular appeal. International labour movement divisions, between those subordinated to 'the free West' and those subordinated to 'the socialist world', meant that international citizen movements (Amnesty International, etc.) were again created on a middle-class, Western and liberal basis. As Feher and Heller (1987: 31, 43–7) argue, the British Trade Union Congress, and various other Western socialist politicians and publicists, were either unsupportive of, or hostile towards, Solidarnosc in Poland. This would have been either because they considered the Communist states as meaningfully socialist or because they understood internationalism in terms of 'peaceful coexistence' – a relationship between states/blocs. Whilst national and international trade union movements are now working more closely with the human rights movement, an intimate articulation between a citizen and working-class internationalism has still to be realized.

It is not possible to discuss all the present or possible subjects of internationalism. There has been a Green International of peasants (Wilczynski, 1981) and I see no reason why it might not revive. A world conference of independent 'fish harvesters' was announced for 1997 in India, where there has been a recent history of their self-organization both locally and nationally (Labour File, 1996). There exist international organizations of indigenous peoples and linkages between regional independence or separatist movements. But it does seem to me that these can be effectively internationalist only in so far as they act, or see themselves, as part of a citizen internationalism. Whilst, further, their territorial identity might seem to lead them towards micro-nationalism and micro-statism, they do represent a current critique or denial of nation-statism (Williams, 1983). In so far, therefore, as they propose inter-territorial relations between non-state communities, they undermine nation-state sovereignty and increase the plurality of inter-territorial relations.

One can imagine the appearance of new mass internationalisms, as common problems are identified, common interests declared and effective forms of national and international communication and organization found. What of the possibility of the development of schoolchildren's internationalism (Stefanik, 1993; Waterman, 1987) into an autonomous children's internationalism?

Purposes or Aims

I want here to talk about ends in a manner that does not reduce the matter to listings or over-generalize in terms that are losing their capacity to explain, inspire and move anything or anybody. The binary oppositions 'utopian:scientific' or 'reformist:revolutionary' neither explain, nor excite – nor even frighten very much any more – but the totalizing projects or world views behind them (for even the infinitely plastic, pragmatic and opportunistic Social Democracy represents these) seem to have had the effect of frightening off. The new internationalisms are marked not only by their plurality but by their often self-limited fields and purposes. The classical example might be Amnesty, with aims, structures and procedures that allow it considerable effectivity but within a limited field. But we also have other new internationalisms *with* a world view, and particularly from certain ecological socialists (Brecher, 1987) and ecological socialist feminists (Bandarage, 1987, 1991; Mellor, 1992; Mies, 1986). It might be in the spirit of a holistic approach to recognize the complementary role of both the narrow/limited/pragmatic and the broad/general/imaginative internationalisms. The problem with the competing traditional international labour-movement or socialist ideologies lay not in their opposition but in the institutionalization of their world views in national or international party and union organizations with hegemonic pretensions, and in the reinforcement of these world views with all the carrots and sticks that the modern nation-state (or inter-state organization) has at its disposal. In so far as the world views of the contemporary internationalists are opposed to capital, state, racism and patriarchy, even the most wide-ranging, far-reaching and compelling world view or utopia can come over only as one contribution to a dialogue, and will have to meet the hard-nosed pragmatism of the little internationalisms.

Having said this, I will put in a plea for more internationalist utopias, by which I mean imaginative and comprehensive models of a world order constructed on radically different principles from our existing one. These utopias are necessary not only because of the stimulation to thought and the inspiration for action that they provide, but also because of the necessity to provide some general guide or framework for the – possibly conflicting – internationalisms of, say, the women's and the workers' movements. This, again, is a matter we will return to in Chapter 7.

Forms

By forms I mean three basic aspects of collective internationalist activity. These are

1   the space or field in which they occur;
2   their organizational type or model;
3   their geographical direction and scope.

I make no special claim for this specification, distinction or order of presentation – except to say that this task has not yet been carried out and that even initial reflection upon them can lead towards sharper analysis and more effective activity.

Space, Field and Target

It may be useful to distinguish a specific space or level of inter-nationalist activity and to then recognize the specificity of the field and the targets at which it is aimed. We cannot simply think in terms of levels (local, national, international). I would suggest distinguishing between at least three different spheres at these levels: the socio-cultural, the political and the economic. Action in the socio-cultural sphere is addressed to citizens, is intended to change attitudes and behaviour, and to increase social power. Action in the political sphere is addressed to the nation-state, inter-state and other statified organs. It is aimed, in the first place, at officials and representatives and is concerned not simply with changing their attitudes and behaviour but at democratization – de-statification, de-bureaucratization. Action in the economic sphere (where separate from the state) is addressed to capital, particularly to its most powerful instances and agents.

The sphere of political action at international level is clear. This would be action within and against the inter-state organs, forcing, for example, the Food and Agriculture Organization (FAO) to get rid of the TNC lobby – or at least to name it as such. The sphere of what I have called socio-cultural action is exemplified by Greenpeace, addressing itself to and creating international public opinion by dramatic activities covered by the international media. The sphere of economic action would, for me, mean action within production, exchange, distribution and consumption; thus, not simply a campaign within the FAO (political) targeting TNCs, nor a film concerned with environmental pollution (social), but action, for example, within TNCs, aimed at decentralization, increased worker rights, better working conditions, socially useful and environmentally friendly products. The different spheres and levels, it should be understood, are determined by capitalist modernization and are therefore themselves instruments of division and control. Popular activity is aimed at breaking these down. 'Economic' action within the sphere of consumption is thus, also, a 'socialization' of consumption and a critique of consumptionism – or of an economistic understanding of consumption. But recognizing a presently existent economic sphere enables us to recognize the specific and essential role of workers – particularly those within TNCs – if the corporations are to be controlled.

Organizational Type or Model

It is evident that in distinguishing our understanding of internationalism from that of the traditional labour movement we also need to develop means consistent with the new definition. It would here be useful to distinguish between four types of organization at international level. These would be the *transnational* (restricted to the TNCs), the *inter-state*, the *inter-non-governmental* (differing from the definition in

Galtung, 1980, by the exclusion of TNCs) and the *internationalist* (pluralistic in membership, democratic in structure and functioning). This typology is evidently value-loaded, with the most dynamic, conservative and authoritarian type at one end and the most dynamic, progressive and democratic type at the other. The spectrum allows recognition of the ambiguous position of the two intermediate types and thus avoids posing either as the centre or goal of internationalist activity. I would want to make the internationalist type the primary category, seeking to further its development and acting through this against, on or within the others. We can already, for example, recognize the progressive and dynamic role being played by internationalist worker organizations and networks,[2] contrasting this with the highly ambiguous role played by the dominant international trade union bodies. We do not have to assume the disappearance of the more conservative types for the development of a more democratic international order. The growth of what I have called internationalist bodies itself already restricts the hegemony of TNCs and the domination of inter-statism.

Another useful distinction for internationalist activity is that between coercion, resource mobilization and legitimation mobilization (Willets, 1982). We may follow Willets in recognizing the existing power of internationalist movements in the last sphere. We might, however, wish to point out that internationalist movements not only act in this sphere, but attempt to enlarge it at the expense of the others. This does not necessarily mean that internationalist movements do or will confine themselves to information provision or persuasion. Armed assistance to democratic regimes (as, for example, to Spain 1936–9), or assistance to armed liberation movements (Hamon and Rotman, 1981; Perrault, 1987) could be included, when carried out independent of states. So must the attempts to create non-capitalist, non-statist trade relations. Such activity can, today, be subordinated to the effort to disarm, to enlarge the public sphere and to reincorporate production and decision-making into the daily life of the citizen. The disbanding of the West European anti-apartheid movements, or their conversion into development aid bodies, after South African 'liberation' in 1994, reflects the old national internationalism rather than a new social understanding of such.

Having recognized that much internationalist activity is initiated by middle-class people and from the West, we must again prioritize the exchange of information and ideas in internationalist relations. This is because of the danger of reproducing the very inequalities internationalism is intended to overcome, or at least of creating patron–client relations between the 'donors' and 'receivers' of international support. This is a problem built into the aid relationship. In so far as we are concerned with social knowledge in terms of its possession by, or use to, masses, then knowledge of the 'other' (including experiences, beliefs and aspirations) is essential to 'us' and of similar value as knowledge of 'us' is to 'them'. This is not, of course, to deny existing inequalities in access to, or control over, information but to draw attention to an understanding of knowledge that already finds some expression in the activities and projects of international movements. If, in Bhopal, 'they' had obtained the internationally available information and experience, then perhaps Bhopal's Union Carbide disaster would not have happened. If 'we' do not learn from Bhopal (including the limitations on the alternative movements there, as shown in Visvanathan and Kothari, 1985) we will have Bhopals here.

Having prioritized communication, it is only natural to prioritize a dialogical relationship. Dialogue differs from debate in that it is non-competitive and is concerned with self-discovery rather than domination of the partner. Dialogue assumes and furthers equality. It assumes and furthers trust. Given the increasing importance of information to power and the extent to which we are moving from an industrialized society to an information society, the priority of communication for and to internationalism become even more evident. This issue will also be returned to in Chapter 7.

Direction and Scope

The populist imperialist Rudyard Kipling talked of the colonized peoples as 'lesser breeds without the law'. He urged his British readers to 'take up the white man's burden'. It is not irrelevant to our subject to point out the extent to which the new internationalism is addressed to those *without* (without human rights, women's organizations, free trade unions) by those *with* (cf. Helie-Lucas, 1991). Those young French radicals who came to help independent Algeria after the French colonial *pieds noirs* (black feet) left were quickly dubbed *pieds rouges* (red feet) by the sceptical lesser breeds. This suggests the crucial importance of axis and direction for the meaning of a new internationalism. If the axis is *limited* to that of North–South and the direction is *only* from North to South, then it is likely to be a lopsided international solidarity, inspired primarily by substitutionism (cf. the charity motivation behind Western aid activities, as shown in Hart, 1987, Simpson, 1985 and Sogge, 1996). On the other hand, it would be idealistic to insist that we can only speak about internationalism when the activity under consideration occurs between and within *all* significant world areas. International problems, international awareness and internationalist organization and action simply do not arise in this way. Yet again, however, 'recipients' of such one-way solidarity are going to be increasingly resentful, suspicious and eventually hostile towards an international paternalism that reproduces the national paternalism of rich and powerful do-gooders. It is therefore necessary to have an ideal or norm concerning direction. The same is true of scope. It might seem that international solidarity between those in a common or similar situation would be the best founded and longest lived. Yet such an international anti-nuclear campaign (European Nuclear Disarmament [END], for example) ran the danger of appearing to represent a *European* common interest separate from or even opposed to a wider anti-nuclear or peace movement. Whilst END might well have represented a solidarity of identity or reciprocity between those involved, a global norm is necessary. Universal norms, in other words, enable us to identify limitations and suggest a direction for development. Let us consider this further.

Concerned primarily with the traditional liberal rights of opinion, speech, movement, organization, fair trial and humane punishment, Amnesty is based on the world area where these are best established and addressed primarily to those in which they are not (although it concerns itself with 'abuses' in liberal democracies also). We saw this pattern (primarily West to South/East) momentarily supplemented by an East to South pattern as human rights activists in Eastern Europe came out publicly and forcefully against loans to Pinochet's Chile (letter to *New York Review of Books*, 11 June 1987). We might not have seen East Europeans come out in solidarity with struggles against increasing surveillance and repression in the West. But it was Yugoslav theorists who first produced a conceptualization of human rights which treated the Western norms as necessary but insufficient, and which rejected any existing model in favour of an international struggle for a possible and necessary alternative (Belgrade Praxis Group, 1978). This case suggests the manner in which direction and scope relate to purpose or aim. Human rights internationalism needs to be based on a radical critique of all existing social models, and on a universalizable alternative, if it is to identify common interests and inspire common activity worldwide.

Internal Relations

Here I want to talk about the role of

1 the 'relational model' necessary for internationalist organization;
2 the role of leaders; and
3 the role of the intelligentsia.

Here again I am simply noting and distinguishing aspects of internationalist activity generally ignored in the limited literature on internationalism. Once again I suggest that even such a pragmatic survey could enrich both reflection and activity.

Relational Model

We must be concerned with the development of an appropriate relational model for a new kind of internationalism. This means certain principles of organization and of behaviour between participants. The earlier distinction between types of international organization (transnational, inter-state, inter-non-governmental, internationalist) are a necessary starting point, but the identification of an organization as internationalist only sets it off from the others. Exactly how are pluralism and democracy to be expressed and ensured? Surpassal of the principal of representative democracy (one member organization for each nation-state) is itself subversive of the traditional model (cf. Galtung, 1980). Another step would be the prioritizing of the international *movement* over the international *organization*. In a sense this is already happening, since there are, for example, too many international human-rights organizations for one to monopolize the field. This suggests two more points. The first is that relations between such organizations would have to be primarily co-operative in nature. The second is that there would have to be recognition that the movement is more than the organizations, since unorganized and unstructured activity can and frequently does lead to innovation.

The development of the kind of openness and flexibility suggested above is favoured by the primary activity-type mentioned earlier – that of communication. It is further favoured by the new information technologies and the increasing centrality of information to social life (Waterman, 1992a). Networking is the traditional and primary form of human communication, continuing to exist today despite the increasing structuring, separation and hierarchization of human relationships (see further in Chapter 7). Informal networking continues within, between and outside organizations, which, indeed, cannot be understood in terms of their formal structures and rules. Whilst those who developed and sell the new electronic media are concerned primarily with control and consumption, the technologies have possibilities that subvert these intentions. The democratic and decentralizing potential of these means of communication are infinitely greater than those of the railways or air transport, both of which imply centralization and concentration in ownership, production and power. The democratic possibilities of the new electronic media are not confined to 'alternative' media uses, although internationalist movements are actively promoting these. It is a matter of the state- or capital-controlled mass media also. It may, for example, be thanks to the capitalist and state media that Peruvian labour activists had to make up their own minds about Solidarnosc in Poland, since much of the Left media in Peru was engaged in ideological concealment or packaging exercises with respect to Poland (Waterman, 1992b). It is difficult, to take another example, to imagine Greenpeace having any significant international impact without the services of the dominant international media (Wapner, 1995).

Alternative *organization* cannot, of course, depend primarily on piggy-backing the dominant media. It requires movement developed and movement controlled means. Examination of the international campaign around Bhopal would show the extent to which this depended on rapid, flexible and co-operative networking between individuals and groups, using movement media as well as those of capital and state (telephone, telex, mail, etc.). The attempt to develop a standard for the manual and computerized recording and transmission of human rights information is inspired by the attempt to increase both co-ordination and decentralization. So are the experiments to create international computer networks for grass-roots oriented groups and movements (Waterman, 1992a).

In prioritizing internationalist organizations we cannot ignore the international non-governmental organizations (INGOs). This is not simply because the two types obviously overlap, but also because of the extent to which INGOs express, stimulate or support internationalist feelings and activities. I think we need to recognize the dramatic growth of the INGO phenomenon as an expression both of the failure of state and inter-state organizations to directly dominate society and an attempt to indirectly do so. The ambiguity of the NGO phenomenon provides an opportunity for national and international social movements. Just as we can conceive of a movement from a charity and aid (Simpson, 1985) to a solidarity relationship (Muto, 1983) on the North–South axis, so can we conceive of a movement from an NGO to a social movement type of organization. Some international organizations combine the characteristics of not simply internationalist and inter-non-governmental organizations but, possibly, of inter-state organizations too. The International Organization of Consumer Unions (IOCU) – which has traded in its pedestrian title for the more activist-sounding Consumers International, or CI – includes state financed consumer councils, independent consumer organizations and others. It represents consumer interests to inter-state agencies. In the Asian/Pacific area, and in Malaysia in particular, however, it seems to take on movement-type characteristics (Sim, 1991).

In discussing organization it is also essential that we talk about money. The ideal, of course, is activity totally financed by the movements and individuals concerned. But self-financing, which may be typical for, let us say, Trotskyist internationalisms, is not a guarantee of solidarity as we have defined it. A Dutch Third World aid and solidarity organization may be totally independent of state funding and still reproduce characteristics of state-dependent aid agencies. On the other hand, there may be organizations, networks and publications that are largely dependent on subsidies from churches, aid agencies and even state or inter-state agencies. This does not necessarily prevent them from developing internationalist activities. Here the crucial issue is honesty and openness about sources of funding. Some Third World NGOs dependent on Western agencies are prepared to talk openly about their funding. This is some guarantee of responsibility. Admission of financial dependence on NGO or state funds may also be an admission that one is involved in internationalism *for* workers or women rather than workers' or women's internationalism. But such an admission at least points one in the direction of a solution.

Honesty about funding raises the question of openness in general. There is a powerful nineteenth-century conspiratorial tradition that still affects some internationalist activity. Conspiratorial activity is inevitably that of an elite or elect. It reproduces the practice of dominant elites, the major communication strategy of which is not 'manipulation' (which all communication inevitably implies); it is denial of access to full or crucial information. A non-international case – but from a formally socialist and internationalist organization – makes the point. The British Communist Party (late, and lamented only by romantic revolutionaries) provided neither the public nor its own members with full information about its Executive Committee meetings. When reconstructing a podium in its headquarters, in the 1970s, it discovered a radio transmitter that must have been placed there several years earlier. The British state security (and possibly its American cousins) had full and detailed information about Executive Committee meetings. Only the party membership and public were denied this (for another British Comunist Party case, see *The Guardian*, 15 November 1991). An ideal or principle of openness does not mean one ignores the necessity for confidentiality or even secrecy. What it does imply is that the areas and types of restriction necessary to protect organizations and individuals in danger are defined and justified. And that energy is primarily directed towards enlarging the possibility for public operation.

Leaders and Organizers

We should here distinguish middle-class membership of international organizations and movements from middle-class leadership of – say – working-class or women's internationalism (cf. Mies, 1986; Mitter, 1986). The nature of the problem that such leadership represents depends on the form of organization chosen, the leadership strategy, and the honesty and openness – again – with which middle-class leaders are prepared to speak and act. The common new organizational form that leadership of mass internationalism takes is that of either the general resource-group, or the specific media or education group. Adoption of such a role by professional or technical specialists is customarily a conscious rejection of the role of Leninist vanguard or Fabian elite. In so far as it is such an option, middle-class leaders will provide technical expertise but refuse to act as spokespersons, organizers or representatives. They will concentrate, further, on consciousness-raising, skill-creation and self-empowerment amongst those they are working with. This is, of course, still an intermediary role and often a crucial one. Resource groups can, in practice, reproduce the traditional elite roles, substituting for the masses, speaking in their name. It is probably, therefore, helpful if we distinguish the internationalism of *socialists* (who tend to consider themselves as leaders even when they have no followers) from the internationalism of *workers*. Similarly with feminists and women. This is evidently not to disparage either middle-class, socialist or feminist internationalism. It is a matter of recognizing the difference of position and interest between middle and working classes, socialists and unionists, feminists and housewives. In the case of Bhopal, internationalism was largely a matter of communication and support between middle-class leaders or intermediaries. If there have been any significant international contacts between rank and file activists from Union Carbide plants or communities worldwide, they have not come to international attention. On the other hand, international labour resource groups have managed to set up meetings and networks of factory-level leaderships within certain industries or particular TNCs. Such experiences require full recording and analysis.

The Intelligentsia

It might seem invidious to distinguish intellectuals from organizers – who often anyway have a university education. This is not a matter of denying the intellectual role of organizers, nor the capacity of ordinary women, workers and citizens to generate knowledge and understanding autonomously. It is a matter of recognizing the division of labour within which are created specialists in thinking, specialists in specialization, specialists in generalization. It is also to recognize the possible role of intellectuals as a socially critical and independent category – the meaning of the nineteenth-century Polish word, 'inteligentsja'. The major institutional base for such people today is in waged work within increasingly commercialized and industrialized education and research institutes. This differentiates them from their largely self-employed nineteenth-century forebears and brings them marginally closer to other working people. In so far as these intellectuals do not confine themselves to the production of ever more specialized and isolated pieces of information (Horne, 1986: 38–42, 76–81), and in so far as they do not confine themselves to creating national or racial meaning (Scottish nationalism, Black nationalism), their vision can be historical and international. Even arch-anti-internationalist Tom Nairn (1980) concedes the international nature of culture and the necessary internationalism of intellectuals. It seems likely that in the Soviet Union of the 1980s the most internationalist force was an intelligentsia starved of the information and dialogue necessary to liberate its society from the stultifying effects of nationalist, collectivist autarchy. Solidarity between foreign and Soviet-bloc intellectuals was probably more effective than any other solidarity apart from that with Jews as an ethno-religious community and certain Christian religions or sects.

Even if culture is more international than capital and class, even if intellectuals are the most internationalist and the most effectively so, this is no guarantee that they will contribute to an internationalism of peoples rather than an internationalism of the intellect and intellectuals. But they could do so, and the organizers and leaders should invite them, or cajole them, to so do.

Towards a New Labour and Socialist Internationalism?

The new understanding developed above should itself enable us to look at labour internationalism in a radically different way. But what is also required is a specification of our new understanding *for* workers, unions and socialist activists. Here I will first do a brief case study using the new understanding, and then try to specify more systematically the meaning of a new labour and socialist internationalism.

Solidarity with Guatemalan Coca-Cola Workers

The case for study is that of international solidarity with Guatemalan Coca-Cola workers. The source is the first English language report to give an overview of the affair (Gatehouse and Reyes, 1987). The case is summarized thus on the back cover of their booklet:

> For nine years the 450 workers at the Coca Cola bottling plant in Guatemala City fought a battle with their employers for their jobs, their trade union and their lives. Three times they occupied the plant – on the last occasion for thirteen months. Three General Secretaries of their union were murdered

and five other workers killed. Four more were kidnapped and have disappeared.

Against all the odds they survived, thanks to their own extraordinary courage and help from fellow trade unionists in Guatemala and around the world. A huge international campaign of protests and boycotts was central to their struggle. As a result the Coca Cola workers forced concessions from one of the world's largest multinational food giants, and kept the Guatemalan trade-union movement alive through a dark age of government repression.

We will consider this case in detail.

First, then, let us see what mileage we can get out of the definitions and distinctions. *Internationalization*: Coca-Cola is, surely, the best-known symbol of capitalist internationalization, economically and culturally; it is one of the world's top 100 companies, operating in 155 of the world's 168 countries, controlling 44 per cent of the world soft drinks market. *Universalism*: it was certain US churches that in 1977 began the international campaign, thus reminding us of the ancient sources of contemporary internationalism. *Cosmopolitanism*: that of Coca-Cola is self-evident, less so that of, for example, Dan Gallin, Romanian-born, US-educated, Geneva-based and multilingual General Secretary of the International Union of Food and Allied Workers' Associations (IUF), who played a key personal role in the solidarity campaign. *Internationalism*: although the solidarity campaign was primarily that of unions and workers, it was the US churches that initiated it, and Gallin first visited Guatemala as a member of an Amnesty – not a union – delegation. *Solidarity*: the concern of both Western middle-class and working-class supporters of the campaign was, presumably, to take the side of, or stand in for, the Coca-Cola workers – i.e. to substitute for them; in the case of the Mexican Coca-Cola workers who took action we can assume identification.

Second, subjects and purposes. *Subjects*: the major mass actors at both ends were workers, but the issue was first taken up in the West as a citizen (human rights) one; whether the Swedish and British Coca-Cola workers considered themselves to be acting as workers, as citizens, or both, would be an interesting matter for investigation; even if the main mass actors were workers, there is certainly no explicit socialist organizational or ideological note evident. *Purposes*: the aim of securing liberal human and union rights for the Guatemalan workers seems simultaneously broad and narrow, broad in its transformatory implications for

Guatemalan society, relatively narrow in those for Western workers and societies (though evidently broader than action restricted to wages and conditions within the company or industry); within the West the energetic and effective union action represents a labour claim for recognition as a force for human liberation internationally.

Third, forms. *Space*: the Western unions acted forcefully at local, national and international (TNC) level; they also acted in all three earlier-noted spheres, addressing themselves to public opinion (using union-made films), to the Guatemalan state (threatening arms, aid and tourist boycotts) and to the company (hitting production through strikes, and sales through consumer boycotts). *Organizational type*: the main international actors were such non-governmental organizations as the IUF and Amnesty, the presence of what I have called 'internationalist' organizations not being prominent; action in the economic (TNC) and socio-cultural spheres predominated. *Direction*: the axis and direction was West–South; Western union and solidarity organization funds (War on Want in the UK) were evidently essential to the Guatemalan workers, but so were solidarity messages and union visits to the occupied plant (i.e. communication); there is no evidence that the Western unionists involved gained anything from the Guatemalans, that they even had in their minds the same questions which the action raised in the admiring but puzzled mind of Ron Todd, then General Secretary of the Transport and General Workers Union in the UK:

> How did the Coca Cola workers in Guatemala, against all odds, manage to win substantial concessions from a giant American company? Why did they receive so much support from other workers in their country? How was international solidarity action mobilized, and why was it so effective? (Gatehouse and Reyes, 1987: inside front cover).

Fourth, internal relations and leadership. *Relational model*: the campaign suggests effective exploitation of the dominant (as well as of alternative) media, national and international networking between concerned individuals and organizations; it suggests that where such networking involves mass mobilization it takes on social movement characteristics; whether the costs of the campaign were directly contributed by individual unionists and others, covered from organizational funds (and whether these were member donated) requires investigation. *Leaders*: we must recognize the initiating role of the middle-class church and human rights organizations, as well as the extent to which initiative and control remained in the hands of full-time international or national union officers; within Guatemala and in exile, Coca-Cola union lawyers (two being seriously injured, one having her daughter raped by state thugs) played a crucial supporting role in the international campaign. *Intelligentsia*: Miguel Angel Reyes, co-author of the report, was not only a former legal adviser to union and Indian organizations but author of a longer Spanish work on the case, a university lecturer, and later a graduate researcher in the UK.

I fear that the condensed analysis above robs the case of its horror, its heroism and its human qualities more generally. There are also elements in the brochure which cannot be handled by the concepts so far developed. There is, for example, the particular vulnerability of Coca-Cola as product and company (Gatehouse and Reyes, 1987: 16). There is the fact that this was a campaign on essential human rights, not on union rights, or worker wages and conditions more narrowly. The handling of these and other elements requires a conceptualization drawn directly from the literature on labour internationalism historically and contemporaneously. This follows immediately.

Thirteen Propositions on a New Labour Internationalism[3]

My understanding of the new labour internationalism (NLI) follows from the arguments in this and earlier chapters. It assumes, more specifically:

1   the weak position of the labour movement in a period of world economic crisis, the introduction of new technologies and products, and of the repeated restructuring of the labour force nationally and internationally;
2   a rejection of the general response of the state and inter-state organs to these crises;
3   a critique of the inadequacy of the dominant traditional union, labour and socialist organizations and ideologies in confronting this situation.

It comes, more positively, from reflection on the successes booked by the internationalism of the ASMs and such labour cases as that of Coca-Cola. Rejecting much of the form, content and procedures of the traditional labour internationals, I would argue that the NLI implies:

1   moving from the international relations of union or other officials towards face-to-face relations of concerned labouring people at the shop-floor, community or grass-roots level;

2   surpassing dependence on the centralized, bureaucratic and rigid model of the pyramidical international organization by stimulating the self-empowering, decentralized, horizontal, democratic and flexible model of the international information network;

3   moving from an 'aid model' (one-way flows of money and material from the 'rich, powerful, free' unions, workers or others), to a 'solidarity model' (two-way or multidirectional flows of political support, information and ideas);

4   moving from verbal declarations, appeals and conferences to political activity, creative work, visits, or direct financial contributions (which will continue to be necessary) by the working people concerned;

5   surpassing an 'export solidarity' model by practising 'international solidarity at home', combating the local causes/effects of international exploitation and repression;

6   generalizing the solidarity ethic by combating national, racial, political, religious, ideological and gender discrimination amongst working people locally;

7   basing international solidarity on the expressed daily needs, values and capacities of ordinary working people, not simply on those of their representatives;

8   recognizing that whilst labour is not the privileged bearer of internationalism, it is essential to it, and therefore links up with other democratic internationalisms so as to reinforce wage-labour struggles *and* surpass a workerist internationalism;

9   overcoming ideological, political and financial dependency in international solidarity work by financing internationalist activities from worker or publicly collected funds, and carrying out independent research activities and policy formulation;

10 replacing the political/financial coercion, the private collusion and public silences of the traditional internationalisms with a frank, friendly, constructive and public discourse of equals, made available to interested workers;

11 requiring of involved intellectuals, professionals and officials that they are open about their own interests, motives and roles, that they speak with workers and take on a service and training role, rather

than that of political leaders or official ideologists;

12 recognizing that there is no single site or level of international struggle and that, whilst the shop floor, grass roots and community may be the base, the traditional formal terrains can be used and can also be influenced;

13 recognizing that the development of a new internationalism requires contributions from and discussion with labour movements in West, East and South, as well as within and between other socio-geographic regions.

This detailed specification could, possibly, be used for further reflection on the Coca-Cola case (described but not analysed in Frundt, 1987). It could also, possibly, be adapted and applied to the study of other (would-be) internationalist subjects, organizations and campaigns.

The Possible Meanings of a New Socialist Internationalism

It seems to me that there are three possible faces of a new socialist internationalism. These would be either

1 simply the internationalism of labour;
2 the internationalism of socialists; or
3 *the* internationalism.

Whilst I have a particular problem with the last of these, I see them as possibly complementary but each of them as internally contradictory. What this means is that we have to make choices respecting each of them and respecting relations between each of them. What I am concerned with, obviously, is developing a positive dialectic between the three, but let us initially consider each of them separately.

First, then, *socialist internationalism as the internationalism of labour*. Let us consider an argument by analogy: a socialist internationalism which did *not* prioritize the labour–capital conflict would, surely, be like a feminist internationalism which did not prioritize the struggle of women against patriarchy. Hypothetically, such a socialist internationalism might evolve into some kind of general ethical or political internationalism. But it would then, surely, be no longer a particularly socialist one. Let us consider the matter more positively. A prioritization of the labour–capital conflict internationally would not only continue the distinct socialist tradition, it would provide a major necessary addition to the internationalisms of the ASMs. In the past two decades, socialist organizations, intellectuals and activists have failed to take labour internationalism seriously, either in providing theory, proposing strategy or carrying out political activity. Developing a new kind of labour internationalism would allow, moreover, for the possibility of a reciprocal or complementary internationalism, instead of – or in addition to – the substitution internationalism implied by Western socialist solidarity with Southern nationalist or Eastern democratic struggles.

Second, *socialist internationalism as the internationalism of socialists.* Here we may again consider an argument by analogy. What is called 'international solidarity between women' or 'the international women's movement' is largely, and primarily, the international solidarity of feminists. The conferences, communications and campaigns identified as the three crucial aspects of women's internationalism by Bernard (1987: chs 7, 8, 9) are largely organized by feminists, or they are mediated by feminists, even where they may be directed to poor urban, working-class or peasant women. This relationship (in point of fact, as Chapter 6 will show, a number of varied and complex relationships between different kinds of feminists and feminisms) represents in the first place an affinity solidarity – an international community of ideas, feelings and desires. Socialist internationalism has always contained this element, for decades obstructed by the identification of socialists with a 'state of affairs' (a nation-state) or an 'ideal' (ideology), rather than with the 'real movement which abolishes the present state of things' (see Chapter 2, note 3). Since the collapse of one such state of affairs and ideals in 1989, international discussions on the future of socialism internationally have been taking place energetically,[4] though often in traditional fora (the Fourth International), or treading the traditional pedals (Miliband, Panitch and Saville, 1990). The sense of defeat or defence that hangs over *these* international debates suggests the need for socialists to learn more explicitly from the organizational forms and working style of the feminist movement. Without idealizing the latter (which is sometimes marked by the reproduction of Leninist practices), the fact is that feminists internationally have felt required to address themselves explicitly to their relationships in a way that socialists have rarely done (see Chapter 6 again). With the increasing abandonment of grandiose illusions and deadly delusions, socialists will probably find their relations with each other internationally to be less fraught, more tolerant and even affectionate. They might even eventually recover that sense of community, and the ability to celebrate, that marks both the early socialist and many of the contemporary ASMs. Understanding that socialism is for the world, rather than vice versa, may eventually enable socialists to mock their own past attempts to fit the world into a socialist straitjacket – and therefore to come more to peace with both the world and themselves.

Third, *socialist internationalism as **the** internationalism* – as the 'vanguard' internationalism, the 'general theory' or 'most advanced form' of internationalism. I have already said that socialists have a particularly rich – though obviously complex and deeply contradictory – tradition here. I have, further, to recognize that I am, both here and elsewhere, trying as a socialist to contribute to just such a general theory and strategy of internationalism. I see, however, a major difference between wishing to be in the vanguard and being a vanguard*ist*. I can see no reason why socialists should not *attempt* to provide a general internationalist theory, or strategy, or political leadership, as long as they do not consider these an 'ontological privilege' (to borrow a potent phrase from Laclau and Mouffe, 1981: 22). They would, then, of course, find themselves on an equal footing with Internationalist Liberation Theologists, or with Feminist Internationalists. Or with the Alternative Social Movement theorists. Or 'even' with those from the tradition of World Federalism. All of these are making serious and significant contributions to the 'critique of international relations', or the creation of a new 'international civil society', or even to working-class internationalism. In the current situation, any assertion that socialist internationalism is more general in nature, or superior in quality, to those of others would seem spurious – and that is putting it with an excess of caution.

Conclusion: The Option for Radical Engagement

Perceptive readers, particularly if actually involved in efforts at labour internationalism, may be puzzled at the limited reference to political economy even in my section on internationalization above. This is not because I underestimate the necessity of such theory and analysis to an understanding of internationalism in general and labour internationalism in particular. Reference to the specificity of the Coca-Cola case above, and to that of cargo-handling in Chapter 4, indicates the importance of an equally specific understanding of the nature of individual industries and types of capital, as well as the changing nature of capitalism in general.

I have here, however, been primarily concerned with what political economy considers the 'subjective factor' or 'superstructural' (politics, ideology, culture, ethics, language, psychology). This is not simply a matter of bending the twig away from the dominant political-economic discourse. It comes from a conviction that – even in so far as industrial capitalism was 'economically determined' – other determinations are of increasing importance as we move towards a globalized information capitalism.

In an increasingly interdependent capitalist world order – one in which an increased necessity for trust is everywhere undermined by economic competition, ecological dangers and military threats – the possibility and necessity for choice is dramatically increased. Both liberal and Marxist ideologues continue to preach about the determining force of the world market (although one considers this a good thing and the other a bad one), but anyone who watches television can also see the visible international hand that directs (but repeatedly and miserably fails to control) the invisible one of world capitalism. We are therefore increasingly obliged to choose our attitudes, understandings and forms of action/inaction. The attitude of either a Candide or a Cassandra are obstacles to that which Giddens (1990: 136–7) considers necessary. In the face of a precarious situation full of life-threatening dangers, he proposes as appropriate the attitude of 'radical engagement'. Those taking this attitude hold that

> although we are beset by major problems, we can and should mobilise either to reduce their impact or to transcend them. This is an optimistic outlook, but one bound up with contestatory action rather than a faith in rational analysis and discussion. Its prime vehicle is the social movement. (Ibid.)

It is, I would add, the *international and internationalist* social movement. So far this movement has lacked not so much a capacity for political-economic analysis but historical knowledge, appropriate language and convincing argument. I hope to have provided some of the latter elements here.

Now we have to see how these work in analytical and political terms. Chapters 4 and 5 apply the understanding developed to two labour cases. The first represents an in-depth analysis of an attempt at 'shop floor internationalism'. The second represents a political intervention into an ongoing situation and discussion – and an in-breadth analysis. After we have considered the limits of the first case and the potential of the second we will consider the understanding of international solidarity coming out of one of the ASMs, that of feminism (Chapter 6). Playing that chapter off against this one will require and enable us to move forward theoretically also (in Chapter 7).

Notes

1. Tony Elger and Peter Fairbrother suggest in correspondence that we need to distinguish between 'affiliation', as taking the *part* of the other, with 'substitutionism' as taking the *place* of the other. I like the distinction here between part and place. But I think this can be covered by distinguishing rather between substitution and substitution*ism*. One could also distinguish between *part* and *place* by using 'adoption' for the first. The matter deserves further discussion.

2. For a sophisticated comparison of the relationship between worker networks and unions in advancing internationalism, see Kidder and McGinn (1995). On the basis of an analysis of transnational organizing in the North American Free Trade Agreement (NAFTA) area, they conclude:

   > Networks – based on interdependent relationships – are effective
   > in workers' transnational organising because they permit rapid decision-making,
   > exchange of timely information, and grassroots relationship-building among partici-
   > pants. However, to sustain campaigns and infrastructure, transnational organising may
   > benefit from some centralised organisational forms that include greater accountability
   > and a firm financial base. (Ibid.: 21)

3. I believe I may have been the first person to try to define the meaning of a new internationalism (Waterman, 1986: 20–1). At that time there were only six points. Since then various other authors have tried to do this, either in terms of alternative national labour foreign policy (Cantor and Schor, 1987: 77–82), or of a new internationalism more generally (Brecher and Costello, 1991; MacShane, 1992a, b; South African Labour Bulletin, 1991a, b). I do not think these specifications differ from each other in essence. Denis MacShane's 'Eight Theses on Trade Union Internationalism' (MacShane, 1992a) may be of most significance, coming as they did from a leading officer of the International Metalworkers' Federation (IMF) in Geneva (not necessarily in his official capacity). They are brief enough to present here: 1) The Cold War is over and a curtain could be drawn on 70 years of

international trade union rivalry; 2) Regional labour internationalism will develop; 3) Multinational finance and production will hasten labour internationalism; 4) The last bastion of national sovereignty will be the trade union; 5) Effective international labour organization does not yet exist; 6) International labour activity will be horizontal not vertical; 7) There will be a growing role for the organic intellectual; 8) Internationalist culture in unions is still weak. Given MacShane's position, and his presumed address to the traditional unions, it may not be surprising that scepticism of the intellect is as much in evidence here as optimism of the will.

4. Quite some time ago Heller and Feher felt obliged to point out the historically developed differences between the Eastern left and Western left. More recently, with communism in ruins, they felt able to both reconsider the tradition (including internationalism) and propose new common principles, ending with the reminder that 'It is socialism that exists for the world, not the world that exists for socialism' (Heller and Feher, 1989: 375). Michael Burawoy has implied, in the context of an international discussion about the future of socialism, that the invention of such a new socialism requires contributions from all over this world: 'The end of Communism, far from being the end of socialism, opens up debate in the West and the East, in the North and the South, about what we might mean by socialism' (Burawoy, 1990: 172). With socialists marginalized, or facing incalculable odds (South Africa, Brazil) all over the world, the chances for a serious and friendly international debate on internationalism will, I believe, be better in the next century than the present one.

4

BEYOND THE BUREAU: THE WATERFRONT INTERNATIONALISM OF THE SPANISH DOCKERS

Introduction: A Force to Be Reckoned with?

The attempt to create a network of European dockers, free of the traditional national and international trade unions with their bureaucratic structures and procedures, began in the late 1970s, at a time when numerous European initiatives were taking place to create some kind of shop-floor internationalism between workers in transnational companies. The basis of the network was the Coordinadora (co-ordination) of Spanish dockworkers. In calling this a 'waterfront internationalism' I suggest both an analogy and a distinction. The idea was certainly to create horizontal linkages between ordinary workers. But these were not factory workers, employed in the same international capitalist company or industry (e.g. Coca-Cola, the automobile industry). Ports are (or were) a mostly state or municipally controlled sector of the international transport industry – and one of a particularly archaic type. Dockers are also a very specific type of worker, historically known for their collectivism (which can include collective petty criminality) and militancy (which can include collective violence), but also for their frequent isolation from other workers and from the surrounding society. Docker awareness of international linkage goes with the job, and union internationalism here has a long and rich history. But this experience and history is a complex and contradictory one. There may be parallels with coalminers, and with the miners' union internationalism, mentioned in Chapter 2. Each country, industry, worker type and community has its own experience, awareness and activity. There can therefore be no alternative to detailed, theoretically informed case studies.

This is such a case, though dependent on study of limited time and depth.[1] It is therefore not possible, and perhaps not even necessary, to apply to the case the full conceptual apparatus suggested by Chapter 3. What I rather do here is to draw on the specification of the new labour internationalism (NLI) in that chapter and then set up the study in the form of a limited number of related hypotheses.

The understanding of the NLI to be employed here is therefore:

1 cross-border solidarity activity by or between wage-workers at shop-floor, grass-roots or community level;
2 expressing their daily-life concerns and aspirations;
3 based on their resources and efforts;
4 in opposition to the major forces or expressions of international exploitation and oppression (e.g. capitalism, statism, patriarchy, racism, imperialism, militarism);
5 tending to create a global community of interest and activity;
6 complementary to those of other mass popular and democratic interests, identities and movements (e.g. of women, oppressed national/ethnic communities, human rights, the environment).

In originally carrying out this study, my major hypotheses were:

1 that the Coordinadora finds itself between an old and new model of labour internationalism;
2 that this is because of its isolation from alternative internationalist labour experiences, ideas, techniques and expertise; and
3 that the reason for this lies in the nature of the industry, its workers and the tradition to which the Coordinadora belongs.

Before beginning, it is worth while reminding ourselves of both the general and the specific tradition from which the Coordinadora springs. A Danish study reveals the general tradition of labour internationalism in the most dramatic possible way:

> [T]he flow of financial support from foreign trade unions – often raised from voluntary individual subscriptions by union members – was vital in enabling financially weak unions to conduct long strikes against well-entrenched foes. International strike support assumed *proportions comparable to the flow of capital in governmental development aid today*. To cite only one notable example, during the Swedish General Strike of 1909, Danish trade-union contributions amounted to about three days pay per unionised Danish

worker; projected onto the current American labour force, *that rate of voluntary contributions is on the order of four times the current US foreign aid budget*. In both symbolic and concrete terms, international labour solidarity was a force to be reckoned with. (Logue and Callesen, 1979: 1, emphasis added)

International solidarity actions of this type were not exceptional in the heroic period of mass union organization. One of them provided the very real basis for the creation of the International Transportworkers' Federation (ITF) shortly after.

This brings us to the *specific* labour tradition to which the Coordinadora belongs. During the historic London dock strike of 1889, Australians sent £30,000 sterling or more to the strike committee, the first instalment arriving at a crucial moment for the movement. Although this money came from public as well as union collections, it was Australian unions which were behind it, 'interested, perhaps for the first time, in international solidarity' (Walker, 1981: 15). £30,000 was an enormous amount of money at that time, equivalent (according to my own calculation) to several days' pay for each striking London docker. When the equally historic Australian maritime strike broke out, and spread to other sectors, one year later, 'the London dockers responded with the greatest alacrity to the Australian appeal (ibid: 19). The union immediately voted £1,000, following this up with a levy of one shilling and further ones of threepence a week – or even per day. By this time the union had 25,531 members on the Thames (Lovell, 1969: 119), earning a minimum of sixpence per hour. We may assume that all dockers paid the levy, since those who were reluctant to pay were forced by others to 'brass up' (Walker, 1981: 20) or were even the cause of strikes. Let us assume that each union member paid three levies of threepence in addition to the initial twelve. If we add this to the ninepence or more per member (the first £1,000), we come to 30 pence per member, equivalent to five hours' pay each from what were still amongst the poorest workers in Britain.

We will have cause to return to this financial face of solidarity after considering our case. The study will move between the Spanish dockers' organization and the European network because much of the initiative was taken by Spain, and because the Coordinadora was the most active internationally. The case also pays particular attention, within Spain, to the Port of Barcelona. This is not the port with the most tonnage but it was the point of gravity within the Spanish organization. Attention to the national and local level will also bring us closer to the dockworkers themselves.

The rest of this chapter presents: the Spanish background; an overview of dockworker internationalism, old and new; the internationalism of the Coordinadora itself; some historical and contemporary comparisons; and a conclusion on the case. I am hoping that the case study will suggest both the extent and the limitations of attempts to create a new kind of cross-border solidarity limited to workers and dependent on the nineteenth-century tradition of labour and socialist internationalism.

Background: Spain, Its Docks, Dockers and Their Organization

The Normalization of Spanish Labour Relations

By 'normalization' I mean the incorporation of Spain, its industries, workers and unions into the West European dispensation of the 1980s and 1990s: an open economy, privatization, job destructive modernization and rationalization; complex restructuring of the working class; individualization of workers; trade union incorporation into collective-bargaining industrial relations and social pacts; the self-subordination of socialist parties to capitalist understandings of the economy and statist understandings of government. We will see how the Coordinadora attempted to resist this pattern, drawing on earlier traditions of worker collectivity, autonomy and militancy. Just as part of the normalization project was the creation or reinforcement of a nation-state identity amongst workers and unions (this despite the institutionalization of both sub- and supra-national identities), so did the Coordinadora's resistance draw on pre- and anti-Franco traditions of internationalism amongst Spanish workers and unions. The word 'resistance' is here used deliberately, since it will be shown that the struggle of the Coordinadora was more to preserve and extend a traditional anti-capitalist status than to assert a new post-capitalist one.

The labour movement played a major role in the anti-Franco struggle in the 1960s and early 1970s but it became decreasingly organized and active after the transition to liberal democracy in 1977. Its rate of organization fell. The strike rate similarly declined. But, given the continued attack on traditional working-class rights and standards during the later period of economic growth, the level of combativity rose again, with increasingly dramatic and effective general strikes in 1985, 1987, 1988 and 1992. One Spanish writer (with Third World as well as Spanish experience) criticizes, however, the 'politics of resistance' (Naves, 1988: 17) to which even the most militant activists are limited, considering that it implies no alternative strategy. He considers a radical alternative vision necessary, this consisting of the following elements: the creation of modern small-scale industries under control of workers and local communities; establishment of human control over new technologies; a pacifist unionism rejecting military budgets and arms production; rejection of sexual discrimination; defence of the environment; extension of trade union autonomy; a rethinking of all strategies in contemporary international rather than outdated national terms. In sum, he proposes 'the necessity of a reconversion of the old traditional unionism into a new workers' movement that is autonomous, anti-militarist, ecological, feminist, anti-discriminatory (in relation to sexual option, age, race), and self-managing (Naves, 1988: 17). Whilst this perspective must be an exceptional one within even the 'anarcho-syndicalist' left of the Spanish labour movement, it was published in a periodical co-sponsored by the Barcelona dockworkers' organization and provides a useful lead-in to our consideration of the Barcelona dockworkers and their union.

Dock Work and Dockworkers[2]

We may, perhaps, begin with the recognition that cargo-handling – an industry crucial to the development of commercial capitalism internationally – has been one of the last industries to be effectively industrialized. The cargo-handling industry has until today been divided vertically into numerous distinct functions, the names of which evoke the days of sailing ships: shipping companies and agents, clearers and forwarders, chandlers and stevedores. In terms of capital accumulation as a whole, transportation is the weak link, representing a dead period between investment and realization. The dead period for capital accumulation also represents a weak link in the control of labour. In the increasingly global assembly line, with 'just in time' supply strategies replacing 'just in case' ones, transport workers have an increasingly strategic position. This is not only a position in the supply phase. In some cases they are apparently even being incorporated into the production process, with partial assembly of car parts from different sources taking place in the port.

At the centre of this transformation lies the container. The container is a standardized and increasingly all-purpose module: it can carry liquids, grains and cars as well as crates and packages. Around 80 per cent of world cargo is now containerized. Container size has increased from the standard 20-foot unit (20 × 8 × 8) to the 40-foot one. Ship size has also been increasing dramatically, from those capable of handling 1,000 TEUs (twenty-foot equivalent units) in earlier days to those handling around 7,000 today. The standard module is both a requirement of and a contribution towards industrialization and computerization. The industry, and those other industries it serves, have been reshaped around the module.

So, the port labour process internationally is at last undergoing Taylorization, with the decomposition of tasks and the possibility of calculating each operation of every worker. Productivity has increased dramatically as labour has dropped via natural attrition, forced retrenchment, 'golden handshakes', reductions of retirement age, etc. In Barcelona, around 1978, there were some 2,000 workers. In 1988 there were 1,052, with plans for a reduction by 50 per cent. The total of some 11,000 dockworkers in Spain was likewise expected to fall to some 5,000–6,000 in the near future. Bearing in mind that this is a peninsular country with two archipelagos (Balearic and Canary Islands) and over twenty ports, this will be a remarkably low figure.

Dockers, traditionally the pariahs of the urban labour force, valued only for their brute force, have been increasingly transformed into skilled workers. They now manipulate massive lifting equipment requiring delicate control, this equipment itself often being computerized. The transformation has its costs as well as its benefits for the remaining dockworkers. One is loss of knowledge of what they are handling (arms? dangerous pesticides?). Another is loss of collective control over the labour process as each individual is increasingly isolated in his work and under computerized instruction and surveillance. A third is that physical stress is being replaced by mental stress. A last major cost would seem to be the sheer reduction in social weight. Even within ports it is often difficult to actually see the few workers left. Within the community they have usually become as anonymous or invisible as modern factory or office workers.[3]

But, if the number of dockworkers in Barcelona has dropped and the residential community has disappeared, the sense of occupational community is still strong. Despite ten to fifteen years of increasing government and employer attempts to break it down, the Organizacion de Estibadores del Puerto de Barcelona (OEPB, Barcelona Port Dock-workers' Organization) had managed, until 1988, to defend certain procedures that preserve collective identity at work. Crucial here were the hiring hall, rotation of work and the impossibility of either workers or employers controlling the distribution of dockers to companies or tasks. Whilst the OEPB had been unable to prevent some workers being taken away from daily reporting at the hiring hall, even those assigned to certain companies were obliged to return there after a fixed period of time. Most of them still had to report daily when they wanted a day's work, providing an opportunity for them to meet each other and be reached by the union. Rotation of available work was assured by a highly visible board in the hiring hall. The board was covered with numbered and coloured tags, the latter indicating the different occupations. Those who had obtained work for the day, or failed to report, got shifted to the end of the queue. Distribution of workers between companies in Barcelona was done by placing numbered balls in an ancient bottle-shaped calabash, held together by sticky tape. Assignment to companies depended on the luck of the draw.

The Coordinadora and OEPB[4]
The immediate origins of the Coordinadora lie in the assemblies and workers' commissions of the period before and after the death of Franco. Alienated by the Communists and their bureaucratic behaviour within the Comisiones Obreras (CCOO, Workers' Commissions) the dockers also kept their distance from the anarchist Confederacion Nacional del Trabajo (CNT, National Labour Confederation), to which they were much closer. In 1979 the different port unions met together and set up the Coordinadora Estatal de los Estibadores Portuarios (CEEP, State Co-ordination of Port Dockworkers). It is noteworthy that, like the OEPB, this body eschews such words as 'union', 'centre' or 'confederation' in its title. The CEEP represented, in the late 1980s, some 80 per cent of the dockers in Spain's twenty or more ports, and above 90 per cent in the major ports of Barcelona and Las Palmas. The UGT (Union General de Trabajadores, General Workers' Union) and

CCOO – backed by state favour and finance – had not ceased trying to woo, undermine or directly sabotage the Coordinadora, but each dominated only one of the minor ports. It must have been in part because of its political autonomy and its consequent openness to workers of all affiliations that the Coordinadora was the one united industrial union in the country.

The basis of the Coordinadora, and therefore of the OEPB, was the *asemblea general* (general assembly), with power to override any other body, to elect and dismiss *delegados* (delegates). Delegates served on *comites de empresa.* Any unelected dockworker could attend and vote in the OEPB's *comite de delegados* (which were anyway answerable to the *asembleas*). Above the port level were five zonal councils, with meetings monthly or more often, as necessary. Representatives were usually the *delegados* but may be other dockers. The National Co-ordinating Committee consisted of the National Co-ordinator himself (in 1988 the Barcelona activist, Julian Garcia) and one representative from each zone. The National Committee was responsible for national-level communications and negotiations. Representation at zonal level was weighted against the major ports. To ensure that he had a base on the waterfront, the National Co-ordinator was elected first at national level and then confirmed in his own port.

Since the end of the Franco period the dockers had been heavily and repeatedly involved in local and national strikes. Juan Madrid, a local and national leader, claimed to me in 1987 that they had been on strike for two or three months a year since 1980. The strike movements were often prolonged – 18 months in 1980–1. They were also frequently bitter, with thugs brought in by employers, scabs thrown into the harbour in Barcelona, and a demonstrating docker's daughter run over and killed in Las Palmas. In this essentially male industry, wives and children have taken part in strikes on a number of occasions in Las Palmas as well as – less frequently and dramatically – in Barcelona. In Barcelona, striking dockers have driven heavy equipment out of the port and parked it in main squares and streets to block the traffic. They also, on one occasion, invaded a major department store until it agreed to stop dealing with a blacked container company. Despite their energetic and often successful struggles, the single national port labour authority was eventually broken up. The principle of employment through the pool was diluted, with 10 to 30 per cent being taken into permanent or semi-permanent employment by the stevedoring companies. Agreements that the Coordinadora signed with its back finally against the wall gave rise to disagreements between ports and amongst activists. There was even a complaint in the Coordinadora's paper, *La Estiba* (No. 33, 1988: 4), that the Coordinadora's negotiators had made unnecessary and dangerous concessions and had overridden the intentions of the assembly.

The Politics of Militant Resistance

Despite its evident anarcho-syndicalist sympathies, the Coordinadora was an organization firmly rooted in its own time, tied neither organizationally nor ideologically to some golden past of anarcho-syndicalist unionism in Spain. Its radical-democratic practices not only made the Coordinadora a model that other militant unions could well learn from. They also make it compatible with the grass-roots democracy, informality and flexibility that hallmark the new alternative social movements. The Coordinadora, moreover, had been able to mount a prolonged and powerful resistance to a concerted attack by international and national capital and the Spanish state over a period of a decade or more, and it had done this without being either defeated and crushed (like the US air controllers) or defeated and split (like the British miners). If it was forced to retreat, this was a fighting retreat, made with minimal concessions and with its troops – at least until the end of 1988 – still in good spirits and good order.

To recognize that the struggle was primarily defensive, and that a retreat had been forced, is not to criticize the strategy followed. But it does raise questions about other possibilities that might have to be considered. Here we come back to the argument of Naves (1988). In identifying the problem as the 'politics of resistance' Naves reveals something common to militant unions or militant union action of quite different traditions (as with the US air controllers and the British miners). It is not, however, only their strategy they might have in common. It is also their constituency. This is defined in all three cases by the parameters of a single capitalist – or capitalist-oriented – industry. If these industries provide a basis for workplace community they also can and do isolate their primarily or wholly male workforce from other potentially anti-capitalist or anti-statist communities. It would be worth while investigating the extent to which the problems of all the above mentioned unions are not due to their failure to preserve a relationship with, or integrate themselves with, workers and unions in other industries, and/or with local residential and geographical communities, and/or with the new social forces identified by Naves. This is a matter of the politics of coalition and alliance we see increasingly practised within or between the ASMs – and by the new 'social-movement unionism' internationally (Waterman, 1993b).

Dockworker Internationalism[5]

Traditional Dockworker Internationalism

We must start with the traditional organization responsible for the co-ordination of dockworkers internationally, the ITF. This has included dockers since its predecessor was founded in 1896 by such men as the leaders of the London dock strike of 1889, Tom Mann and Ben Tillett. These were militant and internationalist activists, quite capable of crossing the North Sea to organize a strike in Rotterdam if they thought it necessary. This early internationalism, however, was also a 'national' one, in a number of senses. Before the international organization was created, in the first place, the British organizers not only assisted strikes in Holland, Belgium, Germany and Scandinavia, they also tried to set up branches of the British dockers' union there. When the new international was created, in the second place, they conceived of it as a single union, which the British pioneers would evidently lead. When the organization eventually settled down, in the third place, it was as a federation of national unions, with all the problems this implied for distance from actual dockworkers, for formal recognition, representation, exclusion, hierarchy and bureaucracy.

In the inter-war period, the ITF was bedevilled by the ideological split between Social Democrats and Communists, and then severely undermined as an international organization by the loss of its powerful affiliates in countries that fell to fascist rule. It saved its internationalist soul by a heavy engagement in underground solidarity work with unionists in such countries. During the war it naturally identified itself with the Western allies in the struggle against Hitler. The post-war period saw a renewal of Social Democratic rivalry with Communism, with the former now fully incorporated into the Western side in the Cold War.[6] This meant both a continuation and a reinforcement of its identification with the liberal-democratic states in the struggle against

Communism and revolutionary nationalism. At the height of the Cold War, in 1951, the ITF had a Mediterranean Anti-Communist Vigilance Committee, which collaborated with US diplomats and, no doubt, the Central Intelligence Agency (CIA), in combating Communists in the ports. The latter were seen as undermining the Atlantic alliance and as aiding the Vietnamese struggle against the French.[7] The ITF continued to be tarred by CIA connections in Latin America in the 1960s and marked by a paternalist, developmentalist and class-collaborationist role amongst port and dockworker unions in Africa in the 1970s (Waterman, 1980, 1983). At the same time, of course, the ITF carried on with its bread-and-butter work of holding meetings, publishing bulletins, and attending conferences of the International Labour Organization (ILO), but it still excluded not only unions affiliated to Communist national trade union centres but also those that – like the Coordinadora – failed to affiliate themselves to national unions or federations (usually of social reformist plumage) recognized by the ITF.

In the 1980s the ITF was a typical West European based International Trade Secretariat (ITS). The name says it all: it had an anonymous London office, its leaders were bureaucrats, not working-class heroes, it organized and attended meetings of national and international union leaders, and its existence was little known to dockworkers internationally. Even in Britain, where the ITF is based, dock shop stewards – and even Liverpool dock officers of the Transport and General Workers' Union (T&GWU) – did not, in 1989, know the name of the ITF docks officer. And they did not receive the informative *ITF News*.

Although the ITF may have been becoming more active on dock strikes and boycotts, it has been subject to repeated criticism by the Coordinadora and its friends. The ITF was found seriously wanting on four separate occasions: in relation to an official boycott of Chilean ships in 1977, during the unofficial Rotterdam strike of 1979, during the unofficial general strike of Danish dockers in 1982, and during the official dockers' strike in Rotterdam in 1987. The most common complaint was of ITF refusal to support dock strikes not endorsed by its national affiliates (often general transport workers' unions distant from ports and dockers). But, as criticism of the Chile boycott suggests, the ITF was considered ineffective even when it did take a solidarity initiative. Despite its particular criticisms – justified or not – the general attitude of the network towards the ITF was one more of disinterest or dismissal than of active hostility or opposition. Its supporters turned their backs on the ITF and instead concentrated on building their own international linkages at waterfront level. The disinterest was more or less reciprocated by the ITF.

A major test for traditional union internationalism was provided by the British dock strike movement of April–August 1989. This dispute was, however, a test also for the waterfront internationalism of the British dockworkers. The strike was caused by the abolition of the National Dock Labour Scheme, which had provided British dockers with protection against the evils of casual labour for some 40 years. That the British strike collapsed just a few days before the one hundredth anniversary of the great London dock strike added irony and poignancy to this failure. That historic strike, which began in London on 12 August 1889, not only signified the massive appearance of unskilled labourers on the British trade union scene, it was also – as already stated – the subject of significant international support from Australia and the primary stimulus to the creation of the ITF itself.

Official Union Internationalism

The ITF had prepared carefully for the looming strike, sending out circulars to its dockers' and seafarers' affiliates as early as 12 April. Between then and the end of the strike it sent out at least six such circulars. It also reported the efforts extensively in *ITF News*. On 17 July, the ITF convened in London a meeting of its North Sea Ports group, consisting of dock officials from its Belgian, Dutch and German affiliates. These agreed a six-point declaration, including the following elements: unions would warn employers that accepting diverted cargoes could 'endanger social peace'; unions would take all possible action, taking account of the 'practical and legal situation' locally; priority would be given to whole cargoes from or to strike-hit ports in the UK; perishable goods would be handled normally; the ITF should receive and transmit all relevant information concerning ship movements and, finally: 'delegations of trade union officials or shop stewards from the UK to other countries should receive full cooperation from the unions concerned only where they have first been cleared by the TGWU and the ITF'.[8] This last point was evidently addressed to the unofficial activity to be dealt with below. To judge by the Netherlands, however, the official approach of the ITF was taken seriously. Kees Marges, then Docks Secretary of the Dutch Transportworkers' Union

(Vervoersbond or VB) of the FNV (the broadly social-democratic Netherlands Trade Union Confederation), approached both the port shop stewards (*kaderleden*) and the port employers. Whilst encouraging the Dutch dockers to give force to the ITF recommendations, he also warned against unofficial solidarity activities:

> In order to ensure that so-called strike tourism does not show its face again (see the experiences with the [British] miners' and seamens' strike), and that, in this manner, uncoordinated actions take place that could bring both the TGWU and the continental unions in legal difficulties, the TGWU will, in a letter to all ... Shop Stewards ... urgently request that no visits to European ports be carried out on their own initiative. If and when possible, an attempt will be made to enable such visits to take place in an organised manner. (Vervoersbond FNV, 1989)

The polite letter to port employers apparently also had effect, with the Rotterdam port employers' association, Samenwerkende Vervoersen Zeehavenondernemingen (SVZ), advising its members, in the interests of social peace, to avoid unloading diverted ships. Whilst recognizing the end of the strike as a defeat for the British dockers, the ITF considered the solidarity effort to have been 'remarkable' (*ITF News*, August 1989: 11). Boycott action was reported from Rotterdam and Amsterdam in the Netherlands and from Antwerp in Belgium. Swedish dockers' and seafarers' unions, and the International Longshoremen's Association on the East Coast of the USA, were prepared for solidarity action.

The Unofficial Internationalism of the Shop Stewards

This effort was made by the National Ports Shop Stewards' Committee (NPSSC) of the T&GWU in the UK. Much of the activity came from Liverpool, where unions in general, the T&GWU, and the dockers in particular, had been involved over the years in a range of solidarity activity comparable to that of Barcelona. Mike Carden, one of the local shop stewards, had been to the Philippines for a conference on free trade zones (Liverpool has had a free port for some years), and to an international trade union school in Spain. He was also responsible for getting local leaflets translated into foreign languages for European distribution. Jimmy Nolan, a longtime leader of the Liverpool dockers and equally longtime Chairman of the NPSSC, was also an old friend of the Coordinadora. But the activity this time seems to have been organized by the British directly and without contact with the old network. Three London dockers went to Zeebrugge in Belgium and to the northern French ports. Three Liverpool men went to Antwerp, Rotterdam and Bremen. In Bremen they were hosted not by the local dockers but by BUKO (Bundeskongress Entwicklungspolitischer Aktiongruppen), an anti-imperialist action group that – like the Liverpool dockers – had been involved in action against importation of Namibian uranium. In Rotterdam it appears that Kees Marges had obtained permission from the container company, ECT (European Container Terminal), for British TV men to film him addressing dockers – provided he was informing them of the situation and not calling them out on strike. The arrival of dockworker activists from Liverpool not only caused the ECT management to turn on the Dutch union but almost led to physical conflict between officials of the latter and the Liverpool dockers. It may have been this incident that led to the warnings issued by the ITF and the VB-FNV. Whilst the latter organizations were clearly extremely annoyed by the unofficial activity, the Liverpool dockers were prepared to treat it as an unfortunate misunderstanding. At an ITF meeting in London, Jimmy Nolan made a point of expressing his appreciation to Marges, and Marges both reported this to his own members and incorporated a Liverpool leaflet (translated in Liverpool into a somewhat awkward Dutch) into his mailing to the Dutch shop stewards.

Evaluation

The British dock strike of 1989 shows both the extent and the limits of official trade union internationalism. It implies activity carried out by or through national and international officials. It implies diplomatic caution and legal finesse in avoiding laws against solidarity strikes, and in then specifying particular ports, particular ships, particular cargoes – or even part cargoes – to be boycotted. It implies hostility to direct contact between dockworkers internationally, this only being conceivable with approval from above. The policy is one that the ITF officer responsible for dockworker unions is proud of:

> [W]e did attempt (and succeed) in stopping some rank and file UK dockers running around and undoing the solidarity action that was being successfully

organised by the Dutch union. I would do it again any time. Successful
strikes are run by unions, not by ad hoc and often unrepresentative groups
of shop stewards.[9]

Since it is registered under British law as a trade union, the ITF itself
has to take care that it does not breach the draconian British legislation
on illegal strikes. The high profile then adopted by the ITF on international solidarity seemed to have been much oriented towards the
national and international media. Whilst this did lead to impressive TV
and press coverage, we must note the price the Dutch union was
prepared to pay for this. We must also ask ourselves whether the British
dockers were right to feel so charitable towards a Dutch union leader
who considered their efforts at creating worker to worker solidarity
internationally 'strike tourism', especially when one recalls that it
was on the basis of such activity that the ITF was created in the first
place (Aubry and Vermote, 1983). Given the formalism, legalism,
ideological/political bans, and the low priority apparently accorded
dockers by the ITF (which has been changing more recently), it may be
understandable that dockers have tried over a number of years to create
their own informal network of international solidarity at waterfront
level.[10]

Building an Alternative Network
The base for the alternative network of the 1980s was the autonomous
or semi-autonomous organizations of dockworkers at the waterfront.
Such organizations have sometimes represented the lowest level of a
formal national union structure (UK), sometimes the committee of
those elected to works council structures (Germany, Spain), sometimes
informal or temporary types of self-organization, often identifiable only
by an occasional newsletter (Denmark, Rotterdam, Antwerp). The most
significant of these, in terms of their size, independence from the
formal union structures and longevity, were those of Spain, of Arhus in
Denmark and Hamburg in Germany.

The active agents of this new internationalism were a number of
individual waterfront activists. These were generally men who had been
through, or in any case rejected, the Social Democratic or Leninist
traditions. Their inclinations were more towards traditional anarcho-
syndicalism, the Italian *autonomistas* of the 1970s or the Greens of the

present day. Such inclinations were not doctrinal, otherwise it might have been impossible for them to have collaborated over a period of some ten years. What united them was probably a radical-democratic orientation, prioritizing the direct and active expression of collective self-interest by the workers, whilst being open towards other democratic ideas and movements (feminism, ecology, peace, Third World solidarity, etc.). The core group were mostly working-class intellectuals, with homes full of books and records. Some were involved with audio-visual or music groups. They usually knew foreign languages, sometimes several, and could use them effectively to interpret or translate. They were often individualistic, sometimes to a trying degree (at least for a researcher seeking systematic information), but if they had not been so they would have probably been incorporated into the bureaucratic trade union structures. They evidently enjoyed foreign travel. They sometimes paid their own way to conferences, visited each other's homes on holidays, even attended each other's weddings. They evidently enjoyed the adventure of their project. If they had not, the network would never have got off the ground.

Around these five or ten key figures could be found a small number of professionals or academics. These related to the group through their presence at conferences, through their translation work for the network, through their analyses and journalism. These were by no means the *eminences grises* of the movement, nor its consultants (on the model of KOR, the Committee for Workers' Defence, in Poland), nor – with one exception – even its service providers (on the model of the Transnationals' Information Exchange, TIE, in Amsterdam). They were simply people who had earned some respect and trust for such work as they might have done. On this basis they may have had their material used or reproduced, or been invited to attend one of the conferences. It should, finally, be noted that these intellectuals related to the Coordinadora as industry analysts rather than as political strategists or theorists.

The network developed out of contacts and solidarity activity not between dockers but between Spanish seamen on the one hand and British dockers on the other.[11] The Free Union of Merchant Seamen (Sindicato Libre de Marineros Mercantiles, SLMM) was set up under the Franco regime in 1975, established an international office in Genoa (with the help of the Italian unions) in 1976, and actively pursued contacts with foreign trade unions from the local to the international level. This policy continued after democratization, with active assistance to foreign seamen and the reservation of 1 per cent of union funds for aid to those under dictatorial regimes. In 1977 Spanish seamen in Southampton struck over redundancy payments when their ship was being sold off to Libya. Southampton port officials blocked access to them by union representatives from Spain until the Chairman of the Port Shop Stewards' Committee 'simply asked them to reconsider their position' (*Southern Echo*, 19 May 1977). He also threatened a firmer line if any attempt was made to break the strike. The SLMM apparently attended the network conferences until at least the Gothenburg conference of 1980. Indeed, discussion about whether the network should not be one of dockers *and* seamen (again recalling the origins of the ITF) continued for some time. What brought an end to this more ambitious project was the normalization of the Spanish labour movement under the liberal democratic regime. This implied not only the formalization of industrial and national union structures but also of international union relations. The SLMM apparently became increasingly involved and interested in the traditional internationals, first the Social Democratic then the Communist, finally with attempts to create some kind of 'peaceful coexistence' alternative to them. The informal network thus became confined to militant autonomous dockers' organizations.

There seem to have been around nine international dockworker meetings, beginning with one in Birmingham in 1978 and ending with one in Barcelona in 1986. The first meeting seems to have arisen out of the contacts between seamen in newly democratized Spain and dockers in the UK in the late 1970s. One or two meetings were held each year, till around 1982. These were in London (No. 2, 1979), Barcelona (No. 3, 1979), Gothenburg (No. 4, 1980), Las Palmas (No. 5, 1981), Arhus (No. 6, 1982). The major force behind these meetings was the Coordinadora itself, but considerable effort was put in by radical dockworker committees in Arhus and Hamburg. At various times there was considerable activity by the Swedish union or the Port Shop Stewards' Committee of the British T&GWU. The meetings discussed a wide range of international dockworker problems, of working-class problems more generally and of even wider issues. Let us consider these in turn.

With regard to the *dockers themselves* we may note the following: the boycotting of ships in dispute; containerization; shortcomings of the official national and international unions; comparative pay and conditions; reservation of jobs for registered dockers; employer disciplinary measures; mutual visits by activists and rank and file dockers; whether minority worker organizations within ports should be supported; computerization; privatization and restructuring; implications of the European Economic Community (EEC) for dockers. Concerning *working-class solidarity* more broadly, we may note the boycotting of coal cargoes and discussion of a one-day strike in solidarity with the British mineworkers.

As for the *wider democratic issues*, there was discussion of boycotting arms shipments and Chilean cargo, of action in support of worker and general human rights in Uruguay and Argentina. Under the same heading of broader interest might be noted the participation of leading dockworker activists from five countries at the Alternative Ports and Harbours Conference, Hamburg, 1985. This conference, which was co-sponsored by the Hamburg dockworker organization, discussed not only port labour issues but also pollution, regional development, the rights of Third World seamen and migrants, the export of arms and harmful products. There was, finally, much discussion on the principles and practice of the network itself. This was evidently always a complex and sensitive issue: should seamen be in or out? What should be the rights and role of the dockers' wives who were present at several of the events? Should there be a permanent and structured organization (as favoured by the British at one time) or only an informal network (favoured by the Spaniards)?[12]

Despite all this activity it is significant that the names of the conferences changed from one to the other and that the network (my term not theirs) never had a definite title. The planned 1983 conference of what was to have at last been formally called the Dockers' International Organization of Solidarity never took place, and the name never came into use. There is no complete account of what happened or did not happen at this moment. It may have been at this time that there was an initiative by Communists in one of the dockers' or seamens' unions within the network to set up a new 'peaceful coexistence' international, affiliated neither to the Western nor Eastern trade union internationals.[13]

There was a seventh meeting in Hamburg (1984), an eighth in Rotterdam (1985) and a ninth in Barcelona in 1986. Throughout the years there have continued to be pleas for the supply of information, and references to the necessity for consultations and some kind of organization. In December 1988 both a Danish dockers' leader and a German academic supporter of the network talked to me of the necessity of another European conference. As for the Coordinadora, it seems to have settled for the creation of an effective network with its French and Italian neighbours. Whilst union leaders from these three countries did occasionally meet at each others' conferences, it does not seem as if there was systematic co-ordination within this region. The 1987 Rotterdam strike revealed that there was none between two major dockworker communities that live an hour or two from each other and speak the same language (Rotterdam in the Netherlands and Antwerp in Belgium).

The problems of networking between dockers at port level were suggested by an event in early 1989. This was a three-day meeting of dockers, called in Amsterdam by TIE. Concerned with 'Restructuring and Union Power in the Ports', this meeting seemed to be carrying on the task of the old network. But it was doing this without making any reference to it, and without any apparent knowledge of its achievements and failures. The meeting involved dockers from Amsterdam and Rotterdam, Bremen and Hamburg, but it included none of the leading figures from the old network and its reports and recommendations showed no advance (Transnationals' Information Exchange, 1989a; Waterman, 1989b). The problems of networking are also shown by the British dock strike of 1989. As I have shown above, the international solidarity effort on this occasion seems to have owed little or nothing to the network.[14]

Organizing Solidarity Action

Despite the inability to build some stable and effective organization, there has been impressive international protest activity since the late 1970s, some of it being quite effective. Amongst the different forms of solidarity we can identify are the following: protest messages to employers or state; supporting ones to the dockers themselves; the supply of information about working conditions and rights, or about ship movements during strikes; the sending of delegates to or from striking ports; the provision of publicity about strikes abroad; collections of money; go-slows and boycott actions. On the most dramatic occasions, these forms combined, as with the Danish dock strike of 1982.

Although hopes for common international action in solidarity with the British miners' strike of 1984-5 might not have materialized, individuals and groups within the network were prominent in its support. This was particularly so for the Arhus group led by Ib Lund, which was not only one of the two major support organizations in Denmark but was also responsible for the most famous poster of the miners' strike. We will see below that the Coordinadora also played a role in this activity. As far as solidarity amongst dockworkers is concerned, however, my impression is that it declined in intensity after the Danish strike. An exception to this decline might have been the Spanish strike in 1986. If, however, we also take into account the major Rotterdam strike of 1987, then there does seem to have been a decline from the 1982 peak. Whilst we have no record of how much was received in solidarity funds by the Spaniards in 1986, we do have records of the $11,736 received by the Danes in 1982, and the apparent zero received by the Dutch in 1987! It would seem that the breadth and depth of boycott and other forms of solidarity activity were greater in the first case than in the second, again being zero in the third. Some implicit recognition and even acceptance of the difficulty of organizing international solidarity seems to have been expressed at the last meeting of the network, in Barcelona in November 1986. This emitted a downbeat note, with a call for each country to 'organise internal resistance without abandoning the coordination of international action' (Waterman, 1990c: app. C).

The Internationalism of the Coordinadora

Given that the Coordinadora was in many ways the driving force behind the international network, it might be thought that its activity had already been dealt with above. This is not so. Some of its actions or relations have been unilateral or bilateral. In some cases it practised where the conferences preached. In yet other cases it might have taken action that was broader or more forceful than the other groups. We have information on some eleven or twelve actions over a period of ten to eleven years. Seven or eight of these are of solidarity by the Coordinadora and three or four with it. When we divide these actions into major types we can distinguish the following:

1   those between dockworkers themselves;
2   those with other workers;
3   those in support of Third World liberation struggles; and
4   those in support of Third World disaster victims.

Let us consider these in turn.

Solidarity between Dockworkers

The solidarity between dockworkers was the only type that went in both directions (i.e. both from the Coordinadora and with it). It was also by far the most common single type of activity. We have already mentioned the solidarity with the Danish strike. We can further mention that with Swedish portworkers in 1981, with the Coordinadora recommending members to go-slow on or boycott Swedish ships. It was probably this strike that Juan Madrid was referring to in 1988 when he mentioned to me the approximate 1 million pesetas (about $9,100) collection in solidarity with Sweden at one time. In 1982 solidarity was declared with a 24-hour strike of British dockers, Las Palmas boycotting ships to and from the UK. As for solidarity with the Coordinadora, this case comes from the prolonged struggle against the restructuring law in 1986:

> Coordinadora receives supporting letters from the Oslo Bryggearbeiders Foreniging, from its Danish friends and from the British NPSS Committee. On May 8 Coordinadora appeals for the blacking of ships diverted to Bordeaux and Fos in France and to Palermo, Italy. On May 19 it reports the refusal of Gibraltar dockworkers to handle Maersk Line containers diverted from Algeciras. In the Canary Islands, dockers' wives demonstrate and picket. On May 27 the new decree is made public. It undermines dockers' conditions and unity in numerous ways. Coordinadora declares opposition and prepares for a bitter struggle. On June 9 is reported another blacking action by the Gibraltar Transport and General Workers Union. The British Ports Shop Stewards sends £200 (about $293) and the assurance that diverted ships will be blacked. Ib Lund, from Arhus, attends a Coordinadora meeting, bringing solidarity and money from Danish dockers. Coordinadora continues to request international support and information on current docker employment status and rights. Letters of support come from the London dockers, from the Transport Workers Union of the CGIL [Confederazione Generale Italiana del Lavoro/General Italian Confederation of Labour] in Liguria, Italy, and from the Federation Nationale de Ports et Docks of the French CGT [Confederation Generale de Travail]. (Waterman, 1990c: app. C)

Solidarity with Other Workers

We have one record of Coordinadora solidarity with other workers, this being during the British miners' strike of 1984–5. The 1985 Rotterdam conference of the network had reported the boycotting of coal exports to the UK by dockers in Denmark, Germany, France and Sweden, and discussed the idea of a one-day international solidarity strike. This did not come off. But when two workers from the Hatfield Main Strike Committee turned up in Barcelona (brought over from France by local Trotskyists or anarchists), they were welcomed and supported by the OEPB and the Federacion Autonoma de Colectivos (FAC, Federation of Autonomous Collectives). The FAC organized a press conference, produced a poster and organized a fund-raising campaign. The OEPB collected 158,700 pesetas ($1,290 at 1988 rates), and the union later sent a message of support to the Coordinadora during the 1986 strike wave mentioned above. Saunders gives a more dramatic account of the visit to Barcelona, suggesting that even more money was collected:

> The visit was a huge success. When Alan Robe and Danny Ostle spoke at the docks, they were applauded enthusiastically. Dockers almost came to blows as they vied for the honour of depositing their money in the strikers' collection buckets. Here was recognition indeed of the British miners' long struggle. Within a few days £1,000 had been raised. As a token gesture of support, the dockers refused to load two British vessels waiting for consignments of fruit. Telegrams were cabled to other European dockers suggesting European-wide boycotting of coal. But before anything had transpired, the miners returned to work. (Saunders, 1989: 240)

Solidarity with Liberation Struggles

Solidarity with Third World liberation struggles can be identified on three or four occasions. The first was a tragi-comic event, the boycotting in 1981 of a ship carrying Fiat tanks, in the belief that they were going to El Salvador. The boycott was ended on the captain producing convincing evidence that they were only going to Peru! The action none the less brought considerable press coverage, overwhelmingly sympathetic. The second case was the 1984 decision of the Coordinadora to load and unload goods for Nicaragua free of charge. The action brought a letter of appreciation from the Nicaraguan ambassador. In 1985 Barcelona dockers declared a South African ship unwelcome, threatening further action if it did not disappear with all due haste.

Solidarity with Disaster Victims

Solidarity with Third World disaster victims was shown twice in 1985 when the Barcelona dockers collected and loaded foodstuffs for Ethiopia free of charge. In this case they were apparently responding to an initiative originally taken by a Catalonian NGO and endorsed by companies both inside and outside the port.

(Whilst, finally, I have excluded meetings from 'activities', we should not forget that Spain hosted three of the international conferences, more than any other country. Britain hosted the first two, but after 1980 no other country besides Spain held more than one).

Historical and Contemporary Comparisons

In considering the nature of the Coordinadora's internationalism, we need to return to the definition at the beginning of this chapter. Here were listed six different aspects of NLI, which we will now examine in turn:

1 *Cross-border solidarity activity at grass-roots level:* since there was no level other than the grass-roots one, this criterion is self-evidently met;
2 *Expression of daily-life concerns and aspirations:* the activity was overwhelmingly related to the specific working-life concerns of the dockers. Where it was broader (Ethiopia, South Africa, Nicaragua), it seems to have expressed their humanitarian and democratic ideals or aspirations;
3 *Based on own resources and efforts:* once again, there were no others that they could draw from or wished to appeal to;
4 *Opposition to major forces of exploitation/oppression:* if their workplace struggles opposed them to capitalism and statism, their internationalism was evidently not limited to this, confronting racism, imperialism and militarism (if only occasionally). Whilst not confronting patriarchy in their public activities, they did at one time do so in relation to their own organization (allowing women into their previously all-male conferences);
5 *Creation of a global community:* whilst this was the aim of the project, it was achieved in respect to the key activists rather than to the mass of the workers involved;
6 *Complementing other democratic internationalisms:* whilst complementary to

certain other democratic internationalisms, the internationalism of the Coordinadora was neither integrated nor seriously articulated with these.

By considering the Coordinadora in relation to these criteria, we can see considerable achievements as well as critical shortcomings. But the exercise does not permit a full evaluation of its internationalism. This requires comparison with other historical and contemporary experience. In evaluating the Coordinadora we will be able to simultaneously evaluate the international network of which it formed the most active part. The easiest way to evaluate their joint effort is by putting it in the context of other European efforts at creating a new labour internationalism.

The core activity of the Coordinadora and its international network, solidarity between dockworkers, can be compared, as mentioned earlier, with the shop-floor internationalism of workers in TNCs. The TNC worker internationalism was the origin of the new labour internationalism. Where the Coordinadora's activity differs from the more general phenomenon is, first, in lying outside the TNC sector, although evidently in one confronted by transnational capital. Since only a minority of the world's workers are within the TNC sector, the international solidarity efforts of the dockworkers show the possibilities, and the problems, of industrial internationalism beyond the TNCs.

However, the efforts of the Coordinadora also go beyond the increasingly recognized limitations of TNC worker internationalism (Haworth and Ramsay, 1984; Humphrey, 1988a, b). One original feature was the role played in some of the international conferences by dockers' wives. Although this activity had a base in Rotterdam as well as in Barcelona, it was probably the militancy of the Las Palmas women that provided the greatest stimulus. Second, by supporting the British miners, the Coordinadora was reasserting the tradition of general working-class internationalism, this solidarity being mostly organized outside (if not despite) the traditional trade union organizations (Howells, 1986). The Nicaragua, El Salvador and South African actions not only revived an old labour and socialist tradition of solidarity with nationalist, anti-imperialist or anti-authoritarian uprisings, they also gave the Coordinadora a place within the democratic internationalism of the ASMs. In the case of famine relief they took part in an international activity close to that of traditional bourgeois-liberal charity and relief efforts, and one that was joined by local capitalists. Whilst the implications of the 'international aid movement' are much debated on the left (Hall and Jaques, 1986; Hart, 1987), the range of the Coordinadora's activities suggest breadth and generosity of spirit. Another unique feature of the network's activity is that it was done without the customary 'support group' of church, socialist or other radical intellectuals and financial supporters.

We must, however, also point out the limitations of the efforts of the Coordinadora and the network. Dockworker solidarity was always limited to Western Europe, whereas that of the TNC networks has often included the Third World. When Gdynia (Poland) dockers played a significant role in the Solidarnosc strikes of August 1988, this was not even noted by *La Estiba*. US strikes might have been known of and reported but there were no contacts with working dockers or union officers in the USA. And when I myself suggested, at the Alternative Ports Conference in Hamburg, 1985, that it would be possible for the network to get in touch with Indian, Pakistani and South African dockers, a German activist said, 'If and when they feel the need for international contacts they will find us and we will do what we can for them'. As for the 'non-dockworker' solidarity activities of the Coordinadora, these were usually one-off actions, provoked by a particular incident. Whilst consistent with the general policy and practice of the organization, they were more symbolic gestures in the direction of international solidarity than expressions of a well thought out strategy. The solidarity of the Coordinadora and the network represented, moreover, a 'national internationalism', in the sense of being customarily addressed to worker struggles in a particular country, rather than being a common international activity for a common international end – such as the campaign at the turn of the last century for the eight-hour day. To mention the eight hour day campaign is to also remember its positive and assertive nature (Foner, 1986) and to contrast it with the essentially defensive international activity of the Coordinadora.

We have, further, to recognize that however significant and welcome the collections of funds were, they were extremely modest in comparison with the 1889 and 1909 cases quoted earlier. In the one case, it may be remembered, London dockers first received the equivalent of three days' pay via the Australian unions, then contributed the equivalent of five hours' pay to an Australian strike fund. In the other case, Danes contributed to the Swedish workers the equivalent of about three days' pay per unionized worker. Now, let us assume that the $9,100 collected for the Danes by the Coordinadora in 1982 represented $1 per member. In 1988–9 the minimum hourly earnings of a dockworker were about 1,000 pesetas, or $8. Even if the earnings had, in 1982, been only $4, $1 would have represented but a fraction of an hour's pay. This was, in other words, certainly more 'symbolic' than 'concrete' aid.

We also need to consider the multiple isolations of this internationalism. That the Coordinadora and its international network functioned without a support group of intellectuals has been mentioned as a strength, but was it not also a weakness, denying the network a technical infrastructure that has enabled the TNC networks to survive despite their shortcomings? The Coordinadora being isolated from the TNC and other internationalist networks meant it was unable to learn from their achievements and mistakes. Was it not, further, a mistake for the Coordinadora to isolate itself from the Social Democratic and Communist organizations for – if not of – dockworkers? This isolation is, once again, something that has been mentioned in a more positive way. There can be no doubt that if the network had succumbed to the blandishments of either of the traditional trade union internationalisms it would have been tied up in endless meaningless conferences and committees. But by turning its back the Coordinadora and its friends remained in a sometimes crippling ignorance of them. The role of the old unions and the new networks in building an effective internationalism has been a matter of political debate (South African Labour Bulletin, 1991a, b, 1993). Other international labour networks, such as the Transnationals' Information Exchange, have developed their independent shop-floor activities whilst remaining open to the traditional unions, which have been themselves making awkward movements in an internationalist direction (cf. Transnationals' Information Exchange, 1989b, c; Niemeijer, 1996).

One last reflection, addressed to the defensive, 'national' and 'Eurocentric' nature of the Coordinadora's internationalism. Do we not need to surpass this with an assertive, internationally addressed and globally inspired internationalism? Some projects hinting at such a broader and deeper strategy have been suggested (as we will see in Chapter 5) in writings on or from North America, Latin America, South Africa and even Australia (Burbach and Nunez, 1987b; Lambert, 1992; *South African Labour Bulletin, passim*; Sulmont, 1988a). The example I have in mind is more modest in the constituency addressed but just as original in the challenge suggested. This is for what might be called a worker, community and democratic plan for the world cargo-handling industry.[15] Such an alternative project would seem overdue. It would be utopian in the positive sense of that word: a humane, ecologically sound, collectively planned alternative that as yet exists nowhere. The seeds of such an alternative were present in the Alternative Ports and Coasts Conference in Hamburg, 1985, but this remained without a follow-up. The project might be utopian in the negative sense, of not being practically realizable in the foreseeable future, but in so far as such a proposal would address worker, local and democratic communities, and in so far as it linked them internationally, it might have the same kind of consciousness-raising and inspiring effect in this area as socialist, ecological and feminist utopias have had or are having internationally. It would, moreover, put before dockworkers, port communities, their democratic friends and intellectual supporters, an attractive and positive task, rather than the defensive and essentially negative one of always reacting against the latest capitalist/statist project for cargo-handling internationally. Finally, it would wrong-foot an enemy whose essentially profit-oriented and destructive ideals, 'more, faster, bigger', are today unchallenged even on a local basis.

Whilst the international activities of the Coordinadora and its friends might seem feeble in comparison with the late nineteenth century, or underdeveloped in comparison with some of its contemporary opposite numbers, the most relevant points of reference should be other national organizations of dockworkers (of which we have been able to present no evidence) and the international organizations (of which we have presented a little). Bearing in mind the extent to which these major traditional forces have been hamstrung by nationalism, bureaucracy, Cold-War diplomacy or other earlier mentioned ills, then the international dockworker network should be seen as a pioneering effort to revive a long-buried ethic and practice of labour internationalism. If this was not a force to be reckoned with, then it is certainly one to be taken into account by socialist and democratic elements within the labour movement internationally, both for what it achieved in concrete terms and for what it symbolized.

Conclusion: Between the Old Internationalism and the New

I think that some of the hypotheses formulated in the introduction to this chapter can be said to have been largely and broadly confirmed. More importantly (given that hypotheses are primarily a rhetorical device), they have been fleshed out in succeeding sections. The hypotheses were the following:

1 that the Coordinadora found itself between an old and new model of labour internationalism;
2 that this was because of its isolation from alternative internationalist labour experiences, ideas, techniques and expertise; and
3 that the reason for this lay in the nature of the industry, its workers and the tradition to which the Coordinadora belonged.

Hypotheses 1 and 3 may have been better established than hypothesis 2. The latter implies that contact with the alternative international solidarity activists and activities would have enabled it to surpass its ambiguous position between the old and the new. But does this 'new' have any more reality than an ideal defined and posed by myself? If it does, does it have sufficient power to overcome the very real weight of the 'old' – the nature of wage-labour status, of dock work and workers, of the Spanish anarcho-syndicalist tradition? And what evidence do we have, anyway, that an intimacy with other such projects would lead to an overcoming of the present impasse?

I do not think that we can give satisfactory answers to such questions in this particular case, for Spain, or even for Europe in general. New experiences of labour internationalism are under-discussed and even under-reported. Waves of internationalism rise and fall (Western Europe in the 1970s–1980s?; the Americas in the 1980s–1990s?). The NLI is, in many ways, as much an ethic and culture as a set of institutions, making it difficult to recognize and evaluate. The NLI can reveal itself outside, against and even within traditional international labour organizations. New national trade union organizations, and even 'alternative' international labour groups, can make simultaneous gestures in the direction of the new and the old (Waterman, 1992a).

Reflecting on this experience almost ten years later, I am inclined more to scepticism of the intellect than optimism of the will. This is largely due to the difficulties of creating a new kind of labour internationalism around the Liverpool dock dispute of 1989 and that which started in 1995 and is continuing as I write (see above and note 10 in this chapter). Even if this last dispute is won, or at least settled to the satisfaction of the Liverpool dockers, I would not expect it – despite the innovatory, adventurous, imaginative and courageous efforts of the dockers and their friends – to permanently impact even on those dozens of dockworker organizations involved in the impressive international solidarity network created. The absence of a new discourse relevant to the new internationalism is crucial here. This requires the 'radical engagement' of intellectuals, with which I closed the last chapter. Armed, however, with that language and the knowledge so far accumulated, let us radically engage with labour internationalism in what many would see as a more promising world area.

Notes

1. The chapter is extracted from a detailed study of the international relations and communications of the Spanish dockers' organization (Waterman, 1990c) which includes eight appendices, giving further details of the case and its sources. That study was based on a one-month visit to Barcelona in 1988, supplemented by contacts with the European dockers' network 1985–9. Since this chapter is not intended for specialists on ports and docks, references have been reduced to a minimum. *Aficionados* can consult the original.
2. I am here able to draw heavily, if not solely, from the analysis of changes in the international cargo-handling industry produced by the Coordinadora's Centre of Studies in Barcelona (Coordinadora, 1988, 1989).
3. Dockworkers are exceptionally well paid in comparison with other Spanish workers. There are three or four grades of docker, from the least-skilled *confronta* (labourer) to the *capataz* (headman). Minimum earnings in 1988–9 were around 200,000 pesetas per month. The maximum of a *capataz* was about 300,000 pesetas per month. We can compare the minimum of 200,000 pesetas (about $1,620) with the cross-industry average in Spain, 1987, of some 122,500 pesetas (El Pais, 1988: 427). The willingness and ability of dockers to engage in prolonged and isolated battles must have rested in part on their comparatively high wages. As far as dockworker lifestyles are concerned, I was dependent on casual impressions. One local leader told me in 1987 that it was not possible to get dockers out on 1 May celebrations. It would therefore seem to be more than idle speculation to ask whether, in their non-work lives, dockers had

not been absorbed into a privatized and individualized pattern of residence, culture and consumption which, whilst incorporating them into
the urban population more generally, distanced them from any more
specifically working-class culture that may previously have existed.

4. Here there is no shortage of material, produced by the Coordinadora itself
and either translated or written independently by its foreign friends in
English, German, Portuguese or French. Much of this is usefully summarized and updated in Fitz (1988), from which I primarily draw.

5. I am here referring to the general phenomenon of international dockworker contacts and protest actions. My major source is the Coordinadora
archives and a number of interviews with its supporters and sympathizers.
But I have been able to supplement these inevitably partial and sometimes
partisan sources with others. The Eurocentred account that follows needs
to be compared with such independent traditions as those of the USA (for
which see International Longshoremen's and Warehousemen's Union,
1949, 1963a, b; Scipes, 1985; Wright, 1990).

6. For a detailed account and original interpretation of the relationship of
another international trade secretariat to the Cold War, see the study of
the International Metalworkers' Federation by Denis MacShane (1992b).
He traces union anti-Communism back to the foundation of the Comintern after World War I. He argues that the reformist unions, nationally
and internationally, were as much a source as they were pawns of Western
anti-Communism after World War II (ibid.: 1–12, 79–82).

7. See File 159/1/18 in the ITF Archive at Warwick University, listed in
Baldwin 1985: 18; Koch-Baumgarten, 1988: sect. 2.3.3.

8. ITF Circular No. 85/S.28/D.16, 19 July 1989.

9. Letter from David Cockroft, ITF, 13 November 1990.

10. The attitude of the official national and international unions to waterfront
internationalism seems to have been reproduced during the prolonged
dock dispute in Liverpool, 1995–7 (Lavalette and Kennedy, 1996). This
time, however, effective solidarity activity, often involving strike action, was
being undertaken by dockers in Australia, Canada, France, Spain, Sweden
and the USA, as well as in the UK. Dave Cockcroft, promoted from his
earlier position, was now accused of trying to prevent a major
international-dockworker solidarity conference:

> A number of European ports have pulled out of this weekend's conference in Liverpool
> at the last minute after receiving faxes from ITF General Secretary David Cockcroft.
> Apparently Cockcroft is upset that direct links, international picketing, occupations of
> gantry cranes in Montreal etc. are taking place without his advance knowledge. The
> stewards are in possession of a fax alerting them to a claim by the ITF that the T&GWU
> will now move to end the dispute. (Email from chrisbailey@gn.apc.org, via LabourNet,
> received 31 August 1996)

This time information was not confined to the narrow network of waterfront activists and their friends. News and mobilization efforts were being 'narrowcast' via computer-mediated communication (CMC), and broadcast by the British press and the BBC. The CMC was by email, electronic conferences and a World Wide Web site. I received most electronic information via the Forum on Labour in the Global Economy, in Canada. This was receiving the material from LabourNet and automatically forwarding it. Chris Bailey, in the UK, seemed to be the active communicator here. Noted British director Ken Loach made a documentary of the strike for the BBC. A more modest video, *Port in a Storm*, was made for and with the dockers themselves. I received some 30 messages on the dispute via the Forum, March–August 1996. I also noted a continuation of some healthy internet competition between the friends of the dockers on the one hand and the ITF on the other. Both of these parties, however, seemed to be having trouble at that time sustaining their publicized World Wide Web sites.

11. Interview with Javier Lozano, Bilbao, 21 June 1990.

12. To get the flavour of the meetings at the peak of the network's activity, we may consider the Fifth Meeting, in Las Palmas, 1981. There were, before the meeting, repeated appeals from the Congress organizers for contributions to the agenda and preparatory documentation. These appeals were apparently without success. None the less, the Congress decisions were extensive and detailed, covering the major issues, forms of organization, the role of women in the struggle, the question of involving other sectors of the working class, and means of communication. The issue of whether dockworkers' wives were to have full rights at the Congress was postponed till the following one. But it was recommended that they have full access to port union facilities for their own work. On communication it was proposed: 1) that there be visits of contact and information between ports, including by rank and file dockers; 2) that there be created research groups by the dockers themselves; 3) that the information flow on wages and conditions be improved; 4) that Congress information be spread to the base; 5) that such information also be provided to the mass media of the different countries; and 6) that an international periodical be created (Waterman, 1990c: app. C).

13. Plausibility is lent to this supposition by the later creation of the International Mineworkers' Organization, with the support of the British National Union of Mineworkers, the French Communist-led miners' union, and the state-controlled miners' unions of the Communist countries. It is also evident that even six years later, Jimmy Nolan, Chair of the British NPSSC, considered linkage between 'the two European trade union movements' as the key to effective dockworker internationalism (Smith, 1989: 2).

14. Despite all the information provided by the computer network mentioned in note 10 to this chapter, it was not clear to me to what extent the old international dockworker network was involved in the Liverpool solidarity action.

15. Although one might have expected such proposals to be formulated by the 'new labour internationalists' on the fringes of the movement, the seeds of such an idea have actually been sown by the ultra-corporatist Japanese autoworkers' unions. Confronted by the multiple crises looming over 'their' industry, these proposed a far-reaching strategy for the motor manufacturers to come to terms with their overworked employees, critical consumers, an overstressed environment, and an increasingly hostile outside world (Confederation of Japanese Autoworkers' Unions, 1992). This document proposes profound challenges to the capitalism it wishes to preserve. At international level its implications would seem to lead in the general direction I am proposing.

5 BEYOND WESTOCENTRISM: NEW WORLD, NEW UNIONS, NEW LABOUR INTERNATIONALISM?[1]

Introduction: Responding to Third World Internationalism[2]

This chapter deals with Third World proposals for a new kind of labour internationalism. These began to emerge in the 1980s and continued into the 1990s. The proposals came from Latin America, from Asia and from Africa. Within these continents we saw in the 1970s or 1980s – at least in certain parts – not only a growth of the industrial working class but also of new radical union centres that, in most cases, were radical-nationalist and/or socialist in orientation and action. They also tended to declare themselves independent of the old Eurocentred and Eurocentric union internationals, and to express themselves in quite independent ways.

There existed at this time an idea, both within the Third World and beyond it, that this newly industrializing world area, and particularly its new union movements, provided not simply a subject of solidarity activity but a source of renewal for the jaded or faded unionism of the North, and even a base for a new kind of labour internationalism. These groups, networks and organizations not only gave support and publicity to the new movements but also information and ideas. This chapter is therefore also concerned with the response to the new Third World unionism and internationalism of relevant political actors within the First World.

These preliminary remarks are necessary because, in the 1970s and 1980s, I shared the idea that a new labour internationalism would come with the new unionism in the Third World,[3] and because I am going to now argue that the existence of this new world of labour, and the development of new union movements, has not led to such a breakthrough. I am also going to suggest how such a breakthrough might yet occur.

If the last chapter was an in-depth one, this is an in-breadth one. First, and as necessary background, I will present a sketch of contemporary institutionalized trade union internationalism. Second, I will consider a number of documents or projects that have come out of the new radical union movements in the Third World. Third, I will look at the response to such movements of some of their significant partners in the North. Fourth, I will present my own suggestions for a new internationalism in, from and for the Third World. The conclusion will deal both with the problems and the potentials of new internationalist initiatives from this world area.

Background: The Old Internationals and the New Unionism[4]

For many decades the international trade union movement has been dominated by a small number of organizations – not all of them international. The best known are or were the Communist-controlled World Federation of Trade Unions (WFTU) in Prague,[5] the social-reformist International Confederation of Free Trade Unions (ICFTU) in Brussels and the ex-Social Christian World Confederation of Labour (WCL), also in Brussels. But a major international role has been played by the American Federation of Labor–Congress of Industrial Organizations (AFL–CIO). This has been not only a major influence within the ICFTU, but an independent international operator, acting through state-funded agencies for each of the three Third World continents – which is not to speak of its past or present clandestine activities in Europe and the Third World (Newsletter of International Labour Studies, 1989; Sims, 1992).

Despite their very considerable mutual differences, these organizations have always shared a number of common characteristics. They are distant from workers on the shop floor, who, indeed, are usually unaware of their existence (the latter holds for the AFL–CIO's international agencies, if not the organization itself). They are still marked by their past participation in the Cold War. They tend to reproduce the structure and behaviour of the nation state and inter-state agencies. They are Northern based and Northern staffed. The internationals are inspired by nineteenth to mid-twentieth century Euro-US labour strategies and ideologies – Social Democracy, Communism, Business

Unionism, Social Christianity. They have tended to reduce the complex reality of working people worldwide to the model of the unionized (or unionizable) male worker in lifetime employment in large-scale capitalist or state enterprise. They are deeply involved in the tripartite structures and ideology of the International Labour Organization (ILO), recognition by which is their badge of international legitimacy. Where they *have* adapted Western unionism and ILO tripartism to allow for the recalcitrant Third World, they have generally adopted the developmentalist ideologies current in the North – ideologies which are not themselves necessarily democratic, even if they assume the possibility of reproducing Northern experience (Pieterse, 1991; Lumis, 1991a). The 'free' Western internationals have long been heavily dependent on state funding for their 'development' activities, here taking on the role of state-funded development agencies.[6]

One reason for the Western internationals taking on this role is financial. In the 1990s, the ICFTU was receiving from the affiliation fees of its 113 million members only some £7 million a year. But Amnesty International was receiving from its 1 million or so members and donors some £12 million per year. In the same period, the ecological international, Greenpeace, with 4.3 million members, had an income of some £110 million a year! Neither of these two latter organizations received state funding. We seem to have revealed here the difference between, on the one hand, an international confederation of national and nationalist organizations and, on the other, movement-oriented internationalist organizations. The impression is further endorsed when we compare the proportion of income national affiliates pay to the ICFTU and Amnesty respectively. For the ICFTU the principle is 1 per cent of membership fees. Yet the Dutch affiliate of Amnesty was paying, in the mid-1990s, some 38.6 per cent of national income to the international office. Given the alternative between reinventing itself as an international solidarity movement and incorporating itself into state-dependent development co-operation, it is hardly surprising that the ICFTU has taken the easy option (Waterman, 1993c).

The structural problems of the old internationals, and the possible alternative, have been presented as follows by an international union officer of the social-democratic tradition:

> [T]he traditional pyramid organisation of unions with international contacts
> carefully controlled and monitored at the very peak runs counter to the most

useful forms of international contacts, which are horizontal, between workers employed by the same company (or industry) in different countries. Fax,
E-mail and cheap travel are also enabling horizontal network-building
between workers in different countries, which contrast with traditionally
hierarchically-organised trade-union activity. These new developments facilitating international labour contacts will pose a challenge to existing
trade-union structures and internal communication links. At the same time,
they open immense possibilities for labour to regain power and influence.
Unions could ride the globalisation process by becoming repositories of
information about international developments as they emerge from, or
impact on, the workplace. (MacShane, 1992a)

Something of a psychological turning point for the ICFTU was
reached with the UN's Social Summit in Copenhagen, 1995. This was
an initiative of the United Nations Development Programme (UNDP),
and consisted of the now customary interstate Conference and NGO
Forum. The ICFTU was not prepared to see itself reduced to the latter
status and therefore tried to demand that representatives of trade
unions *and of employers* should be seated in the official conference
alongside governments. The model it evidently had in mind was the
tripartite one of the ILO. Had the ICFTU succeeded, which it did not,
it would therefore have defined itself as outside a space in which some
kind of 'international civil society' (see Chapter 7) was being represented or taking shape. It was only after the ICFTU had played a
modest, and internationally invisible, role within the Forum at Copenhagen that it began, for the first time, to describe itself in its own
periodical as an NGO.

When the Japanese trade unions decided, quite recently, to become
more systematically involved in the Third World, they largely reproduced the traditional AFL–CIO pattern (Williamson, 1994). Thus the
Japanese International Labour Federation (JILAF), whilst carrying out
training programmes in Asia, has been concentrating on its invitation
programme for foreign union leaders. The nature of the programmes
offered makes it clear that these are simple, even naive, exercises in
propaganda and corruption. Visits are made to the Ministry of Labour
and to the 'participant's embassy' (Williamson, 1994: 190). Guided
tours are arranged. Visitor initiative is limited to a presentation of the
labour situation in the participants' countries and the filling in of JILAF
evaluation questionnaires. Different groups of participants are isolated

from each other and have difficulty seeing the smaller-scale enterprises that employ the majority of Japanese workers. The JILAF provides its visitors with business-class return flights, expensive hotels, and first-class rail travel on the famous Bullet Train. Williamson calculates, for one case, that the expenses granted were, at $720, equivalent to two-thirds of the participant's gross monthly pay (ibid.: 191).

Where Third World regional organizations, such as the International Confederation of Arab Trade Unions (ICATU) or the Organization of African Trade Union Unity (OATUU), have been set up, this has been on the initiative of states or groups of states.[7] These new organizations have – like the Third World states and inter-state agencies themselves – reproduced rather than challenged the traditional model. Where state-approved and/or state-oriented Third World union conferences did occur in the 1970s–1980s, they tended to produce little more than Third Worldist rhetoric. This customarily forgot any conflict between workers and their labour-repressive regimes. The practical implications have tended to be limited to the holding of more conferences (Confederation of Trade Unions of Yugoslavia, 1986: 96).

Even the best (meaning most useful to recipient) cases of Western solidarity with Southern unions have borne the mark of such ideologies, structures and practices. This is clearly shown in a study of solidarity with South African unions during the apartheid era (Southall, 1995). A chapter entitled 'The Content of Solidarity' is devoted entirely to finance, its flow, its impact and its donors. Southall here points out that the total annual amount of union – actually largely *state-provided* – financial aid never exceeded what a British football club might pay for the purchase of a single player (ibid.: 179). This is an odd but striking comparison. A more appropriate one is that given in Chapter 4 above, with what British or Danish workers gave to Australian or Swedish strikers in the heyday of union internationalism before World War I. It is clear that that money represented a considerable proportion of the donors' subsistence income. But such donations differed from contemporary Western union aid to Third World unions also in other important particulars:

1   it came directly out of their own pockets;
2   it came out of a sense of identity;
3   it created a sense of community;
4   it was sometimes reciprocated.

So far the story is sobering, if not depressing. Taken in conjunction with the account in Chapter 4 of one of the lower-level, or more specialized, International Trade Secretariats, we would seem to be looking at the decline and fall of the international trade union movement. We have, however, seen over recent decades the development of new working classes and organizations in the Third World (MacShane, 1992b, c, 1994). Some of these have given rise to broad and militant labour movements, in intimate relationship with other democratic ones. Whilst we have also seen unions in the (ex-)Communist world sometimes making major contributions to democratization movements, the future pattern of unionism there is by no means clear (Buketov, forthcoming; MacShane, 1994). We have, finally, seen in the industrialized capitalist West both the rise of 'labour-community alliances' (for the USA, see Brecher and Costello, 1990c), and the impact on unions of such new alternative social movements as those of women and ecology (Munck and Waterman, forthcoming).

In a number of significant cases the new Third World movements have been obliged, or chosen, to remain independent of the traditionally dominant internationals. They have tended to develop international relations from the bottom up, or to prefer bilateral relations, or to develop a variety of international relations – with unions, with solidarity groups, or with NGO funding agencies. It is from such unions, rather than others, that new ideas about labour internationalism have been coming.[8] These ideas and proposals are not, however, the first and are therefore not being presented in a political or theoretical vacuum. The major original source of the 'new labour internationalism' was radical elements within the Western trade unions, and movement linked or Third World oriented activists or academics, often working with workers at company, industry, factory or community level (*Newsletter of International Labour Studies, passim*). Whatever the Third World writers or organizations might or might not have drawn from other sources, we will see that their thinking is quite distinctly their own.

Globalization, however, means that the new Third World unions find themselves standing on a moving carpet, confronted by moving targets. Since 1989, the Eastern unions, once a possible source of countervailing power, moral inspiration and material assistance, have more or less disappeared. Confronted by world economic crisis, globalization processes and neo-liberal policies, the Western unions, which previously dominated the field and presented a uniformly Westocentric, paternalistic and reformist front, are now themselves in crisis. They find themselves, moreover, peripheralized in the public arena by the alternative social movements (ASMs), potentially outnumbered by the influx of new Eastern unions – and challenged morally and politically by the radical unions in the Third World themselves. The disappearance of the Communist threat, moreover, has made it possible for differences between and within Western unions and internationals to be expressed more openly (Gallin, 1994; Thorpe, 1994). Any Third World initiative therefore has to take account of this spectrum of possible foreign actors and attitudes rather than the previous monolithic ones. How they have been trying to respond we will see later.

A New Third World Labour Internationalism Takes Shape

Here we will consider four cases, taken from Latin America, Asia and Africa. The first is from Peru, the second from South Korea, the third from South Africa, the fourth from the Philippines. The choice is due to force of circumstances (available published information, personal research opportunity). These are countries of widely different size, history, political condition, insertion into the global economy, size of labour and wage force, of union development and labour or popular movement tradition. We will, however, see that there is considerable coincidence, or at least overlap, between internationalist projects formulated under such differing circumstances. It is for this reason that I concentrate on the projects, at the possible expense of specific national background information. The reason for the overlap will be suggested when I deal below with the extent and limits of Third World labour internationalism.

A Latin American Internationalism

In 1984 two intellectuals closely associated with the most militant unions in Peru produced a background paper for a three-country meeting of Latin American mineworkers. This went much further than the conference itself (Giguere and Sulmont, 1984, 1988).[9] After criticizing the past subordination of the Latin American union movement to local capitalist and political elites, nationally and internationally, they proposed the necessity for a labour and popular internationalism based on the following principles (Giguere and Sulmont, 1988: 46–8):

1   *Defence of class independence and union democracy*: that international
    activity must be based on the autonomous interests of the unions,
    independent of the bourgeoisie and state, and that the unions must
    themselves express the interests of the workers at the base;
2   *Complementarity of nationalism and internationalism*: that there can be
    no real national development without a new international eco-
    nomic, social and political order, and that confrontation with
    imperialism demands international solidarity of the peoples;
3   *Non-alignment and Latin American identity*: fighting for a working-
    class and popular position on these matters, inside and outside state
    or inter-state fora; solidarity with workers and peoples of the USA
    and Western Europe, against the Cold War, union repression and
    imperialist intervention in Latin America.

Giguere and Sulmont also identified distinct areas of activity for
international solidarity. These were:

1   *On immediate issues*: concrete matters around which it was possible to
    mobilize international trade union organizations and public opin-
    ion;
2   *Political and union rights*: this speaks for itself;
3   *Defence of natural resources*: this included international union partici-
    pation in interstate bodies like OPEC;
4   *Action against TNCs*: this included the imposition of Codes of
    Conduct, strengthening TNC-based World Concern Councils;
5   *Action in relation to regional and international organizations*: using
    bodies like the Andean Pact for struggle against the IMF and
    debt;
6   *Action against imperialist ideological domination*: this included develop-
    ment of new kinds of national and international union educational
    materials, as well as of the unions' own means of documentation
    and communication.

Sulmont developed his ideas in contributing to debate on the debt
problem (Sulmont, 1988a, b). Whilst endorsing earlier Latin American
declarations by the traditional national and international unions concerning the debt, Sulmont also proposed an international campaign on
the right to work and the reduction of the working day (i.e. the sharing
of available work). Referring back to the historical struggle for the
eight-hour day, Sulmont argued that this was a demand meeting the

interests of workers in both industrialized and industrializing countries, and that it was a positive and progressive demand, not a defensive one (Sulmont, 1988b: 57).

The Giguere and Sulmont initiative came out of a revival of *clasista* (class) unionism in Peru (Waterman and Arellano, 1986) that was, or was to be, matched in a number of other Latin American countries in the last years of the military regimes. It was independent of the institutionalized Communist, social-democratic or populist traditions that had long dominated Latin American unionism at national or regional level. But, even if not marked by vanguardism, their argument does reproduce the Leninist tradition within the Third World, proposing a labour-popular alliance against local capital and state, and even assuming some cross-class national/regional interest in the struggle against imperialism and for a new world order. Whilst many of the specific proposals would need to be part of any new internationalism, perhaps the most interesting one was the one for a contemporary version of the historical international struggle for the eight-hour day.

Whatever the old and new elements in the proposals, however, what is striking is their lack of impact either amongst mineworkers, within Peru or regionally. The tri-national mineworkers' meeting had no follow-up. Even ten years later Peru's workers, unions and labour-support groups revealed little international engagement of any kind. And, in so far as there was a new labour internationalism in Latin America, this appeared to be less intra- than trans-regional (for example, Mexico with the USA and Canada, Brazil with South Africa and Italy). This failure cannot be understood simply as one of Giguere and Sulmont's policy: their original and comprehensive document will surely take its place in the history of Latin American labour internationalism. The failure has to do more with the combination of de-industrialization, de-proletarianization, impoverishment and union decline consequent on the rise of neo-liberalism. The demise of *clasista* unionism in Peru itself is explained by the subtitle of a book on workers there at that time. Quoting an interviewed worker, this stated that 'to be a worker is a relative matter' (Parodi, 1986). Moreover, the establishment or re-establishment of some kind of liberal democracy throughout the region also led to a dispersal and disorientation of labour and other social movements, as left political parties and NGO organizers moved from the public into the parliamentary arena. Ten years and more later, the Latin American labour movement still seems to be reeling from the impact of globalization, a transformation that only slowly began to take shape – and get a name.

An Independent Third World Labour Internationalism

The Latin American perspective was in general accord with that of the new unions in South Korea (for which see Asia Labour Monitor, 1988). But the Korean position had less of an ideological profile,[10] and it certainly had elements to add. This is evident from the document produced for an international solidarity conference with the new unions in South Korea (International Conference on Korean Workers, 1988; Spooner, 1989: 58). This document identified the following common interests amongst Third World workers: improved living and working conditions, exchange of information on union organization, safety, etc., international publicity for joint action, solidarity strikes, etc. It prioritized solidarity relations within the Third World, particularly with neighbouring countries. The Koreans also favoured a certain *style* of work:

> The kind of solidarity relationship will have to take the bottom-up approach. That is, it should start from simple things like the exchange of information and discussions and updates on the plans and strategies of the labour union movement for the exchange of educational programmes, the cooperative execution of common tasks, sympathy strikes, etc. (International Conference on Korean Workers, 1988: 11)

The notion of a shop-floor based internationalism is here turned into something more like a principle. And so is the idea of starting with exchange of information. Here, again, we can find echoes of ideas being discussed amongst the new labour internationalists in Europe at that time (*Newsletter of International Labour Studies, International Labour Reports*).

An Autonomous International Union Policy and Organization

The Congress of South African Trade Unions (COSATU) was one of the fastest growing national union movements of the early 1990s. It took shape in the 1980s independently of the African National Congress (ANC), of its trade union affiliate, the South African Congress of Trade Unions (SACTU), and of the ANC's strongest political constituent, the South African Communist Party (SACP). Whilst it developed alliances with these, and has both membership and leadership overlaps with both of them, the independent origin is significant (Southall, 1995). The new South African union movement has also grown, from early on, independently of the AFL–CIO, the ICFTU and the International Trade Secretariats (ITSs) associated with these (Webster, 1984). Whilst COSATU seems to have had no major problem with the SACTU, the ANC or WFTU, it has had to struggle against the paternalist, colonial or neo-colonial traditions that continue within the Western internationals. At its Third National Congress in 1989, COSATU therefore passed a resolution, worth considering at length. COSATU noted its own failure to develop a consistent international policy, as well as its lack of relations with unions in 'the socialist bloc', the Third World and the African frontline states. It criticized the Cold War spirit motivating the intervention within the South African movement of the ICFTU and certain ITSs. It argued that they were using their financial resources to split unions, or to promote them as a ' "third force" alternative to the ANC and SACTU' (South African Congress of Trade Unions, 1989). It finally took a number of decisions to ensure its autonomy (particularly from the Western internationals), its linkages with both Western and Eastern trade unions, to develop worker-to-worker contacts internationally, and to strengthen the work and control of the COSATU leadership over international funding and contacts.[11]

Since this congress, reflection on foreign and international union issues has continued within publications associated with, if formally independent of, the trade union movement, such as *South African Labour Bulletin* (*SALB*, also known simply as the *Labour Bulletin*), and *Workers' World*, from the International Labour Research and Information Group (ILRIG). These give depth and breadth to the somewhat formal decisions of the organization, as well as having a significant if incalculable influence on both its leaders and activists. We may concentrate on the keynote article in a special supplement on labour internationalism in the *South African Labour Bulletin* (1991a: 12–43). This anonymous article,[12] entitled 'Towards Worker-Controlled Internationalism!', is the most extensive critical treatment of the subject from a union-oriented publication in the Third World *or elsewhere* in several decades. The article repeats many of the criticisms of the old internationals made already in this book. What it was, however, primarily concerned to argue was that COSATU should remain outside the ICFTU, establishing relations with progressive forces within it as well as with unions, workers and international solidarity networks outside it. Referring to other Third World unions and federations such as those of Brazil (Central Unica de Trabalhadores/United Workers' Centre, CUT), the Philippines (Kilusang Mayo Uno/May First Movement, KMU), and the African continent (OATUU), it argued that

> COSATU enjoys enormous prestige with worker-activists everywhere . . . The ability to link with these layers of activists inside and outside the ICFTU would be seriously undermined by affiliation [. . .] On a continental level COSATU is committed to strengthening OATUU . . . A concerted input from COSATU could help the organisation to emerge as a powerful tool for South–South solidarity, and challenge the domination of the Northern centres/federations [. . .] The new emergent and largely non-aligned trade union movements such as COSATU, CUT, OATUU, KMU, and others are potentially in a powerful bargaining position. Their strength includes the support of extensive networks of worker activists in the established unions of Europe and North America. (Ibid.: 39)

If, it was argued, these strengths were to be shared, the non-aligned trade union movements, together with the union activists within unions affiliated to the ICFTU and WFTU, could play a decisive role in campaigning for:

1   the establishment of an 'international democratic trade union alliance which brings together all those . . . who agree on the need for a single, unified, democratic and accountable world federation, and are prepared to openly campaign for it' (ibid.);
2   the free flow and exchange of information about solidarity assistance and resources;
3   the planning of specific campaigns meeting the needs of the working class internationally.

It is hardly surprising that this document, directly criticizing the old internationals and in practice proposing an alternative to the ICFTU, provoked the expressed anger of top ICFTU officials.[13]

However, as the apartheid regime crumbled, the ICFTU made major efforts to woo COSATU, despatching to it a large delegation of top leaders in 1992. Now, in his own house publication, the ICFTU General Secretary claimed that it had 'throughout its history' supported democratic independent unionism (*Free Labour World*, January 1993). Yet in South Africa the previous year the General Secretary admitted

1   that union financial assistance had gone into the pockets of dicta-
     tors – or even supported dictatorships more generally – in Africa,
     Asia and Latin America;
2   that the ICFTU had hardly challenged the World Bank and Inter-
     national Monetary Fund; and
3   that criticism of its past association with undemocratic unions in the
     South was legitimate (Holdt and Zikalala, 1993: 67–71).

This still did not satisfy COSATU, which has remained outside ICFTU
ranks, preferring to develop relations with other African unions, particularly in neighbouring countries, with those in the Indian Ocean
(Lambert, 1992: 66–73; Holdt, 1993a: 76–81; Meecham *et al.* 1993:
76–81), and which at one moment had extensive negotiations with the
Italian CGIL (ex-Communist) and the Brazilian CUT, linked with the
Workers' Party. During a forum the three union centres agreed

> to work for a new form of labour internationalism which could challenge the
> global domination of capital by building an alternative to the neo-liberal proj-
> ect. Such an internationalism should be based on a pro-active or strategic
> unionism which engages in industrial and social restructuring in each coun-
> try. At its centre is a project for democratisation and social justice [. . .] Once
> the project of strategic unionism is adopted, it has to be extended into the
> international arena. It has to commit itself to the tough, ambitious fight for
> social regulation of the global economy. (Holdt, 1993b: 72–9)

Whilst the 1989 COSATU conference document (COSATU, 1989)
represents a forceful rejection of interference by rich and powerful
outsiders, I do not think its understanding of the nature of such forces
is adequate. The problem, surely, is not simply that the old internationals are rich and powerful, nor their Cold War involvement. It is
also a number of other earlier sketched characteristics. A failure to take
these into account led the COSATU to favour relations with the unions
of 'socialist' countries, and the WFTU, at a time when their political
bankruptcy had been already exposed and they were either in crisis or
about to disappear. Without a more profound and extensive analysis,
there is surely a danger of constructing a Third Worldist international,
or of favouring some kind of trade union United Nations, that would
reproduce the state-like characteristics of the old internationals.

This danger is still present in the much more analytical document in
the Labour Bulletin, produced two years later (*South African Labour*

Bulletin, 1991a) – and after most East European unions had already joined the ICFTU! It may be that the proposal to set up some kind of new 'international democratic trade union alliance', as a successor or alternative to the existing ones, was intended to guarantee against incorporation, or to demonstrate COSATU independence from Western domination. One supposes that the model in mind here was that of the OATUU. Whether this is the case or not, the suggestion of such a successor or alternative

1   fails to reflect on the extremely problematic history of such projects in Africa;
2   fails to deal with the contradiction between a) seeking Western recognition and support and b) rejecting the ICFTU that represents an increasing number of the world's unions;
3   implicitly puts the social-reformist ICFTU (which was growing, if disoriented) in the same category as the (ex-)Communist WFTU (ailing and bankrupt – at least politically);
4   fails to consider to what extent a 'new worker-controlled internationalism' *can* be expressed or furthered within one 'single, unified, democratic and accountable world federation' (South African Labour Bulletin, 1991a: 32).

The tri-continental meeting seems to me to have been a much more exciting and original event, in so far as it involved both a South–South and a South–North axis, and apparently on an equal footing. There is here the implication of a common global predicament and a common working-class interest, North and South. Even more promising was the radical and assertive tone, proposing the necessity of an alternative to neo-liberalism both nationally and internationally. The problem here lies in the nature of this alternative, conceptualized as 'strategic unionism'. This notion, drawn from Swedish and Australian union experience, had much impact in South Africa as the unions began to redefine their role for the post-apartheid era. It represented a new and assertive strategy for national industrial modernization and social welfare, based on such conditions as those of Sweden and Australia. But, as a critic pointed out in *SALB* (Torres, 1994), not only were these conditions highly specific but the strategies had *failed* even before the idea was reproduced in South Africa. There is also a question about whether, in the age of globalization, one can follow the classical Keynesian strategy of moving in stages from national social reform to an international one, rather than seeing the two as mutually determining.

A Tri-continental Labour Dialogue

The Kilusang Mayo Uno (May First Movement) was, in the early 1980s, the most dynamic union centre in the Philippines. Set up under the martial law regime of President Marcos in 1980, it rapidly established itself as a militant, mass-based and radical-nationalist union. It was intimately associated with the 'national-democratic' project of the Maoist-inspired Communist Party of the Philippines, implying total opposition to imperialism, the 'comprador' regime and support for a revolutionary transformation of society. The KMU was internationally unaffiliated and sought solidarity much in the manner of other new labour and other social movements in the Third World. Its ideology and declarations, however, placed it clearly in the state-socialist tradition.[14]

Although the KMU had a distinct national – and nationalist – colouring, its identification with international or Maoist Communism became quite evident during this period. Around 1989–90 – and just as they were collapsing – the KMU became involved in negotiations with the state-controlled national and international trade union organizations of the Communist world. However, the clearest expression of its statist conception of socialism was at the time of the bloody suppression of the democracy movement in Beijing. The KMU first expressed its 'full support to the Chinese people under the able leadership of the Chinese Communist Party'. It stated its belief that the CCP had 'been able to moderate the conflict' and was 'moving towards the resolution of the underlying issues' (Kilusang Mayo Uno, 1989a). Partly under pressure from its international supporters (see below), the KMU later modified its position, whilst still declaring it 'our proletarian internationalist duty to ... support the Chinese people and their socialist system' (Kilusang Mayo Uno, 1989b). Even in its third and final statement, in which it did condemn the massacre, it still suggested a common identity between the regime, socialism and the people in China.[15]

In 1990, however, the KMU produced a proposal for a trilateral conference of major new and internationally autonomous union centres from South Africa, Asia and Latin America (Kilusang Mayo Uno,

1990).[16] This proposal was, again, broadly consistent with those mentioned earlier. It also suggested tentative moves beyond its isolation from union developments elsewhere. The KMU paper began with an analysis of the conditions that gave rise to the new unionism in the Third World. It saw this in terms of the new international division of labour relocating labour-intensive manufacturing to certain Third World countries, this itself implying cheap labour, labour-repressive regimes, indebtedness, massive worker, nationalist and democratic struggles, and finally the tendency to replace dictatorships with limited democracies.

The document innovated at two places. First, it made an issue of developments (though not of current mass struggles) in Eastern Europe, which it saw as having major implications for global capitalism. The suggestion here, although it was not spelled out, would seem to have been that East Europe was going to become some kind of new Third World (competing with and further peripheralizing the old Third World?). However, the political implications of this for Third World and international labour struggles were not spelled out either. The second point at which the KMU innovated was in its address to the future of the traditional trade union internationals. It saw the old Cold War division as crumbling and speculated on what Third World affiliates of the WFTU would now do.

The purpose of the planned conference was evidently to discuss such matters, as well as to consider common aims, common interests and forms of future collaboration. As possible topics for discussion, the KMU proposed:

1 the new union movements themselves;
2 the state, including repression, 'democratic space' and options confronting legal unions;
3 union relations with parties, national, community, peasant, women's and tribal struggles;
4 'The future role of independent unions in a progressive socialist state. Visions of the future';
5 TNCs;
6 debt;
7 international union relations and their 'implications for independent anti-imperialist union centres',
8 a 'Joint Statement of Accord' (Kilusang Mayo Uno, 1990).

I do not want to go into a detailed critique of this initiative. The document is clearly marked by its national Communist origins but also reveals an effort to go beyond this. Previously, for the KMU, 'international solidarity' had meant, basically, the receipt of foreign support, whether material or moral. It had also occasionally made declarations of support for labour or popular movements in other countries – though never with those even in the pro-Soviet part of the Communist world. The document contains an interesting collection of theoretical or analytical elements, including a 'cheap labour' vision of the Third World and an effort to understand the reincorporation of the Communist world (but not its workers or unions) into the capitalist one. Most important, however, is the intention to – for the first time – have a dialogue with other Third World partners. Unsuccessful itself, this notion was taken up more successfully by the South Africans, who also extended the dialogue to Western Europe.

However, in fact, as we have shown at various points, this North–South dialogue, or at least a North–South dialectic, has been present throughout the development of the new labour internationalism in the Third World. It is now necessary to look more directly at the Northern side of this relationship.

Western Solidarity with the New Unionism in the Third World

It is possible to identify at least three significant Western contributors to solidarity with the new unionism in, or a new labour internationalism from, the Third World. These are

1   the traditional social-reformist unions, national and international;
2   the development funding agencies (DFAs); and
3   the labour and other support or solidarity committees (SCs).

I propose to consider their present or potential contribution in the light of the thirteen propositions on a new labour internationalism set out in Chapter 3 above. Because of my treatment of the unions earlier in this chapter, I will give more space to the DFAs and SCs.

The Social-Reformist Unions

The national and international unions associated with the Brussels-based ICFTU *have* been responding to the new unionism in the Third World, particularly where they have no traditional ally, *or* where such allies have been totally marginalized by the creation of united labour centres that clearly dominate the field, *or* where social-reformist unions in the Third World have either sponsored or joined in such unification processes. But the ICFTU has tended to shore up a traditional Third World member, even when it has been discredited and is in crisis (for the South Korean case, till at least the late 1980s, see International Confederation of Free Trade Unions, 1988a, b). In yet other cases, the Western unions may have been courting the new autonomous radical unions, even if they have Communist links, providing there is no significant local opposition or client union present (*South African Labour Bulletin, passim*; Waterman, 1993c). Western unions, which sometimes recognize the loss of their historical role and socialist vision, in some sense *need* the aura of heroism, social engagement and political significance that has often surrounded the new union movements in Brazil, the Philippines, South Korea or South Africa.

The question remains of the extent to which the traditional international trade union centres are willing to recognize, and to abandon, their traditionally privileged position with respect to Third World unions, and, along with this, the customary behaviour of the rich and powerful. The general collapse of the Communist project has also had the opposite effect, reinforcing feelings of self-satisfaction and self-righteousness. As with the industrialized capitalist states and their intellectuals, elements within the ICFTU may still feel not that the Cold War has been defeated by its spiralling costs, and by popular sentiment and struggle, but that it has been won by the West.[17]

The acid test for a positive Western response to the new unionism was provided by the KMU in the Philippines. Whereas it was easy for the ICFTU and its friends to welcome Poland's Solidarnosc into the social-reformist fold, and may become so with COSATU and certain united Latin American centres, the Marxism-Leninism of the KMU eventually provoked the traditional Western anti-Communist reaction. The case, however, reveals more general characteristics of the relationship between the old Euro-US internationals and the new unionism in the Third World. These have, thus, expressed themselves also in the South African case, giving rise to the forceful COSATU reactions reported above.

The Filipino case suggests that even the most progressive Western social-reformist unions tend to

1   consider themselves as developed and Third World ones as underdeveloped;
2   see international solidarity as something they represent and which others may join or benefit from;
3   use their wealth and power to reward and punish;
4   apply different standards of behaviour to themselves than to Third World unions.

In sum, there is here a reproduction of common Western bourgeois liberal attitudes and behaviour. This does not necessarily mean that they can only play a negative role in the Third World, or even that they will necessarily respond negatively to any new Third World international initiative. This is for two reasons. The first is that the response to the Third World does not take place solely, or even primarily, in ideological terms (conscious or not); it also takes place in terms of political interest (anti-TNC, anti-International Monetary Fund, IMF). The second is that the social-reformist unions themselves respond to pressure from outside and below. This will be more clearly revealed when we consider the impact of women and feminism on the ICFTU in Chapter 6.

The *SALB* material mentioned above, however, reveals significant differences between the international policies of even social-democratic unions within the ICFTU. Such differences also exist between the ICFTU and the associated ITSs, and between the ITSs themselves. There are obviously organizations and leaders here with whom projects for a new Third World internationalism could be discussed. In the early 1990s *SALB* itself provided space for ICFTU supporters to express themselves (Allen, 1991; Fine, 1992: 85). We may, at last, be passing beyond the old dialogue of the deaf.

The Development Funding Agencies

Numerous DFAs in the First World have been providing financial support to trade unions in the Third World, or to non-government educational, publishing, research or legal services associated with them. Some of these are directly associated with political parties, such as the German Konrad Adenauer Foundation (Christian Democratic) and

Friedrich Ebert Foundation (Social Democratic, known by its German initials as the FES). Others are associated with churches, such as the Dutch Catholic Organization for Development Co-operation, CEBEMO (Catholic) and Inter-Church Co-ordination Committee for Development Projects, ICCO (Protestant).[18] Others originate in charity work, such as the UK-based Oxfam, or have a certain preference for mass self-organization. Yet others have been openly sympathetic to armed liberation movements, such as the Dutch X–Y (a full name, not an abbreviation). These NGOs have long been seen as part of an internationally expanding 'citizen' alternative to a world dominated by 'princes' (states) and 'merchants' (capital) (Nerfin, 1986). They must, however, be considered in their complex relationship to capitalism, the state and mass movements, nationally and internationally. Some, of course, are deeply subservient to particular states, or financed by the World Bank and other such agencies. But I am less concerned with this type than with the 'consciousness-raising' European type (for contrasting views on these, see Evers, 1982 and Pinto-Duschinsky, 1991).

Whilst the 'consciousness-raising' organizations may have quite different ideologies, as well as different areas and types of activity in the Third World, they also share certain common characteristics. These would seem to be the following:

1 they are non-state and non-capitalist organizations and to this extent can be considered part of civil society;
2 they are dependent to differing degrees on state finance, or tax exemption, and to that extent limited in their 'civility';
3 they are not usually themselves mass-membership bodies, and to that extent are limited in their democracy;
4 they are mostly staffed by university educated professionals, and to this extent are middle class.

As a result of all the above, they tend to be more involved in the discourse of 'Third World aid' than that of 'international solidarity'. Whilst the above characteristics might seem to disqualify them from developing a positive relationship with the new unions in the Third World, this is not necessarily the case. In so far as they favour democratic grass-roots organization and action, and in so far as they have no institutional or ideological stake in a particular labour movement tradition, they may be more sympathetic to the new unionism than are the old internationals.

Many different kinds of DFA have been active with the new unions of such countries as South Africa, Brazil and the Philippines. In the latter case, we could possibly distinguish between the German FES and such Dutch agencies as the ICCO, Nederlandse Organisatie van Internationale Ontwikkelingssamenwerking/Netherlands Organization for International Development Co-operation (NOVIB) and CEBEMO. The FES is closely related to the German Social Democratic Party. In the Philippines it seemed, in the late 1980s, to have switched its allegiance from the Marcos regime and the Marcos-sponsored Trade Union Congress of the Philippines (TUCP) to the Aquino regime and the Lakas Manggagawa Labour Centre (LMLC). The Dutch agencies were, during the Marcos period, associated in different ways with the KMU and its service bodies. Whilst this may suggest a distinction between the 'right' social-reformist FES and the 'left' social-reformist Dutch – and similar differences between German and Dutch states and societies – the matter is more complex. In the first place, the FES was also a major funder of the University of the Philippines School of Labour and Industrial Relations. This had, in the late 1980s, been making itself increasingly open to all unions in the Philippines, and its facilities had been used by the KMU as well as the LMLC. (The TUCP did not exploit the opportunities offered, possibly because it had its own heavily US-financed facilities, possibly because it was not yet used to trade union pluralism.) Second, the Dutch agencies became increasingly uneasy, after the fall of Marcos, about the relationship between the KMU and the 'national-democratic' movement in the Philippines. This is because the KMU was publicly linked with an insurrectionary project aimed against an at least semi-liberal regime. Moreover, whilst the popular base of the Aquino regime had been demonstrated in a more than figurative sense, the KMU had been notably absent from the public protests which brought Marcos down, having evidently believed that this was not the right revolution. It may also have been because of the KMU's continued self-identification with statist socialism, as shown by the Tienanmen affair.

The question I want to raise here, however, is not simply of who was financing whom, under what understanding and for how long, but on the possible contribution of the DFAs to solidarity. If we restrict the issue to the first – highly material – aspect, then we are likely to end up with Tilman Evers' judgement on the mutually instrumental relationship between the FES and its Latin American partners:

> In conclusion, it is a game of 'who uses whom', which both sides are con-
> sciously playing. Perhaps the basic rule of the game can be summed up as
> follows: Give me opportunities to think that I am using you and I will give you
> opportunities to think that you are using me. (Evers, 1982: 120)

I think, however, it *is* useful to conceive of the DFAs as in some way 'representing' neither the acceptable face of imperialism, nor even that of their particular state, but their different national civil societies (thus the difference between German and Dutch social reformists). Since they are not usually under very direct party or church control, and since the different DFAs share much in common, they are less likely to represent different party/religious affiliations than notes on the same instrument. What they seem to do is to represent liberal democratic society 'in', whilst their states represent it 'to', the Third World. This means they create a certain internal space for the development of mass movements and new ideas which otherwise would not exist. This suggests that they might be able to support new labour movement initiatives in the Third World that the union organizations from the same countries may not. Most of this activity, however, takes place within the confines of development or aid discourse. Solidarity, surely, is something more.[19]

Solidarity Committees

By support, or solidarity, committees (SCs) I mean those voluntary organizations set up with the purpose of providing publicity, political support and financial assistance to foreign peoples, organizations or even states. These committees are a traditional part of the democratic and socialist movement, going back to at least the early nineteenth century in Europe. In the contemporary Western world, they have been particularly associated with struggles against colonialism, and impe-rially supported authoritarian regimes. Such committees have ranged along a spectrum running from fronts of Leninist political parties to reformist development agencies. In the case of the Netherlands, for example, they were, in the 1970s and 1980s, semi-institutionalized as 'country committees' and benefited from considerable state subsidies for development education work (Rahman, 1988). In the spectrum of voluntary organizations that runs from the semi-state bodies to the social movements, however, these were evidently closer to the latter.

We are here again concentrating on the union-oriented bodies and the case of the Philippines. The US committee was, in 1989, an independent, self-financed organization called the Philippine Workers' Support Committee (PWSC). This had its own bulletin, *Philippine Labor Alert*. In the UK, the SC was the Trade Union Committee of the Philippine Support Group. This committee did not have its own bulletin, but it had close political and personal links with the UK-based independent labour magazine, *International Labour Reports*. The *ILR* gave the Philippines and the KMU more attention than any other country or organization except South Africa and the COSATU. In the Netherlands there was at this time no separate union support committee, but the Netherlands Philippines Group (FGN) did have special union-oriented activities and publications, such as its *Worker Information Folder* (Filipijnen Groep Nederland, 1989). There was also a European network of Philippines support committees, and there were European-level labour-support activities. The Philippine worker-support committees of the 1980s differed considerably in their composition, financial sources, staffing and material resources, their relations to general Philippine SCs and to their local labour and socialist movements. They did, however, have a number of characteristics in common.

In the first place, they endorsed, at least implicitly, the general principles of the new labour internationalism as set out earlier. This is because the founders or leaders of the SCs tended to be radical labour, church, socialist or anti-imperialist activists who were deeply critical of the foreign policies of their respective labour movements. It was also because they mostly came to Third World solidarity activity at the time of the alternative social movements and therefore themselves moved easily between labour, socialist, anti-imperialist, peace, human rights, feminist and ecological issues and movements.

In the second place, they endorsed – this time explicitly – the principle of a shop-floor internationalism. They sponsored and took part in direct exchanges at shop-floor or community level, many of them having intimate relations both with local unions or workplaces in the Philippines and with local-level union activists at home.

In the third place, these tiny volunteer committees, with their meagre finances, had rather impressive effects on labour and progressive public opinion in their respective countries. This must have been because they addressed that latent need in First World unions referred to earlier.

They did manage at one time to get the KMU recognized as either *a* or *the* representative of the Philippine working class by local, industrial and even national trade union centres (New Zealand, Australia, Ireland). An indication of the impact is that the AFL–CIO in the USA went to the extent of training union officers, through role-playing exercises, in how to confront PWSC initiatives in the unions.[20] In the USA, Australia, New Zealand and Europe, Cold War warriors, church and lay, put considerable energy into attacking the efforts of the labour SCs, along with the work of the general Philippines SCs.

In the fourth place, however, these were actually *KMU* support committees. Whilst the US one spoke of support to the KMU and 'others', the very terminology it used for the others was that of the KMU – i.e. 'genuine trade unions'. As for the British one, in 1990 it apparently discussed but rejected a proposal that it should address itself to Philippine labour generally rather than the KMU specifically.[21]

Whilst the SCs might generally endorse the thirteen criteria for a new internationalism set out in Chapter 3, they might also have difficulty in meeting criteria 10 and 11. These, it may be recalled, have to do with the necessity for 'a frank, friendly, constructive and public discourse ... available to interested workers' and taking on 'a service and training role, rather than that of political leaders or official ideologists'. The Tienanmen case suggests that the SCs avoided public debate with the KMU, and that they did not provide their members/readers with full information about the case. This would seem to mean that they were reproducing certain characteristics of the old internationalisms. This is all the more striking given the fact that the widespread *confidential* protests of the SCs were admitted by the KMU to have been a factor in changing its position. It is also regrettable because the issues of principle raised by the affair, and by the protests, were not, apparently, further aired in the Philippines labour movement or abroad.

The attitude of the SCs can hardly be put down to ignorance or naivety. It seems to have been rather due to 'a total and continuing commitment and belief' in the KMU (Trade Union Committee Philippines Support Group, 1989) which they would be unlikely to show to any body of people, or organization, in their own countries. This represents what I would call a 'self-subordination to the victim' – the idea that because Third World workers are being starved, imprisoned and killed, one must subordinate one's own (petty bourgeois? Western?) standards and judgement to theirs. What is here taking place, however, is not so much identification with the workers as with a particular leadership claiming to represent these workers. This is, again, not something the same people would accept with respect to their own unions – or to the leadership of Solidarnosc in Poland (see Holland, 1990; Kilminster, 1989). The relationship involved, therefore, a further element, the prioritization of one particular Third World union organization over others, nationally and internationally. In the case of the Philippines, a *loyalty* relationship with the KMU was being prioritized over a *trust and respect* relationship with other union centres or alliances in the Philippines at that time – or with the unions in their own country. Indeed, at the time of Tienanmen, the immediate problem faced by the SCs was precisely that of continuing to assure disturbed or angry local unionists that the KMU was *not* 'little more than a front for the Philippines' Communist Party' (International Labour Reports, 1989: 2). A final element may have been a lack of confidence in the organization being identified with: a feeling that it was not capable of understanding or confronting frank public criticism. None of these attitudes seems healthy, for either partner. Nor would they seem to be consistent with the construction of a new internationalism, however defined.

Of the three types of Western bodies I have listed, the SCs would seem to have been those most able and willing to respond to the new labour initiatives from the Third World, but I think consistency would require that they spell out to themselves *their* understanding of international labour solidarity – or at least debate it publicly with their own members and their Third World partners. Their very marginality in relation to the labour movement did give them the freedom to innovate and the flexibility to adjust. However, just because they were marginal does not mean that they were necessarily 'alternative'. The point is well made by George Katsiafikas, reflecting on the outcome of the post-1968 movements in the USA:

> The alternative movement is progressive insofar as it: provides some activists with non-alienating jobs; creates non-hierarchical institutions; and provides a sense of community rooted in friendship as opposed to the depersonalised mode of life in the corporate world. On the other hand, the alternative institutions serve as mechanisms of integration because they can lead to the commercialisation of previously uncommercialised needs, fulfil unmet needs within an oppressive system and thereby help to fine-tune and

mitigate the worst excesses of the system; and provide the system with a pool of highly skilled but low-paid social workers within 'alternative' institutions. If there are connections to a larger political consciousness, however, they may serve as structures of dual power ... If they work within a context of international solidarity and participatory democracy, co-ops and collectives could be concrete embodiments of a liberated political culture. (Katsiafikas, 1987: 196)

The Extent and Limits of Third World Labour Internationalism

The Third World projects mentioned earlier overlap to a degree that is remarkable given limited direct mutual contact or even knowledge. This is probably due to two factors: comparable situations and experiences; and access to new thinking on internationalism, via the growing alternative international labour media (Waterman, 1988, 1992a) and even particular internationalist activists.[22] The North–South dialogue and dialectic here mean that a critique of Third Worldist labour internationalism is a critique also of those in the North who were promoting such.

There is in my mind, however, no doubt that this independent thinking and activity represents a contribution to a new kind of internationalism, both within and beyond the Third World. I will spell this out later. Here I want to generalize about the limits of these projects.

The Limitations of Anti-Imperialism and Dependency Theory

Most of these proposals are marked, implicitly or explicitly, by traditional dependency theory and radical-nationalist ideology. This is in the sense of seeing a fundamental contradiction between capitalist core and periphery, with some kind of common Third World interest – of workers, people, and possibly of national industry and economy – against imperialism. This explains the continued attachment to the disappearing Communist world (seen as an ally against the imperialist West), even after the latter had been undermined by its own worker-popular alliances. There are many problems with this model of the world, the most important of which is its incapacity to deal adequately with the high-capitalist modernity that was taking shape – if not name – in the 1980s.

The nature and implications of globalization for Third World workers, peoples and nation-states has been better understood by – of all people – the President of Brazil (Cardoso, 1996).[23] Cardoso argues that contemporary capital is escaping from the control of even the most advanced capitalist states, and that it is radically transforming the capital–labour relation. Globalized capital is increasingly looking for countries not with masses of unskilled labour but trained and skilled workers. It is also creating a new kind of putting-out system. There can thus be an increase in those occupied (small enterprise, self-employment, home-working) but a reduction in the number of jobs (salaried workers). This new system, however, implies a growth in unemployment and marginalization, something to which politics will have to address itself. Whilst Cardoso evidently sees 'politics' primarily in terms of governments, he even says the following:

> If one wishes to effectively contradict the negative and homogenising tendencies of globalisation, the area of the political is already more [significant?] than it previously was; I would say, further, that there is in the present moment a field in which values, justice and solidarity have a task. (Ibid.: 7)

He also finds the bearers of such new values to lie not in a specific class but in civil society, where they are being given shape by non-governmental organizations. Cardoso is evidently living in our new social and linguistic universe. If he is also attempting to shape both a nationalist and elitist interest, this at least provides a challenge to labour internationalists – to which I will attempt to respond in Chapter 7.

The Limitations of Workerism

All of these proposals are marked by an implicit or explicit assumption that the working class is the privileged bearer of both social progress and internationalism. If the expression is more implicit than explicit, this may be an indication of the taming of labour and socialist hopes since the Giguere and Sulmont document of the mid-1980s. Their labour-popular alliance was clearly intended to be a labour-led one. If one cannot find similar elements in later documents, however, neither can one find any indication that labour is seen as one interest or movement amongst many, nor that labour needs to articulate itself, nationally and internationally, with the new alternative social movements.

The Limitations of a Third Worldist Internationalism

Fernando Mires (1989, 1991) offers us a radical critique of the 'Third World internationalism' that came out of decolonization in Africa and Asia and anti-imperialist movements and revolutions in Latin America. This is a kind of internationalism that finds echoes in most of the documents we have referred to. Mires recognizes that Third World internationalism was a relationship between states rather than peoples. He sees it as reproducing, rather than surpassing, the logic of blocs and the 'bloc internationalism' of the Soviet Union. Mires also criticizes the reductionism of the old internationalisms, the practice of either ignoring all international contradictions but one, or of subordinating them to one 'totalizing antagonism' (proletarians/capitalists, Third World/ First World). He none the less expresses the hope that the crisis of Third Worldism will create the possibility for raising anti-imperialist positions on the basis of real and concrete antagonisms, and that the crisis of internationalism might open up possibilities for the rise of forms of international co-operation free of determinism and based not only on respect for similarities but also on that for differences. Given the extent to which the documents mentioned assume some kind of natural common basis for internationalism, this is a timely warning. The bases of solidarity are something that must be constructed through dialogue, not assumed to inhere in a common interest or a common enemy: even a single global source of oppression or exploitation presents itself with different faces and differing weights in different Third World regions and countries.

Two Possible Principles and Thirteen Possible Issues for a New Third World Labour Internationalism

The argument below attempts to respond positively to both the Third World projects and those of their Northern partners. What I am also trying to do, however, is to surpass certain theoretical/ideological limitations indicated above, and then to rearticulate elements from the projects with my own earlier expressed ideas.

Two Possible Principles

I would like to first suggest two principles for a new Third World labour internationalism. I call them principles because they break with a binary logic in thinking about alternatives. In other words, they are intended to exemplify a holistic and complex logic suitable to a world of increasing complexity and interdependency.

The first idea is that a new *Third World labour internationalism should be simultaneously addressed to the Third, First and (ex-) Second Worlds*. By this I mean it should incorporate an understanding of the increasing global interpenetration of social processes and the increasing identity of, similarity of, or parallels between worker struggles in different world areas. This does not mean ignoring or repressing Third World worker interests, capacities and aspirations, but of seeing and expressing these in a way that maximizes their relevance to workers elsewhere. If there is a contradiction between an internationalism that is regionally specific and one that is globally oriented, then this should be made explicit and seen as a difference that must itself be part of international dialogue. This principle may seem self-evident or banal but it is not. First World internationalisms (meaning those originating in the First World) either tend or pretend to have a global vision. Without Third World, or, for that matter, ex-Communist World, efforts at generalization or synthesis, these efforts – such as mine above and below – will be left in the hands of organizations or individuals from just one part of an increasingly interlocked world of labour.

The second proposed principle is that of *seeing the alternative to membership of the traditional union internationals as one of being simultaneously within and outside them*. My earlier critique of the traditional institutionalized internationals might have made it seem that these are the steam trains of the age of national, industrial and imperial capitalism, about to be wiped out by an international, informatized and globalized capitalism, and therefore needing to be replaced by the networked internationalism of the new social movements. There are, however, problems here. One is that the radical-nationalist or socialist unions of the Third World seem to want to re-create the old steam trains of industrial unionism, but powered by new ideas or ideologies. This would be likely to reproduce the same law of oligarchy, the same top-down flows of power, the same rigidities in the face of the constant changes and challenges of a globalized capitalism. Another problem is that of whether an either/or logic (for example, *either* the evil existing internationals, *or* the virtuous new ones, *either* the evil organization, *or* the virtuous network) provides for the best educational or self-educational process. It therefore seems to me as if the best strategy, providing the best opportunities for both leadership and mass self-education, would be for the new radical unions to be both inside and outside the historical internationals. This way they could relate actively both to the old working classes and unions that the latter in some way represent, and to the new international structures and processes of social movements that have grown with a globalized and informatized capitalism.[24]

Thirteen Possible Issues[25]

Drawing freely and extensively from the earlier Third World documents, I would suggest the following list of possible issues for discussion and action. They are not necessarily presented in order of priority, nor comprehensive. But there is a certain logic in their order of presentation. The first two address themselves to workers as they exist for and against capital, even if they open out towards other popular interests and identities.

Struggle Against, and Alternatives to, Transnationalization

This expresses recognition of TNCs as the most dynamic force for exploitation, repression and alienation in the world today. The alternatives proposed need to be primarily addressed to positive self-activity by workers and popular movements, not the state or local capitalists. Opposition to transnationalization does not necessarily imply favouring local capitalist or state bureaucrats, nor a blanket opposition to the operation of TNCs. There are contradictions within and between TNCs, as well as between TNCs and workers, TNCs and communities, TNCs and citizens. On the basis of felt grievances and specific capacities and desires, unions can take common international action to 'civilize' TNCs, demand the generalization of 'best practice', and develop democratic controls over, and alternatives to, transnationalization.

Struggle Against, and Alternatives to, Neo-Liberalism

This issue can not only unite workers with other popular and democratic forces in the Third World, but can appeal to workers in indebted
Eastern countries and to unemployed and underemployed workers in
the West. This struggle includes proposals for a reduction of hours of
waged work (Gorz, 1989), for equalizing the conditions of labour
internationally, for some kind of worldwide social charter (Brecher and
Costello, 1990b), or for a global 'social policy' (Shiva, 1996).[26] The
'alternatives', however, need to be addressed also to specific activities
that can be carried out by the labour and popular movements themselves, not simply by the states – or even the unions 'on behalf of' the
workers or the poor (cf. Cleaver, 1989).

The next five issues relate to workers in their identity as citizens,
whether one considers these as national, regional or 'earth' citizens
(see Chapter 7). They also, therefore, evidently relate directly to those
citizens who are not wage-workers.

Women's Rights

This is not only in recognition of the increasing centrality of women's
labour (waged, semi-waged, unwaged) to the accumulation of capital
nationally and internationally. It is also in recognition of the way in
which the self-emancipation of women can undermine relations of
super- and subordination both within society in general and the labour
movement in particular. Whilst this issue may not have much resonance
at present in the East, it will appeal to and reinforce international
women's and feminist movements in the West that often address
themselves specifically to waged women in the South (see Chhachhi
and Pittin, 1996b and Chapter 6 below).

Democracy

This is based on recognition of the limitations of the liberal, Communist and populist concepts of democracy given the increased threat of
concentrated global capitalist or state power in contemporary world
conditions (Held, 1992) and the necessity of an expanded and powerful civil society if workers are to surpass their proletarian condition.
This demand has particular pertinence under authoritarian or semi-
authoritarian rule in the Third World but should have appeal also to

democratic citizen movements in the East, and to democratic forces in the West. The question of democracy evidently extends to the struggle against capitalist and managerial authoritarianism at work, or workers' control (Bayat, 1991).

Ecological Issues

The relationship between ecology, land rights, labour struggles and internationalism in the Third World has been symbolized in the figure of the Brazilian martyr Chico Mendes (Mendes, 1989). The relationship between workplace health and safety, consumer and ecological issues is being increasingly recognized internationally. Both in the West and the East the advanced part of the labour and democratic movements see that production and development must be understood in an ecological manner if they are not to be self-defeating, or even life-threatening (Adkin, forthcoming; Buketov, forthcoming; Mellor, 1992).

Militarism

Masses of people in the Third World are subject (increasingly?) to military violence, both external and internal. With the decline of nuclear confrontation between East and West, the issue of militaristic domination of and in Third World societies may gain more priority in the Western peace movement. But the democratic movement in the East also has a historical interest in demilitarization, expressed in the pre-democratization proposal for an international campaign to ban the tank (Dienstbier, 1988). 'Por la Vida' (For Life) movements in Latin America have expressed the popular opposition to militaristic coercion of the masses and their organizations by the fundamentalist left (Shining Path in Peru), as well as by the right. Opposition to militarism, it should be said, does not mean opposition to all and any armed movement, such as that of the Zapatistas in Mexico, but it does when, as in the Peruvian case, the movement is experienced by the masses as a terrorist or militaristic one.

The Autonomy of Culture and Communication

This is more a matter of creating alternative labour and popular forms of communication, nationally and internationally, than of rhetorically and ritualistically denouncing cultural imperialism. Third World labour movements have been the most advanced in developing their own forms of cultural expression. The new movements have often innovated in forms of international and internationalist communication, such as the KMU's International Solidarity Affair, the use of electronic communications (Lee, 1996), and South African use of a whole range of low- and high-technology cultural/communicational forms (Waterman, 1995).

The next three issues have to do with forms of organization in and around the traditional union movement.

Non-Unionizable Labour

The great majority of Third World labourers, even in urban areas, are non-unionizable despite being involved in petty- or semi-capitalist relations. This is also true of a considerable – and growing – part of the working population in the industrialized capitalist countries. They are, however, often organized or organizable in residents' associations, urban and rural co-operatives, peasants' associations, women's committees, etc. These are, or have been, or could be, also internationally organized. The point is to consider ways in which they could be organized, nationally and internationally, not *under* the unions but in fruitful association with them (Asian Labour Update, 1996).

Trade Union Autonomy and Worker Democracy

The traditional national and international union organizations of the West and East come out of labour movements that long ago accepted a subordinate (if oppositional) status both within the nation state and with reference to the dominant international agencies and ideologies. The new unions have generally had to overcome such subordination and have done so by appealing to the collective self-activity of the workers. A stress on trade union autonomy and democracy nationally, regionally and internationally will not only appeal to progressive forces within unions internationally but may also help guarantee the new unions against political incorporation and bureaucratic degeneration (Barchiesi, 1996).

Relations with Richer Partners

Here we come to the most material face of aid, yet the one which is usually the last to be confronted. Some radical Third World unions may be satisfied if the flow is shifted from the 'yellow' unions to the 'genuine' ones – with the same confidentiality or secrecy maintained. The South African documents show both the dangers and the possibilities of relations between donor and recipient organizations internationally. There are, no doubt, other unpublished experiences that can be drawn on. Rather than playing the market in capitalist style, it should be possible to draw up a Code of Conduct for relations between donors and recipients. In so far as the donors wish to move from an aid to a solidarity model in their international relations, they should be responsive to such codes – which do exist for some donor–recipient relations on the North–South axis.

The final point has to do with the ideological or ethical base necessary if labour internationalism is to go beyond a series of reactive, pragmatic and corporate self-interest activities, which are unlikely to literally *move* either union members or civil society more generally.

Trade Unions and Socialism

The value of a *discussion* on (not an assumption about) the meaning of socialism, and its relationship to unionism today, resides not only in the continuing attachment to socialism amongst Third World unions in a part of the world where the word may still resonate positively amongst workers. It lies also in the possibility of demonstrating internationally that trade unions can have a positive, attractive, ethical, holistic, alternative vision of society and the world. Whilst this might have little immediate appeal to the mass of workers in the North, it could certainly appeal to socialists in the labour movements of West and East and contribute to the rethinking of socialism that is taking place internationally.

Conclusion: One, Two, Three, Many New Internationalisms!

This chapter has provided both a broader view of the new labour internationalism (or of labour internationalism under the new conditions), and an example of an intervention into international policy-making on this question. In a still rapidly changing world, it is possible that the situation, or even the organizations mentioned, might have changed considerably by the time the book is read. This is no reason, however, for not attempting to spell out the political implications of a theoretical position.

The chapter will also, hopefully, have suggested more than this. First, that there already is more than one new labour internationalism. Second, that there is also a dialogue on this new labour internationalism. Third, that any such new internationalism is likely to advance precisely through such locally- or subject-specific initiatives – and by a dialogue between them. What left or progressive person or organization in the world today would repeat Che Guevara's cry for 'One, Two, Three, Many New Vietnams'? For the peoples of the world, the slogan of many new internationalisms would seem to offer a more promising prospect.[27]

Such internationalisms, of course, would be not only be those of the old social movements but also of the new. It is now time to examine one of these in depth, and to find out whether they hold more promise than those of the evidently problematic proletariat.

Notes

1. This chapter is an adapted and updated version of a paper originally drafted in early 1990. It was first written following a research trip to the Philippines in late 1989, a trip which also permitted me to visit Hong Kong, South Korea, Japan and the USA. On my return I was simultaneously approached by both a Filipino working for the Kilusang Mayo Uno (KMU) union federation and a Dutchman working for an funding agency which had been supporting the KMU. Both wanted my opinion on the KMU project mentioned below. I informed both that I had been approached by the other, wrote a long paper for them, dispatched it – and am still awaiting their respective replies. Eventually, part of the paper was published in the *South African Labour Bulletin*, in the course of a debate on internationalism also dealt with below (Waterman, 1991).

2. Such responses include, of course, my own. I am aware, here, of making not simply a theoretical but a directly political intervention into the international politics of Third World Labour movements. But I would argue that such an intervention does not necessarily have to imply intervention*ism* (cf. Mamdani, 1989). It would seem to me that any contemporary understanding of internationalism involves either the invitation or obligation to 'intervene in the internal affairs' of others. Internationalism either assumes or urges the need for a global community, if not instead of then alongside those of particular world areas, nations and localities. Internationalism, at least today, is hardly a subject which can be thought about without reference to the thoughts, interests or possible responses of the Other – however that Other is defined. Past labour internationalisms have been customarily marked by local feelings of superiority, inferiority and guilt. Today a dialogue is both necessary and possible but, as Chapter 7 will show, such a dialogue requires self-revelation, self-critique, recognition and space for the Other, particularly by the privileged partner.

3. I may have also contributed to the spread of this belief, both in my academic work and in the *Newsletter of International Labour Studies* (1978–90).

4. We do not have a post-1989 account of the international trade union movement, any more than we have adequate histories of the major international organizations mentioned below. A useful overview of the unionism internationally, from the social-democratic or social-reformist tradition, is provided by Spyropolous (1991). As for the new unionism in the Third World and its international implications, see Munck (1988), Munck and Waterman (forthcoming) and Southall (1988).

5. This organization is now little more than a phantom of what it was when I worked for it in 1966–9. It is kept alive largely by money from the ex-Soviet unions, which, having abandoned Communism, still like to imagine this is some kind of bargaining chip in dealing with the ICFTU. In 1966–9 the WFTU was also a phantom, but a more substantial one, being generously funded by all the state-controlled unions of the pro-Soviet world. It remained both passive and invisible during the worker demonstrations against the Soviet invasion of 1968. At that time it had a massive headquarters, in a former hotel, right on the banks of the Vltava. When, after some twenty years, I visited Prague again, I went to look for the building but found only a large hole in the ground – preliminary to the construction of a new hotel. I was told that the WFTU had had to move into a small office in a back street. The other factor keeping this body in at least symbolic existence is the traditional anti-imperialism or anti-Westernism of some Third World unions. In Durban, 1994, I even found an enormous WFTU symbol looming over a tiny union office in the central factory

district. Andrew Herod (1997) suggests that the WFTU – still backed by major Soviet and some other (ex-)Communist unions – may be trying to reinvent itself as some kind of Third World international trade union centre. Such a project might have a future if the ICFTU proves incapable of responding to the particular threat globalization poses within this world area. Herod's study is, however, dependent on the statements and policies of WFTU leaders and presents no evidence that WFTU has any more reality amongst workers than it did when I worked for it 30 years ago.

6. This can sometimes take on quite grotesque and pathetic forms. An international officer of the major Dutch trade union confederation has thus tried to justify its international affiliations and campaigns in terms of the latest capitalist and managerial ideology:

> As you know, modern times do not leave the FNV unaffected. Thus, a few years ago, the FNV had to slim down ('become lean'), limit its tasks ('back to core business') and now we are going to work in a 'client-oriented' way. And I find this very good, because we naturally have to be more conscious of whom we work for, of better goods delivery, of the reactions of those who consume our 'products', etc. And in this area we can certainly learn something from employers and their tactics.

The author continues, somewhat surprisingly, 'I want to defend the proposition that children in the Third World are clearly also our clients'. The reasoning here is complex – not to say bizarre. The notion seems to be that the product of this union company is 'a modest scale of social redistribution', and that the clients for this product are workers, or union members. The author then switches from the discourse of business (methods) to that of ethics (purposes), given that this

> little factory is set up because we consider unfair distribution in conflict with basic human principles, or unchristian, or simply irrational or ugly. And naturally because we were and are often ourselves the victims of unfair distribution, that we came and come to resist it.
> And whoever thinks like this naturally finds that a fair distribution should not exclude outsiders.

He ends on a similarly high ethical note, indeed a spiritual one: 'And if we should not believe any more in this, then we will have taken over from the employers more than simply some useful managerial strategies. Then we will have sold them our souls' (IZ Bulletin, 1995). 'Disoriented' would seem to me the kindest word one could use about the combination here of the discourses of the 21st-century Japanese manager and the nineteenth-century Dutch missionary, in function of international trade union solidarity – which apparently has no discourse it can call its own.

7. I know of no academic or even serious journalistic work on these two organizations, but I had numerous contacts with the OATUU in the 1970s

and early 1980s, including visits to its Accra, Ghana, headquarters and collaboration on a joint course in Arusha, Tanzania. It appeared to me then that the OATUU functioned as a regional international of union officers, capable of sometimes protecting them against authoritarian regimes. At that time the OATUU continued the Pan-African and Non-Aligned tradition of its forebear, the All African Trade Union Federation (AATUF). It made great play of the principle of non-affiliation to the Northern internationals, whilst turning a blind eye to the many relationships that existed in practice. It was less happy with my 'new internationalism' than with the developmentalism of my academic colleagues – one of whom went on to develop a major Dutch union-supported and state-funded worker participation project with the OATUU in the 1980s–1990s.

8. I am aware of certain new initiatives from the Canadian public service and autoworkers' unions, which suggests there are likely to be others I am not aware of. The problem here is that there is at present really no publication, or even an email forum, in which such proposals or projects are likely to be found. The increasing number of international email lists and World Wide Web sites may provide such places in the future.

9. Joseph Giguere was from Quebec, Denis Sulmont of French origin. They thus acted as bearers of new democratic socialist and internationalist ideas from the North American and European left of the 1970s–1980s.

10. This was certainly in part due to its existence under an authoritarian and viciously labour-repressive regime, which had its own favoured trade union centre. The radical unions in Korea at this time were themselves under considerable Leninist or Maoist influence. As I was able to observe in 1989, they were very impressed with the Maoist Kilusang Mayo Uno in the Philippines (see below). Some of the leading activists considered Korea to be in a pre-revolutionary situation, like that of Russia in 1905, and they were studying the recently, and illegally, translated work of Lenin, *What Is to Be Done?* (Lenin, 1952).

11. Denis MacShane (1992b) points out that at that time 71 per cent of COSATU's funds came from ICFTU affiliates in North-Western Europe. He also makes clear the extent to which such funds were provided by their respective states. We thus had a paradoxical situation in which Western capitalist states with heavy investments in apartheid South Africa were funding its best organized and most effective opponent, another one in which COSATU was publicly snapping at, if not biting, the hand that fed it – if not the hand that fed that hand! Even more paradoxical is that the Western unions and their government backers were aware that numerous COSATU leaders were Communists, and that leading South African Communists were prepared to be funded by capitalist states. MacShane argues

that the problem is not so much the funding, or its source, but the secrecy that has surrounded it. Whilst his argument for open funding and account-ability is consistent with the principles I have suggested in Chapter 3 above, I have also suggested that money should be collected from workers and the public directly. MacShane sees no reason why it should not come from government taxation of workers, provided there is labour and public control over its channelling. The issue deserves further discussion.

12. I made considerable efforts to discover who the author was but, even after the democratization of South Africa in 1994, editorial staff of the *Labour Bulletin* refused to divulge the name. Given the content and style, I have always assumed that it was written by a non-South African associated with the new labour internationalism in Europe.

13. Personal communication from South Africa.

14. This interpretation would be disputed by Kim Scipes (1996), who has written a book-length study of the KMU.

15. The most convincing explanation I received for the original KMU state-ment was the following. It had been formulated and issued, or imposed on the KMU, by the party representatives the CPP kept in the headquarters of all its front organizations. These party agents were withdrawn and replaced at regular intervals, to ensure they did not become identified with the 'sectoral organization' concerned, rather than with the party leadership. The story was that although the party held the same opinion of Tienanmen as that of its agents in the KMU, it would have preferred this not to have been imposed on the unions. The successive adjustments were due to the combination of international reaction with the protests of KMU leaders independent of the party.

16. This conference never, apparently, took place. Given the lack of success that had haunted previous KMU foreign policy initiatives, it may be that it decided against such a dramatic step, or that the funding could not be found. On the other hand, labour activists and union representatives from South Africa have visited the Philippines, and the KMU has continued to hold annual International Solidarity Affairs. Furthermore, a number of Indian Ocean Basin union conferences have been held on Western Australian initiative. Due, no doubt, to both South African and Australian sympathy for the KMU, the Philippines found itself in the Indian Ocean for the purpose of these events (Lambert, 1992). The Indian Ocean conferences later spread to Pacific Asia, becoming known as the Indian Ocean Initiative. See further note 25 below.

17. For social reformist responses that are either more 'Western' or more 'democratic', see, respectively, Vanderveken (1990) and White (1990).

18. Even in the Netherlands, these organizations are known rather by their initials than their long Dutch names.

19. For a sober and sobering account of the limitations of even the consciousness-raising agencies, see Sogge (1996).
20. Interview with John Witeck, PWSC Co-ordinator, Honolulu, December 1989.
21. Conversation with TUCPSG member, London, October 1989.
22. The media include, or have included: *TIE Reports* or *TIE Bulletin*, from the Transnationals' Information Exchange, Amsterdam; *International Labour Reports* from the UK (now deceased); information and books provided by Asia Monitor Resource Centre (AMRC), Hongkong, including *Asia Labour Reports*; the *Newsletter of International Labour Studies*, edited by myself in The Hague; the internationally circulating *South African Labour Bulletin* and *Workers' World* (International Labour Research and Information Group) from South Africa; also, possibly, *Labour Notes*, Detroit, USA; the Geonet computer network (Kirkless Node), based in the UK; and the Association of Progressive Communicators computer network, based in San Francisco. As for the activists, I have already mentioned the Northern origins of Giguere and Sulmont. The other activists I know of were, significantly, associated with one or more of the above-mentioned projects. The individuals, and the countries or regions in which they were or are active, include: Dave Spooner (*ILR* and Geonet, from the UK) in East Asia; Stuart Howard (*ILR*, UK) in the Philippines; Celia Mather (*ILR*, UK) in South Africa (where she was responsible for the special section of *SALB* quoted); Jeroen Peijnenburg (TIE, from the Netherlands) in Brazil; Dave Figg (ILRIG, South Africa) in Brazil; Jagdish Parikh (AMRC, the Association for Progressive Communication [APC] computer network, from India) in the Americas; Rob Lambert (COSATU and *SALB*, South Africa), in Australia, South East Asia and the Indian Ocean. In Moscow, 1993, I discovered Argentinean and US Trotskyists, busy not only with that I called 'the import of revolution' but also with an international anti-privatization campaign that had apparently reached India. There was apparently also present in Moscow at this time a Brazilian representative of the TIE network. There are certainly other such activists, with no party axe to grind, particularly in the NAFTA area. For reflections, by the producers themselves, on the role of independent international labour publications, see Williamson (1993).
23. Cardoso, the philosopher-prince, is not only an internationally known sociologist but one of the leading theorists of the Dependency School.
24. I first tried out this argument in contributing to the debate on a new labour internationalism in the *South African Labour Bulletin* (Waterman, 1991). I invited responses but received none. I fear that, in the absence of such an understanding of the issue, the new unions will (under the influence of radical nationalism or Leninism) remain in a Third Worldist

posture, or (under the influence of social democracy or pragmatism) both join and adapt themselves to the internationalism of the existing organizations.

25. Too late for working into this section came a fascinating labour movement collection from India (John and Chenoy, 1996). This is not a work about labour internationalism, although there are contributions directly on the topic. It is about the 'social clause' in multilateral trade agreements – the requirement that imports from the South depend on their observance of certain labour conditions. Such clauses are evidently a protectionist device proposed by capital and state in the North – often supported on labour or human rights grounds by Northern unions or human rights bodies. The book, outcome of a conference on the topic, claims to avoid taking a position on the issue, intending rather to record a debate. It may well be the case that the contributions of the national union representatives lean toward a protectionist position. Space is none the less provided for those rejecting a binary logic, on the grounds that this implies identification with either a Northern or an Indian capitalist interest. Amongst those proposing the necessity for a third, independent, analysis and strategy, no single position can be identified. But these are voices from a whole range of thinkers and activists from the labour, women's ecological, children's, human rights and other such movements. What the book therefore represents is a new contribution to what is – or will have to be – an international debate on the international strategy of labour and other social movements in the era of globalization. Why I mention the book here is because it seems to touch on many of the thirteen issues I list below: transnationalization, neo-liberalization, non-unionized labour, women, democracy, ecology, union autonomy and worker democracy.

26. Since I have elsewhere been critical, or even dismissive, of the internationalism of the Indian eco-feminist Vandana Shiva, it should here be said that this item is a powerful critique of the social clause as a top-down and unidirectional device, dividing international social movements, – and a potent argument for a bottom-up policy that can unite them.

27. One such new internationalism has been alluded to earlier. It is the Indian Ocean union solidarity network, now becoming known, because of its extensions, as the Indian Ocean Initiative. This network has a number of new and original features. One is that it links workers in the industrialized and industrializing worlds (e.g. Australia, India, South Africa). Another is that it is based on *unions* rather than workers or worker-support groups, thus including the broadly social democratic Australians with the still-Communist Centre of Indian Trade Unions! A third is that is addressed to shop-floor mobilization. A fourth is that it has led to a dramatic and successful international solidarity activity of Third World workers and

unions with those of a First World country, Australia. A high level of local mobilization, and convincing threats of action from South Africa, India, Sri Lanka, Indonesia and the Philippines, actually forced the West Australia government to withdraw draconic neo-liberal legislation (Lambert, 1996). Without claiming that this initiative represents the 'both in and outside' principle I proposed above in this chapter, it certainly provides an important new experience for analysis and reflection.

6 BEYOND INTERNATIONALISM: WOMEN, FEMINISM AND GLOBAL SOLIDARITY[1]

Introduction: The Very Model of a New Internationalism?

Whether or not the contemporary women's movement is – as some would argue – the prototypical alternative social movement, it certainly provides us with a rich source of contemporary emancipatory social theory and a rich and complex history of international solidarity. In the Introduction to this work I provided further arguments for taking the women's movement as my example of the new alternative internationalisms. I suggested that women's internationalism is a 'subject' one and belongs, like labour, to the tradition of emancipatory internationalisms. I said, further, that the women's movement had shown itself particularly sensitive to the forms and relations of movements, both old and new, and I concluded that the similarities/differences between the labour and women's movements internationally would therefore make for an intellectually suggestive and politically potent comparison.

In comparing women's and feminist internationalism to past or present labour and socialist ones, it is tempting to dismiss, or simply to qualify, the former as 'middle class', or as 'incorporated', or as 'unrepresentative' of any mass base, but this is to forget a number of factors, which this work has tried to make clear:

1 that international activity tends to be either carried out by, or to convert its bearers into, a middle-class stratum, or a mediating group, with an inevitable distance from any mass base;
2 that the same accusations, or qualifications, have been made about labour and socialist internationalism;
3 that the popularizing of internationalism is a task facing all internationalists and internationalisms.

Perhaps the most important question here is, rather, that of why the internationalism of women has today such a public presence and impact compared with that of labour.

The impact of women's movement activity may be due, first, to the coincidence of the new feminist movement with the move from an industrial to an information capitalism, this having both provoked and facilitated international awareness and linkages. This, however, is surely true of the labour and other social movements also. Second, it may be due to the lack of a perceived threat by the international women's movement to the commanding heights of capital or state: this has provided a relatively benign atmosphere for the development of the movement internationally (even if it may meet the utmost hostility or difficulty under authoritarian regimes of right and left).[2] However, the liberal capitalist states have also been prepared to stimulate ecological and human rights conferences and organizations, and the Western trade unions and their internationals have benefited massively from state funding (usually from the same 'development aid' as has funded many women's and feminist projects in the Third World). Third, it may be that the very novelty and energy of the feminist movement – and the absence of any feminist equivalent to the bureaucratic international socialist or union organizations – has provided space for a new wave, and that the sensitivity of the women's movement to the multiple levels and forms of domination has promoted the exploration of new forms and contents for international contacts (Bernard, 1987; Boulding, 1975). Finally, the extent of international activity may be due precisely to the global address of the contemporary feminist movement. By 'global' here, I mean not simply worldwide but holistic (Bunch, 1987a, b). Women's movements are evidently rooted in territorial places – communal, national, regional – and they just as evidently address themselves primarily to the 'region' of gender and sexuality. But, as is evident from the international declarations referred to later, it is common cross-national or global problems that are in the forefront of their attention, and the interrelation of women's emancipation and other emancipatory struggles is often made explicit.[3]

So much by way of introduction. This chapter opens with a review of the literature – or rather a reflection on the scarcity of literature – on either women and internationalism or feminist internationalism. It then considers feminist internationalism at two levels, the global moment of the 1995 Beijing Conference and the historical and contemporary process at regional level in and around Latin America. The chapter continues with reflection on two cases, aspects or issues: the South–North relationship, and the impact of the women's movement and feminism on the labour movement internationally. The conclusion suggests that the political and theoretical successes and travails of women's internationalism have to do with the world historical transition from 'the international' to 'the global' – a matter conceptualized more generally in the following chapter. If there is here an excess of focus on the South, and the North–South relationship, this reflects the fact that most of the writing and reflection has been on this world area and axis. But we should not forget that a concentration on – or reduction of – international women's solidarity to this axis stands in the way of a broader and more general understanding.

Hidden from Herstory (or at Least Hertheory)

Despite the energetic and innovatory activity of the women's movement and feminist academics, it was not possible, up to the 1990s, to find one general theoretical book about women and international solidarity, or one theoretically informed history of this. International surveys and articles with titles like 'Sisterhood is Global' or 'Planetary Feminism' (Morgan, 1984; Papandreou, 1988) either assume a shared identity and common response or fail to problematize the relationship between the sisters globally.[4] The same is generally – though not entirely – true of special issues of journals on the topic (Feminist, 1980; Lova, 1986; Quest, 1978; Woman of Power, 1987; Women's Studies International Forum, 1991). Even the documents of – and most papers on – international feminist conferences do not do this (see Anon, 1991; First Women's Conference on Security and Co-operation in Europe, 1990; Mujer/Fempress, 1991; Sternbach et al., 1992; Vargas et al., 1991).[5] Despite the pending Beijing Conference, the situation had not been transformed by the mid-1990s. This strong judgement is based on a reading of two different types of recent Anglo-Saxon literature.

The first, general, literature, is that on 'feminism and the international' (Grewal and Kaplan, 1994; Miles, 1996; Peterson and Runyan, 1993; Pettman, 1996).[6] This can itself be subdivided into that on 'international relations/global politics' and that on 'international feminism'. The second, quite specific, kind of literature deals with women's work and self-organization in relation to current forms of industrialization, migration and new technologies (Chhachhi and Pittin, 1996a; Mitter and Rowbotham, 1996; Rowbotham and Mitter, 1994; Truong, 1996).

These are two important and politically relevant bodies of work. The authors often innovate theoretically or methodologically, either borrowing from or extending the armoury of feminist theory, conceptualization or strategy. The first type reveals innovation also in form, providing both the kind of overviews and teaching texts essential for the international women's movement. In the labour case, this is work which has had – as revealed below – a demonstrable impact on the international trade union movement. But these two types of literature do not, I think, begin to provide us with a framework necessary for interpreting or strategizing women's internationalism. The first, more general, type does not come to terms with globalization, nor with either international feminism or feminist internationalism. The second is highly sensitive to at least economic globalization, and local responses to such, but fails to analyse or strategize on feminist internationalism even within its chosen sphere. The presence within such works of single chapters on the international (chapter 5 in Peterson and Runyan, 1993; chapter 10 in Chhachhi and Pittin, 1996b; chapter 9 in Miles, 1996; the last ten to fifteen pages of Pettman, 1996) is promising but in no way adequate.

This is also my feeling about most (though not all) of the multiple and multifarious feminist responses to Beijing/Huairou, in the form of published and unpublished reports, interviews, diaries and reflections. In this case, the material comes not only from the Anglo-Saxon world but Latin America, Western Europe, China, India and elsewhere (see, for example, Chuan Renyan, 1995; and the often international special bulletins, sections or issues of journals, such as CLADEM, 1996; Cotidiano Mujer, 1996a; Debate Feminista, 1995; Indian Journal of Gender Studies, 1996; Lokayan Bulletin, 1995). This extensive and growing literature provides us, in my view, rather with a subject *of* than a means *for* analysis. Where it is – as it frequently is – theoretically incisive or politically relevant, this is customarily in matters *other* than globalization, global institutions and global solidarity. The situation may be changing (see the papers of Eisenstein, 1996; Helie-Lucas, 1996; Melchiori, 1996; Rivero, 1996),[7] but for the bulk of the writers, Beijing/Huairou appears as a place women visited rather than one they

– briefly, partially – occupied. Global activity remains a moment rather than a process. Global space remains detached from rather than informing/informed by local space.

Why is there this blind spot in feminist theorizing? It can hardly be due to a shortage of brilliant and innovative feminist theorists. Consider the intensive feminist debates, and shelves of feminist books, on sexuality, violence, patriarchy, masculinity, technology, history, ecology, human rights, culture, autonomy, development, pornography, nationalism, democracy, difference and last (but not, of course, least) citizenship. There may be an academic as well as a political obstacle here. An obvious explanation lies in the entrapment of feminist political theory within the still dominant nation-state and inter-state paradigm. Another might be the absence of any significant contemporary left (implying *machista* and therefore provocative) discourse on internationalism. A third might be the feminist recoil against earlier notions of global sisterhood. A fourth might be the more general and related fear of master discourses and universalisms – and what can be more so than 'world views', either literal or figurative?

The absence of such a literature represents something of a challenge, which I will attempt to take up in the rest of this chapter.

The International Level: Beijing and Huairou

I begin my analysis with women's movements on an inter-state platform. In so far, however, as the Fourth World Conference on Women (4WCW) had attached to it an NGO Forum, was attended by 20,000–30,000 women from movements and NGOs (as well as in individual capacity), and was prepared for locally, nationally, regionally and internationally by such women, we have to consider relations between women's movements here also. Finally, in so far as the 4WCW was one of a series of global conferences recently, we also have to ask ourselves what implications it might have for the construction of some kind of alternative global civil society.

We cannot simply equate 'the global women's movement' with Beijing, or even with Huairou. A very large number of women, and of women's organizations, covering a great variety of identities, interests and geographical areas, were there. But, of course, millions were not –

and many feminists and women's organizations either refused to attend, considered themselves un(der)represented there or felt they had been excluded from the preparatory process or from national-regional delegations.[8] Others considered it simply a talking shop, without real significance to women on the ground.[9] Latin American feminist activists, working with both the urban and rural poor, from Nicaragua in the North (Bueso, 1996: 13) to Chile in the South, had a more positive evaluation.[10]

Here then are some reflections on the complex, novel, globalizing process, the globalized time and space, now known throughout the international women's movement simply as 'Beijing'. Thinking of this rather as *Beijing/Huairou* reminds us of the NGO and social movement periphery umbilically attached to the inter-state core. Stressing that it was the *Fourth* World Conference *on* Women reminds us both that it is the latest of a series and that these were primarily conceived as conferences on, rather than of, women. What follows will be a series of propositions about the event, rather than a description of it (for which see International Women's Tribune Centre, 1994, 1995a, b; NGO Forum on Women Secretariat, 1996).[11]

The UN international conferences in the 1990s, on ecology, human rights, population, social problems, women and human settlements, represent both an expression of and a response to the civilizational crisis symbolized by the collapse of the Berlin Wall (the victory of the West over East), the Gulf War (the victory of the North over the South), and Rio (the problematic nature of the victory). These conferences are an initiative of the inter-state UN agencies, in their attempt to re-establish control of the processes, problems and movements (intellectual, social) of an increasingly globalized world, in which the nation-state and inter-statism are being challenged from both without and within. The conferences also, however, represent the point at which international development/dependency discourses (essentially Westocentred and/or modernizing) begin to be challenged by global-ization discourses (which *can* also interrogate both the West and modernity). Whilst attempting to create a new global and social con-sensus, these conferences simultaneously highlight growing global problems, reveal deep global contradictions, and provide a focal point for global social discontents.

The fora attached to these conferences (but included within at Habitat II in 1996) are a means by which:

1   (inter-)state bodies attempt to harness the innovatory capacity, energy, ideas and mobilizational capacities of the new alternative social movements and NGOs related to such;
2   the new alternative social movements appear most dramatically on a global stage, define themselves in relation to the state, to other hegemonic forces and to each other.

Such conferences provide the ambiguously alternative global social movements with an equally ambiguous space in which to discover, collectively construct and organize themselves. In so far as the social movement and NGO activists present are overwhelmingly from the (university-)educated middle classes, the fora represent a 'globalization from the middle' rather than one from below. The extent to which such activists/leaders speak for the local and the base at such conferences, and speak to these after them, will decide whether or not there is a dynamic and democratic dialectic between the local and the global.

In the absence of any International Gender Organization, any hegemonic International Women's Federation, any agreed Feminist Internationalism, the 4WCW represented a rare space and time at which the 'global feminist and women's movement' took on a visible, dramatic, effective – if inevitably temporary and partial – existence. Beijing/Huairou provided a privileged moment for agenda-setting for the global women's movements of the next century, but in the absence of any agreed movement declaration, the nature of this agenda, and its priorities, can become apparent only in post-Beijing dialogue. The Conference and Forum, and Conference/Forum interaction, provide one example of multiple democratization at global level, as women's organizations struggled and negotiated:

1   within and against the state at the official inter-state Conference;
2   against (and within) conservative bodies in civil society (churches, religions, ethnic particularisms);
3   amongst themselves within the Forum.

Beijing/Huairou was also a cultural and communication event, both an object and subject of

1   dominant cultural/communications globalism, as exemplified by the extensive daily CNN TV coverage (which cannot be dismissed simply as 'distorted' or 'patriarchal');

2   a global solidarity communications/culture, as revealed by the cultural events within the Forum, feminist demonstrations within the Conference, and the extensive feminist declarations on, training in, and use of international computer-mediated communication.

Recognition of the above dominant/alternative duality as a dialectical relation found expression at the Forum/Conference. It suggests the necessity in the future for priority attention to communications and culture not only from movement specialists but also its 'generalists', both political and theoretical. (See further on feminism and 'communications internationalism' in Chapter 7 below.)

Beijing/Huairou represented the highest point yet reached in the transition from the 'global woman question' to 'women's questions about the global'. Beijing/Huairou put both body politics and feminist theory on the global stage, suggesting the necessity of both of these for a solution to contemporary global problems. Movement activity here, therefore, also provides one example or aspect of the self-organization of an alternative global civil society. In confronting authoritarian states and religions, Beijing/Huairou effectively addressed what might be called 'the unfinished business of traditional modernity' (the women's rights not yet established even in advanced industrialized liberal democracies). The NGO Forum, however, also addressed high or radical modernity – the new, complex, informatized and globalized capitalism and the implications of this for the current reshaping of patriarchy.[12] A final 'Declaration of Non-Governmental Organizations' (CLADEM, 1996: 123–5) made trenchant criticism of a globalization controlled by TNCs and international financial agencies. It did not name capitalism as such, but it argued for a radical reconsideration and transformation of concepts, assumptions and structures governing economic and social life, and it called for an alternative global economic model based on equality, mutual respect, environmental sustainability, responsibility towards and participation of women.[13]

The propositions above only highlight the need for further information, reflection and dialogue. What follows, therefore, amounts to a research agenda, something definitely required by the importance of the event. This would cover, amongst others, the following issues. (As we will see shortly, some of these issues are already being raised locally in the Latin American region; others are explored in later parts of this chapter; yet others are addressed in the following chapter.)

1   *History.* How are we to understand the rise and fall, or successive waves, of the international women's movements, and the relationship of these to inter-state conferences?

2   *World conferences on women – and women in world conferences.* What is the significance of the successive UN world conferences for relations between women and states, between women and capital, between women and patriarchal institutions/ideologies, between women's organizations and other democratic forces, and between women themselves? To what extent and in what manner did regional or issue movements/networks participate in, learn from and determine the process of the conferences?

3   *Preparing for Beijing/Huairou.* How did the various National/Regional Co-ordinations relate to the movement regionally, to other such internationally, to middle-class and poor/minority women locally, to state and inter-state organs at different levels? How did the Co-ordinations relate to the different 'streams, spaces and knots' (Vargas, 1991) in the different regional women's movements?[14]

4   *Participating in Beijing/Huairou.* Which were the major political forces, forms and actors behind and within the event?[15] Which significant new actors were present? What kind of impact might it have had on such actors, as well as on different kinds of NGOs participating, and what kind of global public impact is it having?

5   *Projecting beyond Beijing/Huairou.* What kind of issues, proposals or decisions came out of the Conference and NGO Forum (during the event, from reports, reflections and follow-up meetings) with respect to the activities of women's movements and NGOs themselves at every level?

6   *Global women's networks.* What role is being played by such networks (apparently structured supra-nationally and addressed to the regional/global), and to what extent do they overcome the traditional limitations and conflicts of territorially based or state-focused women's organizations?

7   *The financial basis for the global women's movement.* In so far as the Southern women's movements consist largely of NGOs, funded by liberal-democratic Northern states, foundations, development-funding organizations and churches, what future financial basis can or should be developed under conditions of global neo-liberalism, and if and as Northern paternalism is challenged by non-Northern movements?

8   *The increasing centrality of communication and culture.* To what extent is it true that the crucial form of the global women's movement *is* that of communication/culture? To what extent would this imply greater possible variety, dialogue, cohesion, flexibility, impact on laws and institutions, mass reach and meaningful participation? To what extent do both imply the necessity to rethink the global women's movement in cultural/communicational rather than political/organizational ones?

9   *The relationship of the women's movement to a global civil society.* To what extent, and in which ways, does the problematic global women's movement both benefit from and contribute to the development of an equally problematic alternative global civil society? In so far as it is recognized that such a global civil society is (unlike a national one) something still to be imagined and constructed, does women's citizenship *globally* have more radical implications than it might *regionally* or *nationally*?

10 *The necessity for realistic global feminist utopias.* In so far as it is recognized that utopias provide an intellectual, ethical and aesthetic position from which can be mounted both a holistic and an effective critique of the existent, and in so far as it is recognized that the latter must today address global society, what kind(s) of realistic/idealistic global utopia(s) does the women's movement already offer, and need?

11 *Women's global solidarity.* Is it not necessary to deconstruct such terms as 'International Women's Solidarity' or 'Global Feminist Solidarity'? Could not this help to avoid reduction or homogenization, to surpass binary oppositions, and to spell out, in more precise terms, what is sometimes now covered by merely evocative terms such as 'transversal politics' (Yuval-Davis, 1995) or 'reciprocal solidarity' (Helie-Lucas, 1996).

Internationalism, it should finally be remembered, is not simply a matter of activity within an international instance, nor is it limited to the international level, nor does it require global reach. Etymologically, as earlier stated, it is a relation between nations/nationals/nationalisms. Historically it has been demonstrated between two specified countries/ regions, or within a particular region. Indeed, it is at the regional, rather than global, level that internationalism is likely to be practised most intensively. Nowhere, perhaps, is this better illustrated than in the case of Latin America, with a long past and intense present of women's internationalism. This will be demonstrated in the next two sections of this chapter, dealing in turn with the rise of internationalism in and around the region, and then with its forward march halted, at least temporarily – with considerable significance for the development of the new global solidarity.

The Regional Level: Latin America and the Caribbean before Beijing[16]

In Latin America and the Caribbean (LAC) there is now a rather developed feminist movement (Radcliffe and Westwood, 1993; Safa, 1990; Vargas 1992a). There is also possibly the most intensive and extensive set of feminist regional internationalisms, which have apparently developed in a fruitful dialectic with a more global one. Up until 1996 it appeared that a long history of informal and formal relations had allowed Latin America to work through and, possibly, beyond the dichotomies that have plagued other regional feminisms. We will see that this has not been the case. But there are lessons for internationalism to be learnt also from this fall from grace.

Let us begin with a little history. Francesca Miller (1990) is primarily concerned with the participation of Latin American feminists in intra-American conferences, themselves attached to the International Conferences of American States (i.e. both North and South America). She argues as follows:

> [T]he transnational arena held a particular appeal for Latin American feminists. There are a number of reasons this was so. Within their national communities, they were disfranchised; and, as elsewhere, the national social and political arenas were characterised by androcracy. Moreover, Latin American female intellectuals were particularly alienated from politics as practised within their countries, excluded from leadership positions by the forces of opposition as well as by their governments. The inter-American arena in the first half of this century proved to be an important domain for feminist activity, one in which women activists from throughout the Americas pursued a number of the longstanding goals of international feminism. Two of the themes that emerge in the examination of women's concerns in this period are ... legal and civil reform and the search for international peace. (Miller, 1990: 10)

Women played an active role in the Latin (later Pan-)American Scientific Congresses which began in 1898. The women who attended these also played a significant role in a first international feminist congress.[17] This took place in Buenos Aires in 1910, was sponsored by liberal, labour and socialist organizations and took up a broad range of feminist and social reform issues. As the scientific congresses became politicized (i.e. diplomatic events), women felt the necessity to organize themselves separately. Eventually there was created an Inter-American Commission of Women within the International Conference of American States. According to Miller (1990: 13–14), the participants in such conferences were neither diplomats nor spouses, nor were the Latin Americans simply endorsing something sponsored by North American feminists.[18] The anti-imperialist Women's International League for Peace and Freedom (Foster, 1989) was heavily involved and influential. One of the conferences specifically attacked North American imperialism. The Latin Americans also attacked their own governments:

> In this era, the women active at the international level had little tradition of identifying with the nation-state. To the contrary, they had historically articulated their position as other, within the home, the society, and the nation, and looked to the transnational arena as the space where they could find mutual support from one another and publicise their agenda. (Miller, 1990: 19)

In so far as these women felt excluded from their national polities, we would seem to have a parallel to labour internationalism before labour was enfranchised, unions and parties recognized, and then incorporated into the nation-state. Miller, in any case, reveals in this period no such feminist identification with states as were to appear during the Second Wave in the 1970s.

This Second Wave seems to have actually begun with, or been preceded by, initiatives of states, inter-state organizations, the Communist and Third World movements. Given that these 'women's organization' initiatives all related to nation-states or blocs of such, it may not be so paradoxical that the blocs actually collaborated with each other, at different places and times, thus providing platforms for major conflicts in Third World/First World, nationalist/imperialist, socialist/capitalist, or revolutionary-women/bourgeois-feminist terms. These conflicts found most dramatic expression at the NGO Tribunal held at the International Women's Year (IWY) Conference, Mexico City, 1975. Here the North American Betty Friedan played the role of (or was taken to represent?) Northern Imperialist Middle-Class Feminism, and the Bolivian Domitila Barrios de Chungara played the role of (or was taken to represent?) Southern Nationalist Revolutionary Proletarian Woman (Greer, 1986; Miller 1992a: 199–202). Cuba, simultaneously Third Worldist, nationalist and Communist, spearheaded state-socialist international women's initiatives, through the FMC (Federacion de Mujeres Cubanas/Federation of Cuban Women). Vilma Espin, revolutionary veteran, wife of Raul Castro and Central Committee member, has led the organization almost as long as Fidel Castro has Cuba. She has also always avoided calling herself a feminist. The FMC, which has played a major role in raising women's issues and changing women's roles within Cuba, also saw itself as the vanguard of the Women's International Democratic Federation – the Communist-front organization for women. A statement by Castro at an FMC congress in 1980 reveals, in all its richness (or poverty), the nature and discourse of an internationalism of blocs as addressed to women:

> Our federation has undertaken a lot of important internationalist work in the Women's International Democratic Federation, and also in the United Nations, with IWY and the International Year of the Child … The FMC has earned a great deal of prestige internationally, in international bodies, in women's organisations in other countries – countries of both the socialist camp and the capitalist camp – liberation movement organisations and organisations of underdeveloped countries. I think that our federation has contributed enormously to the foreign policy of the revolution. (cited in Miller, 1992b: 213)

Looking at the five LAC Feminist Encounters (*Encuentros*) that took place between 1981 and 1990 (Miller, 1992a; Sternbach *et al.*, 1992; Vargas, 1992a), it appears as if the feminist movement in Latin America had been able to avoid or surpass such discourses whilst still addressing itself to the women's experiences they articulated. This might have been because the major social source of the new wave of feminism was neither the traditional political/state elites nor the 'popular women's movement' organized by populist, socialist or Communist parties. The new feminists came largely from the same ranks as those involved in the first wave – educated middle-class women, often academics. Such people had access to the work of people like Betty Friedan and Simone de

Beauvoir, had sometimes studied in Western Europe or the USA, sometimes having been exiled there. Being, moreover, commonly from socialist parties (Vargas, 1992b), they were also open to respect for and co-operation with poor urban or rural women. In so far as they came from the socialist tradition, they also shared its internationalist ethic. Developing this internationalism has been a far from painless process, but, along the way, Latin American feminism has not only demonstrated a considerable pluralism, flexibility and tolerance, it has also earned the respect of Northern feminists:

> Latin American feminisms hold lessons for feminists in industrialised countries. We ... could revitalise our own movements if we tapped the enormous creative energies embodied in our own *movimientos de mujeres* (women's movements). The present vitality of Third World feminisms within the industrialised world is indicative of this potential. Regressive economic policies and rightwing governments in the 'First World' have also created conditions ripe for the mobilisation of poor and working-class women and women of colour ... Just as North American or European feminism has provided crucial insights for the second wave of feminism in Latin America, perhaps now Latin American feminisms can enrich and inspire our own movements. (Sternbach *et al.*, 1992: 433–4)

This is true in more senses than these authors reveal, since they concentrate on the *encuentros*, and then deal with these more as political than intellectual events. But Latin American feminism (either inside or outside the *encuentros*) has also produced theoretical and strategic documents of considerable originality and potency. These not only contribute to the enrichment of Northern feminisms. They also reveal an openness to other social movements, and thus potentially to other internationalisms:

> We are living in a time, not only in Latin America, characterised by the simultaneous emergence of new social subjects, multiple rationalities and identities, expressed in the social movements. This opens up more individual and collective possibilities for transforming social values. It also reflects the fact that experiences of oppression and subordination, and the resistance to them, are expressed in so many different ways that there cannot be one global explanation which encompasses all social conflicts. The acknowledgement of these multiple and diverse rationalities refutes the idea of an

emancipatory process that articulates aspirations within one dynamic only and through an exclusive and privileged axis. (Vargas, 1992a: 196)

Gina Vargas (1992c) has sketched both the extent and limitations of Latin American feminist internationalism. She distinguishes the various streams, forms, themes and actors, suggests significant periods and identifies current problems. The streams are the feminist, the popular and that of women in the 'traditional-formal' spaces (parties, unions, federations). Of these, as suggested above, it is the feminist one that has been most involved in internationalism. The forms include networks of many kinds, themselves organizing conferences and campaigns, keeping in touch through magazines, newsletters or electronic mail (cf. Miller, 1992b: 217–18, 225–7). Some of these networks extend across the Southern continents or are concerned with South–North dialogues. The themes include health and legal services, popular education, communication itself, and issues such as race, sexual option, ecology, etc. The actors, apart from the feminist activists, increasingly include women from different class, ethnic, party, labour, peasant, indigenous and youth organizations.

The two periods distinguished by Vargas are those of the building and unfolding of the sub-continental international movement (1980–7) and that of its expansion and enrichment (1987 onwards). The first period was marked by a Latin-American version of 'global sisterhood' which initially provided a collective identity but also suppressed differences. During the second period such differences have found public expression in the *encuentros* and other meetings. These differences include contradictions between and within distinct Latin American regions (Central America, the Caribbean, South America). There are political tensions linked to nations/regions which have not yet been freely discussed: the failure of Peruvian feminists to take up an imaginative Ecuadorian proposal for demilitarizing and de-nationalizing a frontier dispute; the initial difficulties some Central American feminists had in condemning Peru's terrorist Shining Path movement for assassinating the best known popular feminist leader in Lima (they apparently considered it a revolutionary guerilla movement of the Central American type). It seems that, with the Latin American and Caribbean contributions to, and follow-up from, the Beijing Conference, 1995, we may have to now identify a third phase, in which the regional movement sees itself more globally. It is this new phase that seems to have given rise to the conflicts within the movement alluded to above and to be dealt with below.

The late arrival of the 'popular sectors' (such as indigenous women) in international relations reveals, or gives rise to, a series of problems in the advancing of solidarity relations. One is the existing domination of South–North international relations not simply by middle-class feminists but by those in the NGOs. These have long had a special relationship with agencies, governments and women in the North. This relationship has, until recently, been little questioned either from within the NGOs or from outside. Another problem is the patronizing of the popular sectors by certain middle-class feminisms in Latin America. Yet another is a patronizing of the same by Northern aid agencies or solidarity committees:

> Support from governments and/or women in the North in this case has some vices: their proposals and demands are fundamentally inspired [by] ideological proposals . . . alien to the feminist proposal, and/or that feminism itself aims to surpass: populism and Marxism, generally in their less creative expressions (emphasis laid upon anti-imperialist postures more than on democratic ones). The relationship of women in the North, in the case of the [Latin-American] Domestic Workers' Union, has thrived a lot upon the basis of class (poor women versus petite-bourgeoisie), stemming from a guilty and only economic-minded solidarity on behalf of women in the North. (Vargas, 1992c)

This need not always be the case, as is suggested by the activities of Mujer a Mujer/Woman to Woman.[19] Mujer a Mujer (MaM) is or was a feminist collective of women from Canada, the USA, the Caribbean and Mexico, based in Mexico City itself. The origins and inspiration of MaM are not necessarily those of the regional internationalism in Latin America and the Caribbean. It makes little reference to regional internationalism and I am not sure whether it has been involved with the *encuentros* or other regional networks. It seems to have come out of the tradition of North-to-South labour and women's solidarity movements. But it certainly goes beyond the common characteristics of such movements.

Mujer a Mujer began, around 1984, as an international solidarity project for women workers and seems to have either avoided or surpassed the traditional North-to-South aid/solidarity model. With Mexican and other Latina women growing in numbers in North America, with increasing numbers of US plants shifting there, and now with the North American Free Trade Agreement (NAFTA) confronting the peoples of all three (see Cavanagh *et al.*, 1992; Gabriel and Macdonald, 1994; Moody and McGinn, 1992), MaM appeared to recognize that solidarity is a multidirectional as well as a multifaceted matter.

Mujer a Mujer was involved with labour, community, women's, communication and computer groups in Mexico and North America. It was a major mover in the first Trinational Women's Conference on Free Trade and Economic Integration, held in Mexico, 5–9 February 1992. The activities of MaM reveal, furthermore, that labour networking is not restricted to trade union networking, and that it can be a result, or even an integral part, of the work of an ASM – in this case a feminist one.

An account of the Trinational Women's Conference, by a MaM activist and conference co-organizer, indicates the way this movement was broadening both beyond wage-labour and beyond the initial three countries involved:

> The world is changing so quickly that even as we met the notion of 'tri-national' links was beginning to appear outdated ... Maquilas [cheap-labour assembly plants] have already taken root in countries like Guatemala and El Salvador. Our analysis and solidarity must begin to weave new connections. The focus on women's labour sometimes constrained our insights. While much path-breaking solidarity has been begun through union and other networks, we must not limit ourselves to those sectors. In Mexico, women within the urban poor movement have begun to look at issues of free trade, where it comes from and how it will change their struggles. They have already identified the need to develop an international perspective and solidarity links. (Yanz, 1992: 8)

MaM was primarily oriented toward working women, and it could therefore be understood to be interested only in international solidarity of or with women as workers. This is evidently not the case, since its newsletter, *Correspondencia*, shows that it also took up general feminist issues, such as those of reproductive rights, violence against women, lesbianism, the position of coloured and indigenous women. Unlike most international labour networks, this one was also theoretically minded. It pressed for a gender perspective on all issues – such as the NAFTA. Some of the materials from the Trinational Conference, indeed, seem to suggest that, whilst the event presented women's demands, a feminist perspective was not yet sufficiently developed. Thus, the Canadian report concluded that: 'For the future, we have more work to do to strengthen our gender analysis. We need to be linking theory, research, education and action' (Yanz, 1992: 8).

Mujer a Mujer introduced new ways of conceiving the 'mass', 'members', 'followers' or 'audience' addressed by the activists (whether these be workers or women), in so far as value was given to real-life diversity rather than an abstract unity:

> The concept of 'masses' gives way to the valuing of the diversity of unique 'identities'. Each new emerging 'social actor' ('sujeto historico') claims power in areas of experience damaged or buried by domination. Women, for example, bring the intimate and domestic worlds into public view and action. Indigenous peoples confront and offer alternatives to the spread of a racist and environmentally destructive monoculture. (*Correspondencia*, August 1990: 2)

Mujer a Mujer also innovated by involving women of the popular sectors in promoting internationalism. A one-year project was intended to develop *promotoras internacionales* (actually, promoters of internation-al*ism*). Apart from studying such themes as globalization (again), structural adjustment and the NAFTA, the idea was that these women would actively involve their own working or residential communities in an alternative kind of international relations. Participants had been learning English and computer skills, taken part in international conferences and the hosting of delegations. They were intending to identify and contact partners in the USA and Canada. Mujer a Mujer was hoping to publish the bilingual manual developed during this project (*Correspondencia*, No. 14, 1992: 11–13, 19–27).

Interestingly enough, MaM's activities even raised major strategic issues on *labour* internationalism that had remained little debated in the male dominated organizations or fora – right or left. At the Trinational Conference there was, thus, discussion on whether or not it made sense to demand that the Free Trade Area bring about an 'upward harmonisation' of working conditions and rights, given that it was premised precisely on the difference in costs, rights and conditions:

> We all spoke of the need for further research and exchange of information in order to be able to act strategically in this new world ... There were those who emphasised 'upward harmonisation' as a goal for regional struggle. Others favoured demands which could be immediately achievable within the

logic of the new system, in order to lay a solid foundation for future struggle.
(Trinational Women's Conference, 1992: 14)

One does not have to have a specific position here to recognize the opportunities and dangers opened by both strategies, and therefore the importance of wide-ranging debate on the issue. The activities of MaM, and its reflections on these, revealed connections both with Latin American feminist internationalism and with a new kind of labour internationalism.

We have, however, also to come to terms with the decline of MaM in 1995-6, and the disappearance of *Correspondencia* as one of the most forceful and attractive bearers of the new internationalism.[20] Mujer a Mujer seems to have suffered the fate of so many other internationalist networks: burnout amongst the self-financed founders, lack of the necessary funding, pressure of other occupational and political concerns. It may be some comfort to MaM to know of the Italian concept of the 'biodegradable organization', its activists and experiences being recycled in other activities. MaM still exists as a network of the initiated and interested, and we must hope that the thus far lacking account of its history will eventually appear. Where 'successful' internationalist projects are invitations to praise and imitation, 'failures' are invitations to critical reflection and learning.

The positive Northern evaluation given LAC Feminist *Encuentros*, or its women's movements more generally, should not be allowed to obscure their ups and downs, as just indicated above, and their continuing tensions. There is within Latin America an ultra-radical tendency, which first found international expression at the time of the Sixth *Encuentro* in El Salvador, 1993 (Gargallo, 1993; Pisano, 1993). This presents a sharply differing evaluation of its development. In one case it sets up a binary opposition between the 'fairies' (supposedly in the NGOs, collaborating with local governments, in international networks, collaborating with UN institutions, receiving foreign funding) and the 'witches' (supposedly autonomous from foreign funding, collaboration with states, and patriarchal ideology).[21] This tendency was given the responsibility for organizing the seventh *Encuentro*, in Chile, 1996, and evidently intended the event to be controlled by the witches rather than the fairies (see the interview with Margarita Pisano by Garrido, 1996). A large number of Chilean feminists, from women's organizations and Santiago-based international networks, protested publicly against this (Cotidiano Mujer, 1996b). The ultra-radical feminists in Latin America have, however, been forcefully raising issues about the NGO form, foreign-funding and Northern patronage that the movement more generally has been either observing through rose-tinted spectacles or turning a blind eye to.[22]

Within the experience of feminism in and from Latin America, up till 1996, we could apparently witness a way forward from the paralysing dichotomies bequeathed by the traditional politics of protest. But Latin American feminist internationalism is not a utopia promised to jaded or faded feminisms in other regions. Globalization has also apparently meant a growth in the kind of tensions that have marked feminism internationally.

The Regional Level: Latin America (without the Caribbean) after Beijing[23]

The Seventh Latin American and Caribbean Encounter was held in Cartagena, on the coast near Santiago, Chile, 23–26 November 1996.[24] Organization of this event was, as above stated, in the hands of a small minority of Chilean feminists. These called themselves *feministas autonomas* (autonomist feminists).[25] They were to a large extent lesbian feminists, some being movement veterans, many of them young and new to the *encuentros*. Other lesbian feminists were (self-)excluded from the preparatory committee or condemned in the event itself. Representatives of the majority of Chilean feminists had found it impossible to work with the organizing committee and then issued a call to other feminists in the region to boycott the event. The majority of Chilean feminists did eventually boycott it, although many attended the opening. No one came from the English-speaking Caribbean, thus belying the full name of the event. Latin American attendance was way down on previous encounters.[26] But, even so, the 'autonomous feminists' represented only about one-quarter of the 400–700 (estimates vary between days and amongst observers) present.

The position of the dominating minority found expression in a Plenary Document of the 'Workshop on the Deepening of Autonomous Feminism' (Autonomous Feminists, 1996). This either implicitly or explicitly condemns feminists or feminisms that (in its own words) subordinate or integrate themselves into the system of power and inequality, that reduce feminism to a list of demands, that act within the existing system of legitimacy. It condemns means of communication that create 'thinking and writing elites', here suggesting that the Santiago-based Latin American NGO, Fempress, was arrogating to itself the voice of feminism in the region.[27] It condemns negotiations with national or international institutions that cause 'hunger and misery', such as the World Bank. It condemns the speaking of English as a condition for participation 'in the grand international events of Imperialism' (here apparently alluding to Beijing).

The document suggested that Latin American feminism needed to recover its lost roots, that feminism departed from the personal, the body and the 'I', that its crucial bases were those of 'non-institutionalised imaginary spaces', that its primary languages were Portuguese and Spanish, that it should relate internationally (only?) to 'rebellious European and US women who question everything' and who placed themselves beyond the limits of political or academic power. It also addressed the problem of 'international cooperation' and funding, admitting that the movement needed resources but demanding a questioning of such, and saying that the creation of its own resources was a challenge to the movement's creativity.

Two paragraphs are significant for the intended programme of the event and for its style of operation. The first said that an appeal to young women required that feminism create a new image of the world rather than a series of partial and institutional demands. The other said 'Our tolerance is great but has limits' and that no tolerance should be shown for those who 'sell or deny us'. The first of these apparently expressed the intention that the *Encuentro* should discuss the basic politics and ethics of feminism, rather than dividing into the customary workshops that have dealt not only with such issues but also with the demands of, for example, black, waged or indigenous women, or the issues of the NGO networks, such as health, violence, human rights, ecology or communication. The second of these suggested that tolerance would not be extended at the *Encuentro* to those opposed to 'autonomous feminism'.

The *Encuentro* turned out, in practice, to represent an attempt by the dominant minority to impose its vision on the majority or, possibly, to simply put its major opponents in the stocks. Of the six or eight speakers on the opening day, only two were 'non-autonomous' feminists. An attempt was made to deny opportunity for discussion at the opening plenary. A banner was raised behind the back of Gina Vargas (Regional Co-ordinator for LAC NGOs at Beijing), warning against 'Patriarchy in the Cloak of a Power-Greedy Feminist'. Shouted slogans condemned, as 'corrupt', 'traitors', 'sleeping with the enemy' or 'patri-archal', those, including an internationally active lesbian feminist, who had other ideas. In addition to the attack on Fempress, accusations of personal corruption in use of Beijing funds were made against Vargas and menaces were uttered.[28] Friends of the latter were sufficiently alarmed as to provide her with a personal bodyguard for the rest of the event.

Despite the announced intention of discussing feminist ethics, these were expressed in a certain direction rather than as a principle or an extent. Thus, whilst tolerance was requested from the platform for the banner-raisers, none was shown for the majority demanding its removal. Nor were the issues of development co-operation, of the NGO form, of Northern funding, the relation of the national, regional and international further deepened, although they might have been expressed in more reasoned form.[29] Thus, the Mexican, Ximena Bed-regal, was reported as saying:

> The confusion of the feminist movement with the collection of institutions employing women, even if they have a radically feminist focus, has as con-sequence not only that the political interests of the movement subordinate themselves to the institutional, working and professional interests of their members, but also that the leadership of the movement has become cen-tralised in those institutions that development cooperation defines as most efficient and therefore more worthy of financial assistance. (Leon, 1996: 23)

There remains, however, a significant ambiguity of the ultra-radicals concerning foreign funding. It is unclear from their statements whether it is the nature of the *sources*, the *recipients*, or the *mode of transfer* that is to be politically or ethically questioned (in other words whether dirty or dubious money can become clean or virtuous by giving it to the right rather than the wrong feminists, in the right rather than the wrong way).[30]

Despite considerable pre-*Encuentro* discussion amongst majority fem-inists in Latin America, there was no agreed strategy on how to meet a concerted attack of which there had been long and plentiful warning. At a report-back, organized by the MEMCH (Movimiento de Emancipa-cion de Mujeres Chilenas/Movement for the Emancipation of Chilean

Women) the day after the *Encuentro*, the word 'fundamentalist' was the one most generally used of the *Encuentro* organizers. Others compared its purist ideology and intimidatory style to that of the Peruvian left terrorists, *Sendero Luminoso*. During the *Encuentro* itself attempts were made to conciliate, negotiate, and even make concessions to a group that was apparently interested only in polarizing, condemning and dominating.[31] One workshop, entitled 'Neither the One or the Other', attempted to take a position independent of the 'two vocal tendencies' and their 'dichotomic logic', stating that 'to fragment and divide is ALSO to play the game of neoliberalism'.[32] Another workshop, said to have been attended by 170 women, entitled its final statement (in evident reference to the previous one) 'From Neither the One or the Other to Both the One and the Other', and spoke in more customary and conciliatory *Encuentro* language, of diversity and plurality. But it also recognized the current fragility of the feminist movement in the region, rejected the demonizing of institutions, and called for the revitalization or creation of autonomous feminist spaces that would produce specific feminist policies and practices.

Seventy socialist feminists, friendly to the Federation of Cuban Women and the (ex-)Communist Women's International Democratic Federation, produced their own statement, making no reference at all to what was taking place in the meeting. Neither did a woman from Chile's major indigenous community. But an improvised workshop of black women criticized the *Encuentro* for not dealing with issues of race and ethnicity, and suggested that any final document would be one of white women only.

I am concerned with this event primarily in terms of its relationship with the international and its implications for internationalism. It seems not unreasonable to see the 'autonomous feminists' in terms of an attempted escape or retreat from a world of increasing instability, distance and – particularly – complexity. However, as some kind of feminist fundamentalism, this one appears, from its own statements and actions, to be a weak echo of its historical predecessors (in the North of the 1970s–1980s) and its contemporary equivalents (certain anti-pornography or eco-feminisms). It does show clear parallels with religious, racial, ethnic and socialist fundamentalisms in its reference to some pure original state or source, in its claim to truth and morality, in its Manichaean ethics, in its binary logic, in its representation of the external/surrounding/dominant world as simply, totally and inevitably evil, in its rhetorical invocation of the suffering masses and of privileged languages,[33] in its politics of polarization, its accusations of corruption, treason and betrayal, and in its blindness to the manner in which its own practices reproduce the evils it condemns.

The phenomenon has, however, more specific roots in the dilemmas of contemporary Latin American and Caribbean (and international) feminism in the period of neo-liberalism and globalization, and it is these specific origins that explain, at least for me, its only quasi-fundamentalism, its internal inconsistencies and ambiguities. The tendency is capable of expressing, or at least revealing, certain long-standing and fundamental problems, mentioned earlier in this chapter or in the book more generally. But there is no evidence of a capacity of the ultra-radicals to translate moral outrage into a relevant new ethic or a positive political programme. Far less clear are the lineaments of their alternative feminist culture or civilization – something that is present in other radical feminisms internationally. And any strategy for reaching this, particularly in the light of neo-liberalism and globalization, is equally absent.

More revealing, however, of the crisis in the Latin American feminist movement was the tendency of the overwhelming majority of Chilean and continental activists to either avoid confronting the ultra-radical minority by staying away, or to concede to or conciliate them ('Both the One and the Other'). Mainstream Latin American feminists had evidently thought their movement was free of the negative traits they have identified in the patriarchal socialist movement, or experienced amongst themselves elsewhere internationally. It also seems as if the mainstream had been for too long tolerant of, or even complicit with, unprincipled behaviour, tendencies or leaders. It is clear that some of the criticisms touched a guilty nerve. It also seems as if the majority accepted in practice what previous Encounters have denied in principle: that all women (in the movement?) are sisters. For one or a combination of these reasons, the majority was either unwilling or unable at this *Encuentro* to confront its own millenarians, Machiavellians and matriarchs. The evaluation of Carina Gobbi (1996: 9) adds another note:

> What one can say about this encounter is that the Latin American and Caribbean feminist movement forms part of the social and political map of the region; because of this it cannot avoid bleeding from the wound that

affects the left and all the social and political movements of the continent: the traditional forms of doing politics, self-centred, non-dialogical, punitive, messianic, incapable of confronting strategies, of dissolving spaces of power without fracturing, perplexed before this enemy without a face that is neoliberalism and its postmodernity.

Gobbi's identification of the 'enemy without a face' is perhaps even more pertinent than she realizes. Even *Encuentro* participants independent of or opposed to the ultra-radicals tended to evoke the infinitely complex and contradictory process of globalization only in terms of neo-liberal policies, and then only as threat and negation. The presentation of globalization, by Vargas (1996a, b), in terms of both threat and opportunity did not find significant echo at the event, reeling, as it was, from an attack, unprecedented in *Encuentro* experience, from friends or comrades-in-arms whose faces were familiar to all.[34]

It should by now be more than evident that being a new, women's or feminist movement is no more a guarantee of democratic, pluralist or internationalist character than being an old, worker, union or socialist one. The sobering experience dealt with just above has parallels in the international ecological movement and, as with the ecological movement, the experience points towards the necessity for a theory, analysis and strategy for a new kind of global solidarity that so far have hardly existed. An attempt to produce such a theory, analysis and strategy is made in the next chapter, but before doing so we will consider in more detail some of the problems and promises revealed above. We will start with two of the problems. The first is that of surpassing the binary oppositions that have plagued traditional internationalism (e.g. left/right, liberal/socialist, worker/capitalist, reformist/revolutionary). The second is that of dealing with 'aid' as a highly problematic aspect of internationalism – without, of course, setting up a binary opposition between aid and solidarity!

Problematizing Binary Oppositions within Feminist Internationalism

The problem of dichotomic thinking, or reduction to binary oppositions, is one that has not only been experienced but also recognized and reflected upon elsewhere in the international women's movement.

Many contemporary women's movements, NGOs or networks operate both inside and outside international agencies. One of these is on health and reproductive rights and it has given rise to one of the serious reflections on what it itself calls global solidarity (Keysers and Smyth, 1991; cf. Mies, 1992; Reinalda and Verhaaren, 1990: 279–82; UBINIG, 1989).

The report is primarily on the Sixth International Women and Health Meeting, Manila, 1990, attended by some 500 women from 60 countries. But it also gives an overview of previous conferences, starting with a first one in Europe, 1977. It mentions a movement away from 'individual choice' in matters of contraception, etc., to questions of community-level health needs, and to recognition of the necessity for global organization and action against the powerful national and international population control and health institutions. This movement has been accompanied over time by criticism of Eurocentric discourse within the movement, and insistence that a variety of Third World experiences and voices be heard.

The Manila meeting was concerned precisely with the creation of global solidarity for women's health and reproductive rights. An opening address linked issues of women's health with global economic crisis, militarization, violence against women, and international population-control policies. Two planned workshops, on 'Redefining Global Solidarity' and maintaining 'Feminist Integrity in Mainstream Organisations', were merged, leading to intensive and animated exchanges on research, funding, communication, organizational networking, campaigns, as well as on such issues as co-optation, institutionalization, radicalism versus reformism, racism and classism. Women from the Third World

> raised their concerns over the existing unequal distribution of resources (information and funds) between them and their sisters in the North. Information should not only be disseminated from the established institutes but there should also be an active sharing of experiences, strategies, ideas, etc. amongst all women in the health networks, implying that also South–South and South–North communication should be facilitated. (Keysers and Smyth, 1991: 28)

Both the Third World organizations and their funders expressed a desire to 'attain a more empowering funding relationship' (ibid.).

Despite this apparently advanced agenda, Loes Keysers and Inez Smyth identify the operation of both explicit and implicit dichotomies during the meeting. The explicit one was between the international institutions (World Bank, Population Council, International Planned Parenthood Federation) and the grass-roots organizations. This, however, was underlaid by 'a more elaborate dichotomy', which, 'for the very fact of remaining unspoken, is highly dangerous' (Keysers and Smyth, 1991). They present this diagrammatically as follows:

Institutionalization	*Grass-roots work*
North	South
White	Black
Rich	Poor

In terms of power	
Dominant	Marginal
Powerful	Powerless

Keysers and Smyth recognize the real-world origins of such a dichotomy in the North/South divide, in the death of the early myth of global sisterhood, and in the appropriation of feminist language and concerns by powerful right-wing institutions. At the same time, however, they see it as simplistic, since it implies that institutions are unproblematically evil and the grass roots unproblematically good, and also because it 'carries a heavy burden of personal, individualized accusations and distrust' (Keysers and Smyth, 1991: 29) against feminists working within the institutions.

The authors consider it necessary, with respect to the institutions, to distinguish incorporation from meaningful access, and, with respect to the grass roots, to recognize the danger of self-isolation. They conclude here that

> it is important to realise that the two sides of the dichotomy raise problems and questions which have much in common: the danger of marginalisation on the part of the grassroots groups is mirrored by the risk of cooption on the other. The scarcity of resources and the financial vulnerability ... of the grassroots groups, has echoes in the question of accountability which work within 'mainstream' institutions raises. The problems of efficiency and efficacy experienced by grassroots organisations appear as a carbon copy of

> those which, on the other side, emerge from working in highly hierarchical and bureaucratic systems. (Ibid.)

They propose, as antidote to the common problems, and the asserted or implied dichotomies, the possibility and necessity of co-operation:

> [M]uch can be done to prevent the marginalisation of grassroots organisations by the transmission of information from those located in the agencies/organisations in which such information is produced or simply available. Those working in powerful institutions, on the other hand, would find guidance in the thorny question of accountability if grassroots groups made them answerable to them. (Ibid.: 30)

The mirrors, echoes and carbon copies here, it should be pointed out, are only so from a 'feminist point of view'. They assume, in other words, that there *are* feminists, or a feminist *movement*, in the institutions as well as in the grass-roots organizations. If, and to the extent that, this is established, the injunction above follows. I would only like to add that the positions taken here imply a much more complex and difficult world of solidarity activity, but also one that is infinitely richer. It suggests multiple places, spaces and levels of solidarity work, with these essentially interdependent on each other. It is also subversive of the deeply rooted dichotomizing of 'reform within' and 'radicalism beyond' in national and international movements, suggesting that today each is a condition for the existence of the other. Perhaps they always have been but this has been obscured by past civil and uncivil war between and amongst 'politically correct' progressives, blind to the advantage they were giving to the reactionary and conservative right.[35]

The Questions Solidarity Poses Aid

Let us now try to consider, in the spirit of solidarity, the significance of Western capitalist state funding for women's – and even socialist-feminist – projects in the Third World. What happens to 'the gender approach', to 'empowerment' and 'autonomy' when they not only become part of First World state development strategies but even some kind of 'progressive conditionality' on the basis of which – for example – Dutch state or NGO aid may be granted to 'developing' Latin American or African states or NGOs? If it is suggested that we here have a process by which Western feminists, and even their Third World counterparts, are successfully pressurizing the North American or West European governments to recognize Third World women's interests, what model of representation is operating here, what theory explains this practice, what ethic informs it? How does the concept and practice of the 'pressure group' (from liberal pluralist theory and practice) relate to that of the emancipatory social movement? Should feminists even associate themselves with the Western, racist, capitalist and patriarchal discourse and practice of development, a discourse that excludes emancipation and subordinates democratization (Lumis, 1991b)?

Some of the problems are revealed in an article by Kathleen Staudt, who has written widely on women, feminism, development aid and aid bureaucracies (Staudt, 1985, 1987, 1990). Her 1987 article is on a women's centre in the *maquiladora* zone of Mexico, the cheap-labour export-processing area on the border with the USA. Staudt's study suggests contradictions between 'reformist' and 'radical' elements in its programme. She employs an evolutionary empowerment model, rising from the personal level through networking to an organizational one. Questions not raised in her paper, nor in the whole collection of which it forms part, are the following. How, in terms of feminism or women's solidarity, can we understand the US Inter-American Foundation's role in funding such an evaluation (if not the project itself)? How, in the same terms, are we to understand the relationship of the US feminist researcher to the Mexican (feminist? women's?) project, its organizers and its beneficiaries? Even if one accepts Staudt's empowerment model (many ASM theorists consider the network a higher form than the organization), what are the implications for feminist solidarity of such a North-to-South movement of concepts or models, and their specific institutional or academic channelling?

Supposing that one accepts that government ministries and state-funded development agencies do provide a 'traditional space' (cf. Vargas, 1991) for feminists to contest, by what token can it be demonstrated that they are taming the white, male, capitalist, imperial or bureaucratic tiger, and not just being taken for a ride? Should it not be a requirement of feminist (or union) activity within aid that 'aid' be interpreted within a 'solidarity' discourse, instead of the latter being assumed inherent to the former, and that the struggle should be seen primarily as one of replacing the institutions and procedures of aid (tax-funded, government-controlled, state-administered or supervised, top-down, on a donor/recipient model) by those of solidarity (publicly contributed, publicly and democratically controlled, movement super-vised, on the horizontal axis and an interactive model)? We will consider this point below and in Chapter 7.

In so far as one is here involved in a dialogue with development politicians or administrators (or those major national and international agencies tagged by Graham Hancock (1989) the 'Lords of Poverty') should this not be in function of an autonomous international sol-idarity network of feminists and women (otherwise 'donors' and 'recipients')? How, in a minimally more technical or specialized sense, would we distinguish (or oppose?) 'bad' government aid and 'good' government aid (for a 'good' social-democratic aid agency in Latin America see Evers, 1982). Material on the basis of which such questions could be raised does exist, although little of it raises these questions (Ford-Smith, 1990; Himmelstrand, 1990; Jensen, 1990; Kardam, 1990; Moser, 1991; Wieringa, 1990; Yudelman, 1990).

One is here also involved in often considerable flows of cash, from quite specific sources to quite specific projects, organizations and individuals (and not to others). Should not this aspect of the relation-ship – at once the most material and the least visible – receive more than the passing mention, the occasional footnote? Particularly where a sometimes considerable proportion of the 'aid to Third World women' is actually paying for First World institutes and consultancies, research-ers and consultants, at First World rates? I am evidently not proposing that we limit our understanding of the international relationship on the North–South axis to 'the foreign hand' (Gandhi and Shah, 1991: 303–7), but that it should be treated openly and frankly, according to feminist principle (as attempted by Gandhi and Shah and Ford-Smith). Treatment of this potentially explosive/destructive issue should not be left to the Third Worldist or Leninist left (Karat, 1984; Petras, 1990: 214–18), nor to journalists from the dominant press (Eppink and van Straaten, 1991a, b). Yet, until quite recently (Sogge, 1996), they seem to have been the only ones who actually presented figures or made a serious analysis of the cash nexus. Refusing to face this issue would seem to indicate the guilt and dependency associated with development and aid; confronting it would seem to suggest the mutual responsibility associated with solidarity.

In so far, finally, as many feminist academics, professionals and organizers are simultaneously engaged in and committed to both 'development' and 'autonomy', I do feel there is an obligation to confront the increasing criticism not simply on the political but also on the professional and personal levels. Susan George (1992) argues that in the development domain there are no such norms, measures or ethical standards as apply to other professions. What such a criticism would seem to imply, if it is to be taken on board by those involved in women's development and aid projects at either end of the international relationship, is not simply a sense of responsibility and a practice of openness. It is also criteria for discrimination between particular projects and practices, and the public pronouncement and personal assumption of a feminist ethic amongst development professionals (and, of course, amongst academics such as George and I, to whom her strictures would seem to equally apply).

If the last two sections have revealed general problems or raised general questions about women and internationalism, particularly as articulated with 'development' and the 'development axis', the next one is intended rather to suggest, from a labour-case, feminism's potential for emancipating the old social movements.

Feminist Challenges for Unionism Internationally

In 1995 the International Confederation of Free Trade Unions in Brussels produced a pamphlet entitled *Changing the World Through Equality: The Trade Union Vision Document.* This was not, despite its title and appearance, a general union declaration. It was a women's – even a feminist – one. It appeared to have come out of a conference of or on women workers, although this was nowhere indicated. The document was not, however, addressed only to 'the woman question'. It was indeed about changing the world through equality – with that principle extended from gender relations (my phrase) to racial, national and social ones. 'Sexism', 'exploitation', 'oppression', 'transformed global community' – these are not terms one is accustomed to seeing, particularly in potent combination, in international union declarations coming from Brussels. I quote from Points 17 and 18 of the document:

> We envisage a world which is not divided by sexism, racism and xenophobia: these are divisions which undermine our capacity to work together for a better future. We will only realise our human potential when we create

conditions of freedom and mutual respect that end domination and exploitation. We see a society where women and men, young and old, enjoy an
equal share of power and rights, of work and family responsibilities – in their
communities and nations, North and South, East and West. (International
Confederation of Free Trade Unions, 1995)

... Our vision will not be realised overnight, or even perhaps in our lifetime. It means rebuilding our economic, social and political institutions ...
And, finally, our vision demands a firm and genuine commitment by all of us
– women and men – to create a transformed global community where economic and social solidarity will prevail over human degradation, exploitation
and repression. (Ibid.)

Something similar was produced, around the same time, by the
Dutch trade unions. Their *New Trade Union Perspectives* document,
however, was of explicitly female origin (Women and Development
Project, 1994a, b). The main title was again somewhat misleading
because this project was, as its subtitle revealed, actually limited to
Third World women workers in agriculture, export-processing and the
informal sector. This particular document was the result of a research
project, involving (socialist?) feminists from the two major Dutch union
federations, as well as others from a Dutch development-funding NGO
and from the universities. In this case, the G-word (gender) was used
explicitly, and general principles necessary for a rejuvenation of unionism were forcefully expressed.[36] The many radical ideas here were
reinforced by the conclusion to the discussion paper, entitled 'A world
to be won' (which echoes the last line of the *Communist Manifesto* of
1848):

Trade unions have much to gain when increasing numbers of women join
their ranks: more bargaining power, new policies, new female leadership,
the mainstreaming of reproductive needs, and a general revitalisation.

In concluding, we would like to stress that the issues discussed here are
not isolated problems ... International solidarity and mutual support is
needed to strengthen women's bargaining power and to contribute to the
development of guarantees for human dignity and security for all, women
and men. (Women and Development Project, 1994b: 36)

These declarations are as puzzling as they are welcome. It is not clear
to me whether we should rejoice or weep when the major international
union organization, and a long-established and deeply incorporated

Western union, feel it necessary to go, both for international analyses and visions, to feminism.[37] The documents suggest both the exhaustion of the traditional trade union movement and the vitality of the women's one. They also reveal one of the many ways in which the women's movement operates, nationally and internationally – in the interstices of traditional patriarchal social movements. Questions, however, inevitably remain. Do these two feminist swallows presage a summer of gender-sensitive national unionism and renewed labour internationalism? Or are they simply providing an ethical and internationalist image to a series of pragmatic and jaded national organizations? Can a feminist impact in Brussels or Amsterdam spread to unions in Moscow or Buenos Aires? Can activity at international or national levels, in conferences or documents, filter down to impact on the thoughts and actions of ordinary workers, female and male? And, lastly, can the new international solidarity ethic here expressed translate itself into the theory and strategy necessary to bring the vision into existence, either in relation to labour or to internationalism more generally?

Conclusion: From Women's Internationalism to Global Solidarity

I earlier suggested that the lack of reflection on internationalism in the women's movement has been because it is less interested in relations between nations than in global problems. This is true even if 'global' is sometimes conflated with 'general'. The words 'global' and 'global solidarity' do recur in these pages. Where international or inter-regional documents are produced, they do naturally tend to deal with common global or regional problems. Moreover, they tend to 'cross borders' in their analysis and demands, whether these borders are those of gender, race, class, or a territorial understanding of the region or world.

Thus a European document raises little question of relations between states, nations or nationalities within the Conference on Security and Co-operation in Europe (CSCE) area but declares that

> No European state accords equal rights to all people within its borders [and that] the structure of our society is dictated by the inequality which exists between men and women, natives and aliens, dominant cultures and ethnic

groups and between the rich and the poor. (First Women's Conference on Security and Co-operation in Europe, 1990)

It then addresses itself to the problems of 'all people over and above the nations and borders of the CSCE states'. A South Asian document states that:

Who we are today is as much a product of a common heritage of the legacy of colonialism and the struggle of earlier generations to create a just and equal society. In the post-independence period we share common struc- ture[s] of oppression and exploitation imposed by dominant class/caste and patriarchal rule, reinforced by almost identical government responses to the legitimate aspirations of people. (Anon., 1991)

Whilst evidently recognizing the way in which state-nationalism, ethnic or religious chauvinism/fundamentalism, and militarism divide the peoples of the region, it proposes a broad common orientation, as well as a linkage of the women's movement with others.[38]

The Declaration of Comilla, on reproductive technology, clearly recognizes a 'patriarchal, industrial, commercial and racist domination over life' as a global problem, facing women of all countries, classes and ethnic groups, although with evidently differential (and divisory) impli- cations and effects. It just as evidently proposes a global response, appealing to men as well as to women:

We appeal to all women and men to unite globally against dehumanising technologies and express our solidarity with all those who seek to uphold and preserve the diversity of life on our planet and the integrity and dignity of all women. (FINRRAGE-UBINIG, 1989)

It seems clear, in other words, that the past lack of a feminist focus on internationalism has been due to a shift of gaze toward a broader, if not always named, horizon. That horizon will be both named and explored in the next chapter of this work. In the meantime we would do well to ponder the tragic life of Rosa Luxemburg, who was not only a theorist of an earlier stage of capitalist internationalization but an outstanding female (not feminist) representative of classical labour and socialist internationalism. In a work otherwise thoroughly sceptical of revolu- tionary utopianism, James Billington (1980) reveals a soft spot for the internationalism of Luxemburg. Writing before the collapse of Com- munism, he says that if the revolutionary faith does revive in those lands where Rosa Luxemburg lived and died, it seems likely to be moved by her ghost stalking the stalags of Stalinism and the dachas of its directors. To them, she can speak of forgotten dreams – reminding them that a Jewish woman once argued that Poles should unite with Russians for their common good; that Germans would benefit from revolution in Russia; and that social revolution would directly abolish both the national identities and the authoritarian controls that repress the creativity of working people themselves. (Billington, 1980: 503)

Yet it is my impression that Luxemburg's internationalism went along-side a denial of her identity as Jew, Pole, woman and, in some way, person. Concluding on her unhappy relationship with both her lovers, Elzbieta Ettinger says:

Capable of effecting change in the consciousness of the workers, she believed she could also change an unhappy man into a happy one. The difference between the amorphous crowds she so easily swayed and the individual escaped her. So did the distinctions inherent in divergent cultures and social conditions; she saw humanity but not the individual human being. 'Contact with the masses gives me inner courage and tranquillity', she said, but [her lovers] Jogiches or Zetkin seldom evoked these sensations. With them she felt unloved, unappreciated, and unneeded, or at best was con-stantly afraid of not being loved, appreciated, or needed. Lonely and sick at heart, she increasingly sought in humanity the wholeness and security that her parental home and her lovers had failed to give her. (Ettinger, 1987: 160)

Rosa's internationalism was, in other words, an alternative to identities she could not recognize, or with which she could not come to terms. Most contemporary feminisms argue for the necessity of joining together such divided and denied identities, and most are suggesting a shift of paradigm away from the impossible past of inter-nationalism (which could only be a dream) and toward a global solidarity to be built day by day in our waking hours.

Notes

1. This chapter is no more academic and detached than previous ones. I have had a commitment to, and engagement with, feminism internationally for some ten or fifteen years. I have contributed, often as the sole man, to four or five international feminist events, one of which I myself organized, and

I have benefited greatly from longtime friendships with a number of feminists deeply involved in international solidarity activity. Amongst these has been Gina Vargas, my *companera* and sparring partner, much cited in what follows. She was a founder of the Flora Tristan Women's Centre in Peru in the 1970s, and was the Latin American and Caribbean Co-ordinator of the Women's NGOs for the 1995 Beijing Conference. This chapter is, unavoidably, part of our ongoing dialogue. It goes without saying that neither Gina, nor the organizations and networks with which she is associated, are responsible for what follows. The chapter draws on Waterman, 1993d and 1996c. Motivated readers will find in the original papers extensive literature reviews and bibliography on women, feminism and internationalism.

2. Considering the second wave of the feminist movement in Latin America, Francesca Miller (1992b: 192) supports the first of these arguments, but also reveals how even authoritarian regimes have allowed space for the development of feminist movements.

3. It is, again, Miller who reveals the intimate interconnections of both waves of Latin American feminism to much broader political issues. This is true of the predominantly liberal feminism of the earlier period and the predominantly socialist one of the present (Miller, 1990, 1992a). There are, of course, in Latin America and elsewhere, accounts of national or international women's movements that simply ignore other male domi-nated or mixed movements and processes. But, then, they would seem to be reversing rather than surpassing the phallocentric vision they con-demn.

4. This problem is precisely identified and convincingly criticized in the process of a friendly review of the Morgan anthology by Chandra Mohanty (1992: 83–4). She says:

> Universal sisterhood, defined as the transcendence of the 'male' world ... ends up being a middle-class, psychologized notion which effectively erases material and ideo-logical power differences within and among groups of women, especially between First and Third World (and, paradoxically, removes us all as actors from history and politics). It is in this erasure of difference as inequality and dependence that the privilege of Morgan's political 'location' [in New York City] might be visible. Ultimately in this reductive utopian vision, men *participate* in politics while women can only hope to *transcend* them.

It should additionally be pointed out that Morgan's claim to present an anthology on 'The International Women's Movement' is actually a collec-tion on *national* women's movements, with little reference to any international organizations, activities or ideas – apart from an item on women in the UN (Hedevary, 1985) and her own asserted transcendental ethic.

5. One exception to the rule is the chapter on the period 1974–90 in Latin America by Miller (1992b), which includes 'international feminism' in its title. Another is the conference report and reflections of Keysers and Smyth (1991) mentioned below.

6. For a useful review of the feminist literature on international organizations/global governance, see Prugl (1996). Although Prugl also identifies literature on 'global governance and women's struggle', which includes that on feminist NGOs preparing for Beijing, this is not quite the same as either 'international feminism' or 'feminist internationalism'. I really think that what is going to be necessary is not a feminist international relations or a feminist critique of international relations but a feminist alternative to these. The book by Jan Jindy Pettman may move in this direction and contains, in any case, an excellent overview of the literature on women and international relations (Pettman, 1996: vii–xiii).

7. Both relevant and promising here is the section 'Is feminism global? Is sisterhood global' in Hartmann et al. (1996) Here and elsewhere in this collective interview the responses of veteran internationalist Charlotte Bunch suggest the value to US feminists of engagement with those elsewhere, of the necessity and possibility of a new kind of feminist universalism. Another promising contribution is the article by Gabriel and Macdonald (1994) on women organizing around the NAFTA in Canada and Mexico. This is a model of the kind of theoretically informed case study of which tens or hundreds are needed. It is as strong on revealing differences and obstacles, between and within the two countries, as in revealing how many more activities were going on here than that mentioned below.

8. Gladys Marin, General Secretary of the Communist Part of Chile, complains that Communist women were excluded from the Chilean delegation (Eltit and Richard, 1996).

9. Despite my own scepticism about terrains and discourses created or dominated by inter-state bodies, I was somewhat shocked at the negative attitude toward Beijing/Huairou expressed to me by two British feminist thinkers/activists, during an international feminist conference in London, July 1996. Both of these are deeply concerned with and committed to women in the South. One had been at Beijing, the other not. Possibly their attitudes had been influenced by the relative lack of mobilization around Beijing by the women's movement in the UK. Just as mine had been my different experience, or impression, of activity in Latin America and the Caribbean. For a more positive British response to Beijing, see the report of a well-attended national follow-up meeting in the UK (Ashworth, 1996).

10. This was shared by those at a seminar I attended in Santiago, 29 November 1996. Organized by the MEMCH (Movement for the Emancipation of Chilean Women), it was formally concerned with women and politics in the era of globalization, but represented a follow-up to both the Beijing Conference and the Seventh Latin American Feminist Encounter. More on this below.

11. My propositions are based on extensive reading of documents, press accounts, participant reports, and feminist analyses, as well as on observation of the preparation process in Santiago, Chile and in the LAC Co-ordination Office, Lima, Peru (July–August 1995), and discussion with Conference/Forum participants from Latin America, Western Europe, Africa and other regions.

12. Thus, of 3,328 panels identified, Economic Policies, Science and Technology and Media of Communication accounted for some 21 per cent. Of the 456 panels devoted to Economic Policy, 78, or 17 per cent, dealt with Economic Alternatives. Of the 447 panels (14 per cent) devoted to Government and Politics, 44 (10 per cent) dealt with the world conferences and role of international agencies. This information is extracted from Guzman (1996). As the author herself points out, the identification of subjects is itself arbitrary and tells us nothing about the actual contents, orientation, participation and outcomes. All that it does do is to suggest the extent to which Huariou was addressing itself to contemporary topics, issues and – in the crucial economic case – alternatives. A more meaningful analysis of Huariou could be made by an examination of the increasing number of documents and reports becoming available. Amongst ones I have had access to, but not been able to analyse, are the final NGO report (NGO Forum on Women Secretariat, 1996), a collection of the forum newspapers (Forum '95, 1996) and the extensive report of speeches to Forum Plenaries (Friedlander, 1996).

13. Two comments are here in order. One is that the failure to name capitalism as such risks making it invisible, a failure common to many global reformist projects. The second is that this was, in fact, a draft declaration which, whilst following three days of intensive discussion, was not formally issued as a common document.

14. An edited collection of essays, in Spanish and English, on the Latin American and Caribbean national/regional organization for Beijing should eventually appear, under the auspices of UNIFEM (United Nations Development Fund for Women) and UNICEF (United Nations Children's Fund).

15. Glimpses are provided by NGO Forum on Women Secretariat (1996). This breaks down NGO presence by region, revealing that the LAC region had, at 5 per cent, a lower participation than Africa, Asia or Europe/North

America (which had 40 per cent) (ibid.: 16). It also reveals that the NGO presence was heavily financed by governments and inter-state organizations, which directly provided some 48 per cent of the total $5,795,311 (ibid.: 65). Much of the rest would have been provided by governments indirectly, via state funded NGOs.

16. To call everything in the Americas south of the USA one region (or, in local parlance, *la región*) is to beg numerous questions. The relationship between feminists in the largely Spanish-speaking subcontinent and the largely English-speaking islands is only the most prominent of the multiple linguistic, geographical and political differences to be noted. The region of the subtitle must therefore be seen more as an international feminist project than a political fact. But, in so far as globalization subverts traditional, simplistic political or geographical divisions/oppositions, and in so far as the new feminist internationalisms allow for difference, dialogue and dialectic, the regional project does not contradict overlapping national, sub-regional, supra-regional and global identities.

17. According to Reinalda and Verhaaren (1989: 103), this was not an international but a Latin American congress, although it was attended by women from five European countries and the United States.

18. Does Miller overstate her case? The account of Reinalda and Verhaaren (1989: 103–8) is somewhat more nuanced or complex, since it reveals the rather active role of the inter-state bodies, and certain individual male diplomats, to forward women's issues. This account also gives more space to the energetic pioneering activities of the US women's movements.

19. What follows is largely extracted from Waterman (1992a: 40–4). MaM is one of the few such networks on which such information is available, the case provides us with some depth where we otherwise have breadth.

20. This account is based on email correspondence with MaM activist, Landa Yanz, August 1996.

21. Although the language here is that of Amalia Fischer (1994), this is not to necessarily identify her with the ultra-radicals. At the time of the Seventh *Encuentro* she distinguished herself from them.

22. There is a parallel here with the continuing international feminist debate on pornography. This was begun by ultra-radical feminists, whose slogan was 'pornography is the theory; rape is the practice'. This powerful, if misleading, slogan provoked a much more nuanced and complex response, and led to an important and liberatng discussion about female lust, as well as on broader cultural and political issues such as 'representation', censorship, the relationship between 'speech acts' and action as conventionally understood.

23. Received, regretably too late to work into this chapter, was the paper of Sonia Alvarez (1997). Written – from internal evidence – before the

Seventh *Encuentro*, this provides the outstanding analysis of the Latin American feminist movement in the age of globalization and, more specifically, in relation to Beijing. As someone herself employed during the Beijing process by the Ford Foundation, she grasps the nettle of Northern finance more firmly than heretofore. She also provides something close to a prediction of the disputes that burst out into the open at the *Encuentro*, and she deals more frankly and forcefully with the relationship between the movement's elite and its base than other writings I am familiar with. In her conclusion she writes:

> Though the battles waged by the so-called *'institucionalizadas'* [instituionalised feminists in NGOs or government] within the conventionally defined political arena must be understood as cultural struggles over the meaning of received notions of 'citizenship', 'development', 'the family', or 'gender' . . . the neglect or silencing of other forms of cultural-political intervention – such as local mobilisation and *concientizacion* [consciousness-raising] work with women of the popular clases – might ultimately compromise the very quest for more 'equitable' gender policy. In the absence of such work, feminists might lack the broad social base or political constituencies that would enable them to . . . [realize] . . . the many new rights and entitlements . . . conquered through increased engagement with political-institutional arenas on a national, regional, and global scale. (Ibid.: 36)

24. The account here is based on the following sources: published articles and declarations, particularly in the Uruguay-based *Cotidiano Mujer*, the Chile-based *Mujer/Fempress* and the Mexico-based *La Correa Feminista*; unpublished documents of the conference itself; attendance at two meetings of a Chilean feminist organization immediately following the event; discussion with five or ten Chilean or other Latin American feminists who either took part in or boycotted the *Encuentro*; reports circulated by hand or my email. Given that a number of these sources are women who were involved in the bitter disputes there, I should state that the account below is my own and does not express their – inevitably differing – positions or analyses. I should also say that I have not spoken to any of the 'autonomous feminists' who organized the event and am therefore dependent on their conference documents, as well as articles by, or interviews with, them in the journals mentioned above. These include *La Correa Feminista*, with which some of the leading ultra-radicals were closely associated, and in the pages of which they had recently appeared.

25. A, or the, leading figure of 'autonomous feminism' in Latin America is the Chilean architect, Margarita Pisano, who had set out her ideas recently in a book, interviews and articles. Her contribution to the Mexican *La Correa Feminista*, Winter, 1995–6, reveals a view of patriarchy as a single, timeless, worldwide and total system of oppression. Its domination of the global level explains her hostility to the Beijing Conference. Patriarchy, it further

appears, is capable of creating a 'patriarchal feminism' and of incorporating all but her own. She states:

> The discourse of autonomous feminism disturbs patriarchy because it is an intelligent discourse that fundamentally unveils its system, its values and the dynamic of its domination; it is a knowledge that provides paths to deconstruct it and create a new system, and additionally breaks with the image of the woman dependent on the male, which is always appealing to the masculine, and installs the image of the autonomous and thinking woman. (*La Correa Feminista*, Winter, 1995–6: 36)

This argument – or evocation – continues for many pages, without anywhere even suggesting what 'autonomous feminism' actually consists of, what the nature of the feminist alternative would be.

26. The organizing committee complained that, under the influence of their opponents, Northern funders were also boycotting the event. They presented evidence for one case, and it seems probable that there was Northern reluctance to finance such a disputed event. The organizers did none the less receive such funding. There does seem to be a contradiction here between on the one hand complaining about financial dependence on the North and, on the other, complaining about its insufficiency.

27. Fempress describes itself as a network of alternative communication for women, is based in Santiago, and has been in existence for fourteen years. The last issue of its bulletin, *Mujer/Fempress*, before the *Encuentro*, October 1996, had published, as usual, one report each from most of its country correspondents, press-clippings, book announcements and notices. *Mujer/Fempress* announces on its inside front cover that it is funded by nine bodies, including the Ford Foundation and three UN agencies. Amongst the articles in this Northern-funded but Latin America-wide journal are articles on the defence of young pregnant women, the challenging of a national Public Defender (ombudsman), increasing the number of police stations of and for women, student movements and feminist utopias, the defence of reproductive rights. This issue also publishes, amongst its press-clippings, a full-page statement by the Organizing Committee of the Seventh *Encuentro*. Fempress had additionally just published a professional and attractive handbook on non-sexist journalism, also funded by Ford (Valle, Hiriart and Amado, 1996). If the bulletin reveals the nature of its Latin American internationalism, the book draws on feminist sources worldwide. There would thus seem to be here plenty of material for specific analysis, discussion and debate. None of this is reflected in the condemnation.

28. The accounts of the NGO Co-ordination for Beijing have been made available throughout the region, but critics again made no reference to these.

29. Gobbi provides us with the detailed critique of the NGO form by *Encuentro*-participant Maria Galindo from Bolivia:

> The NGOs and networks of NGOs have provided the form of organisation on the basis of which institutionalisation has been unchained. It is important to understand and repeat that this has been the process [from] a time in which there was a spontaneous coincidence between mechanisms of solidarity with women in the North, the channelling of funds principally in order to advance denunciatory actions, and the present moment in which these structures have increased, have been bureaucratised, have given way, have laid aside the values of solidarity and anti-colonialism, and have been converted into para-governmental, para-party, para-state and in some cases even para-military organisations. (Gobbi, 1996: 8)

There is a serious argument buried within this allegation. But the view of a golden age of spontaneous, anti-imperialist solidarity is, as earlier might have been suggested, romanticized. No evidence was offered of Northern agencies funding para-military NGOs.

30. Further indications of the rhetoric of the *feministas autonomas* can be found in the first issue of the *Encuentro* newsletter, which provides a series of quotes, some of which I reproduce herewith: *Ximena Bedregal:* 'I don't believe in leaders. I believe in the rebellious acts of women'; *Margarita Pisano:* 'I do not want to do politics with a woman who is not committed to another suffering poverty and hunger. I do not want to do politics with a woman who believes that Neoliberalism is leading us to a solution of women's problems'; *An 'Aymara feminist, autonomous and anarchist':* 'The sociologists and anthropologists of the NGOs study the poor and the women in order to sell us to Neoliberalism'. Bedregal, it should be added, publicly distanced herself at the *Encuentro* from some of the most extremist of the 'autonomous feminists'.

31. Thus, in the heat of the debate, Gina Vargas, the prime individual target of the ultra-radicals, announced her resignation from the Gender Advisory Committee of the World Bank. This had been created following Beijing/ Huairou, during which the Bank had been forcefully criticized for – amongst other things – gender blindness. Vargas agreed to take up the invitation to join this committee only after wide consultations, particularly with those Latin American and Caribbean feminsts who had been involved in Beijing. Neither in a post-*Encuentro* interview nor in immediate reports of the event, was further reference made to this dramatic resignation, which evidently remained a delicate issue.

32. One of the nine or ten signatories was the earlier mentioned Amalia Fischer, who has done academic work on the *Encuentros* (Fischer, 1994) and on the policies, activities and leadership style of the Latin American feminist movement.

33. The emphasis on Spanish and Portuguese could be taken as an affront by either the English-speaking Caribbean or the indigenous women. The hostility to English, here reduced to a language of imperial power, would seem to ignore its potential for communication with women in, for example, Africa and Asia. We may also note, by way of contrast, that the common language used by survivors of the Auschwitz death camp, in their post-war anti-fascist political consultations, was German.

34. The Vargas paper, known variously and in different versions as the 'Open Letter' the 'Feminist Odyssey' (Vargas, 1996a) or the 'Radical Feminist Agenda', was widely circulated amongst LAC feminists, in Spanish and English, using the print and electronic media. Despite its relevance, it led to no discussion, at least in published form, either in the months preceding or those following the Seventh Encounter. Yet it remains one of the most specific LAC reflections on the relationship between the national/regional and global. A few quotes from an email version, Summer 1996, may illustrate this:

> I believe it is important to move openly . . .into the discussion of what the Beijing experience and other [international UN?] conferences meant: what they meant to us as feminists; what they meant to the other expressions of the movement, including those sectors that remained on the margins or were opposed; what paths or risks the criticisms may raise for us; what purpose they served or will serve to modify at least some aspects of the multiple subordinations women are subjected to; and, above all, what . . . they mean to a long-term feminist agenda.[. . .]

> We need to analyse the practices, as well as the [longstanding] tendency of the movement to look inward . . . and not to confront [or] share its feminist developments with what is happening in other regions and on other continents'.[. . .]

> Only in these terms can we see the national, regional and global as increasingly interdependent. If the processes of domination operate at all levels then an effective struggle for emancipation has to articulate the struggles happening at all these different levels.

35. For a detailed and more recent account of the international reproductive rights issue and movement see Keysers (1996).

36. The Conclusions and Recommendations to the report include the following (Women and Development Project, 1994a: 149–62):

Can women's concerns be translated into trade union policies?
Multiple identity of workers
The lives of women and men go far beyond their experiences in the workplace and are also determined by their social identity and roles . . . Any redefinition of trade-union

policies aimed at increasing membership must be based on recognition of the multiple, gender-specific identify of workers – men as well as women.

How should women be organised?
Networking and coalitions between trade unions and women's organisations
Women's organisations have developed a great diversity of strategies and organisational forms to address women's needs and priorities in the reproductive sphere . . . such as communal kitchens . . . cooperative stores, housewives' committees . . . women's centres, places of refuge . . . self-help organisations . . .

Trade unions should not try to take over these initiatives. But by forming alliances they can contribute to increased bargaining power of both women's organisations and the trade unions . . . Networking, cooperation or coalitions between these organisations could empower both.

Trade unions should also take more advantage of the results of women's studies in defining new policies and issues . . . Mutual strengthening between trade unions and these groups and NGOs could be promoted by an exchange of ideas, networking and cooperation.

37. National and international union organisations have, of course, made approaches to other ASMs over the last twenty years or so. This may have begun, at the international level, with relations between the ICFTU and Amnesty International, given a mutual interest in rights questions. Amnesty appointed a union officer, if I remember correctly, in the late 1970s or early 1980s. I am not aware of any such close relationship with the ecological movement, despite the apparent mutual interest in issues like the Union Carbide disaster in Bhopal, 1984. National and international unions were here both slow and narrow in response. Given the productivist/consumptionist ideologies of most unions, and the anti-industrialism/anti-consumptionism of most ecological movements, this is evidently a more difficult relationship to develop. The commonly instrumentalist attitudes of contemporary unionism towards alliances with broader communities and on broader issues has been convincingly shown for the USA by George DeMartino (1991). The whole matter suggests the necessity for differentiated analysis of union/ASM relations.

38. There has, thus, been a significant and far from coincidental overlap between South-Asian feminist networks and a Pakistan–India People's Forum for Peace and Democracy, that has been attempting to create linkages at civil society level across the region's most divisive and dangerous frontier. The complexities of even such an apparently local, narrow and simple transborder internationalism are shown by the Indian feminist Amrita Chhachhi (1996) – who was involved in the first formal contact between Indian and Pakistani feminists as recently as 1986. Chhachhi talks of the resistance, within the Forum, to feminist analyses of the connection

between sexism and war – although a feminist one was eventually accepted unanimously. She also reveals (or possibly makes) the connection between women in a border village, transborder meetings and an exhibition in Huairou at the 4WCW.

7 CONCLUSION: GLOBALIZATION, CIVIL SOCIETY, SOLIDARITY[1]

Introduction: A Newly Imaginable Community

It is not so very long ago that the British political scientist John Dunn (1985) was writing of internationalism as an 'unimagined community'. He also evidently thought of it as unimagin*able*. It is less than a decade since David Harvey, in a seminal work on modernity, said the following:

> [T]he capacity of most social movements to command place better than space puts a strong emphasis upon the potential connection between place and social identity. This is manifest in political action ... The consequent dilemmas of social or working-class movements in the face of a universal-ising capitalism are shared by other oppositional groups – racial minorities, colonised peoples, women, etc. – who are relatively empowered to organise in place but disempowered when it comes to organising over space. In clinging, often of necessity, to a place-bound identity, however, such opposi-tional movements become a part of the very fragmentation which a mobile capitalism and flexible accumulation can feed upon. 'Think globally and act locally' was the revolutionary slogan of the 1960s. It bears repeating. (Har-vey, 1989: 302–3)

It is possible to understand why these statements carried weight then and also why they no longer do – or ought not to do. The possibility or necessity of going further than both writers has been shown to us not only by the international women's movements but by the peace, eco-logical and human rights ones. But, as we have seen from Chapter 6, necessity is not always the mother of theorization. A new body of writing on globalization has, however, appeared since around 1989–92 when, as we now know, the twenty-first century began. I am going to try to give it shape here as 'critical and committed globalization theory'. Whilst many new labour internationalists will continue to work within old paradigms, or could make effective use of the initial reconceptualization I offered in Chapter 3, I feel that a specific understanding of globalization, and a critical and committed attitude towards it, could today – for the first time – make internationalism both imaginable and something more than local action.

This chapter therefore represents both a summary and a restatement of earlier ones. In what follows I will, first, critique internationalization/internationalism discourse more deeply than heretofore, second, sketch an understanding of globalization, third, look at the relationship between globalization and social movements, fourth, consider the meaning of global civil society, fifth, propose 'global solidarity' as a successor to 'internationalism'; finally, consider some implications for post-traditional internationalists.

Internationalization and Internationalism as Particular and Partial

Let us first settle final accounts with the old internationalizations and internationalisms. 'Internationalization', in either the liberal or socialist understanding, implies universalization and is accompanied by a related political/ethical universalism. In both cases the internationalization and internationalism mean Westernization. These are, thus, particularistic universalisms in which Western Enlightenment theories, models, aspirations and utopias are offered to, or are imposed on, the rest of the world ('lesser breeds without the law', 'peoples without history'). These are also partial universalisms, in so far as they prioritize/marginalize particular social structures, processes and social movements. They fail, finally, to come to terms with traditionalisms or particularisms – including those they themselves provoke. Stuart Hall (1992: 314) sees the matter thus:

> Both liberalism and Marxism, in their different ways, implied that the attachment to the local and the particular would gradually give way to the more universalistic and cosmopolitan or international values and identities; that nationalism and ethnicity were archaic forms of attachment – the sorts of

thing which would be 'melted away' by the revolutionising force of modernity. According to these 'metanarratives' of modernity, the irrational attachments to the local and the particular, to tradition and roots, to national myths and 'imagined communities' would gradually be replaced by more rational and universalistic identities. Yet globalisation seems to be producing neither simply the triumph of 'the global' nor the persistence, in its old nationalistic form, of 'the local'. The displacements or distractions of globalisation turn out to be more varied and more contradictory than either its protagonists or opponents suggest. However, this also suggests that, though powered in many ways by the West, globalisation may turn out to be part of that slow and uneven but continuing story of the de-centring of the West.

There is another serious common limitation to the old discourses. Both liberal and Marxist concepts of internationalization are two-dimensional: they depend on a planar understanding of space – of space as place – with the politically privileged place being that of the nation-state. Yet the nation-state, or state-nation, is a historically recent phenomenon, it ties rights and community to territory, and rests finally on the use of violence against external and internal enemies. The nation-state evidently has continuing appeal and success in capturing the popular imagination and even mobilizing it for (self-)destructive war. But the primacy of the nation-state as against more local, more particular, more general or non-territorial identities, communities and values (e.g. democracy, pluralism) has always been tenuous and is increasingly in question.

In both the liberal and Marxist traditions nation-state and society are considered as more or less synonymous and provide the essential parameters for sociology. For both 'right' and 'left' specialists 'international relations' tends to mean inter-state relations (and state- or bloc-defined economic ones). These academic traditions are not only unable to deal with globalization, they are of decreasing value in explaining the particular terrain or relation they have abstracted for study. Today, for example, it makes less sense than ever to identify or count the number of 'societies' in the world and examine the relations 'between them'. Society, as it will be argued below, is not a count-noun. There is a multiplicity of social relations – beneath borders, within borders, across borders, without borders. We need a view of the nature of the world that allows us to understand these.

Internationalism, in both the nineteenth and twentieth centuries, subordinated itself to 'a world of nation-states'. For both liberal and socialist internationalism (i.e. inter-national-ism), the projected future was one in which the breaching of borders, the occupation or merging of territories, would lead to the surpassing of the significant differences (read: 'traditionalism', 'particularism') previously marking and distinguishing such places. But such territorial internationalization/internationalism has occurred only in the most contradictory or perverse ways. Two examples follow.

Both the League of Nations and the United Nations were inter-nation-state organizations (regardless of UN references to 'we the peoples'). Both attempts at surpassing national rivalries functioned simultaneously to reinforce and reify state-nationalism. Clinching evidence of the existence of a state – one licensed internationally to kill in its own defence – is UN recognition. This fundamental ambiguity of our supra-state order is being today revealed in ever more dramatic form as the UN tries to reconcile the universality of peace, human rights and ecological care with the particularity of the territorially based nation-state.

The left, pertinently dubbed by Bauman (1986) 'the counter-culture of modernity', made its own supreme effort at surpassing nationalism with the October Revolution of 1917. This created the Union of Soviet Socialist Republics (USSR). The name, it is worth remembering, means 'union of socialist republican councils'. What modesty! What ambition! Unlike the United States of America this title made reference to neither states nor sites. It was an attempt to create a political form at once post-imperial, post-capitalist, post-national and post-parliamentary. It was intended to be open to any who wished to join and any who wished to leave. Within years, if not months, it was bent, or bent itself, to the logic of international capitalism, to the nation-state form and inter-state relations. Those people or peoples who attempted to leave the USSR were repressed with extreme violence. It was only by such violence that peoples were joined to it. The Soviet Union was experienced by its multiplicity of peoples, and its foreign dependencies, as imperial, statist, militarist, chauvinist and anti-parliamentary. In the most bitter and tragic of ironies it now finds itself in the historical dustbin to which it had consigned the capitalist nation-state.

Towards a Critical and Committed Globalization Theory

Working towards a Model

Calderon's (1994) notion of 'living mixed times' (developed later) is quite crucial here, since it subverts conventional binary oppositions and (r)evolutionary schemas/stages which would, for example, have it either that capitalism has not changed fundamentally (globalization as the highest stage of imperialism), or that there is a fundamental break between a national-industrial-capitalist modernity and a global-informational-technocratic/managerial post-modernity. The problem with the first fundamentalism here is the implied corollary, that the alternative is 'the highest stage of nationalism', something that has been tried and failed in either its Communist or Populist variants. The problem with the second is that – at the moment of its global triumph and triumphalism – it makes it impossible to even talk about capitalism.

A critical and socially committed globalization theory can surpass the traditional world views of right or left (e.g. The Spread of Western Civilization, Imperialism, Development, Dependency, Interdependence, Globalism). It can do this without necessarily denying or ignoring such continuing processes as these may connote. I use 'critical and committed' here in the tradition of Marx's *A Contribution to the Critique of Political Economy* (Marx, 1904), in other words as rejection of an alienating social relationship, as criticism of a given understanding of this, as an address to an emancipatory movement.

When I say that such a theory need not, or should not, deny or ignore the processes that other discourses attempt to reflect, express, explain or control, I mean the following: that we should not, for example, reject imperialism discourse whilst abundant evidence of imperialism still exists (e.g. the Gulf War, drainage of capital from the poorest parts of the world, etc.). Critical globalization theory should, thus, rather be understood as both a new map and a transparent overlay, through which old structures, processes and discourses are still visible. Whilst, again, 'imperialism' can still be used in relation to the Western-led war against Iraq, it hardly explains widespread Third World complicity with this war, and even less can it lead us – as left anti-imperialist tradition led some – to identify with Iraqi state-nationalism. And whilst it is hardly logical to use Three Worlds discourse when the Second World has imploded, the common-sense understanding of 'Third World' can be accepted, provided one has at hand an overlay with more explanatory and emancipatory value.

The concept of globalization I am working towards recognizes the limits of Western internationalization projects and universalisms. Exported (r)evolutions increasingly boomerang (George, 1992). Major 'Northern' cities, states and societies reveal 'Southern' traits: Afro-Americans in the US suffer – on average – the same quality of life as the people of Trinidad. Northern states lose the integration and control that previously permitted them to (believe they did or could) control the world. Or even that they can fully control their own multi-ethnic or multi-religious backyards (Forbes, 1993). Consider, here, Quebec in Canada, and then North American Indians within Quebec, between Quebec and Ontario, across the Canada–USA border.

According to the new understanding I propose, the external invests the internal, the local redefines the global.[2] Thus, the global ecological movement discovered the rubber-tapper, rural organizer, unionist, socialist and ecologist, Chico Mendes (1992). In turn, his struggles, and his death in struggle, in a tiny isolated Amazonian community, informs the global ecological movement with a sense of how ecological struggles are life and death ones in a more than cosmic sense. He also provides the world with a new kind of working-class hero,[3] one who is much more than a worker and a socialist. It is now also a local hero that is something to be. And local heroes (and heroines) can today be global ones also.

Radical Modernity as a Complex, Globalized, Information Capitalism

Synthesizing arguments from Ulrich Beck (1992), Anthony Giddens (1990), Alberto Melucci (1989) and Mark Poster (1984, 1990), I would refer to our contemporary period as one of *high* or *radical* modernity, characterized further as that of a *complex high-risk globalized information capitalism*.[4] Globalization (unlike Imperialism, Development or Dependency) must be understood as multi-determined: by the market, surveillance, militarization, industrialism, patriarchy, technocracy, informatism, racism, etc. Table 7.1, which is based on but varies from the model originally offered by Tony Giddens, presents the matter schematically. Row A indicates the continuation of capitalism and its dominant ideology as one of the defining characteristics of modernity. Row B suggests the continuing connection with industrialization and

Table 7.1   Globalization: its discontents, movements and alternatives

	1 Aspects of high capitalist modernity: institutional/ (*ideological*)	2 Dimensions of contemporary globalization	3 Social movements: global, national and local	4 Alternative global civilization
A Economy	Capitalism (*possessive individualism*)	Increasingly rapid movement, intensive penetration, restructuring, capital concentration	Labour, union, socialist	Socialized production, ownership, exchange
B Production	Industrialization (*industrialism, consumerism*)	Ecological manipulation and despoliation	Ecological and consumer	System of planetary care
C Organiza- tion	Administration and surveillance (*bureaucracy, technocracy*)	Hegemonic inter-state regimes	Democratic, political, civil and social rights	Co-ordinated multilevel order
D Violence	Professional army (*militarism*)	Military/police repression and control	Peace, conflict- resolution, pacifist	Transcendence of war via exemplary disarmament
E Culture	Computerization of information and culture (*computerism/ informatism*)	Informatization of crucial international relations and culture	Democratization and pluralization of information and culture	Accessible and diverse alternative information and cultural order
F Gender/ sexuality	Commoditization and manipulation of gender, sexuality and reproduction (*patriarchy*)	Global gender, reproductive, sexual, family commoditization and programming	Women's, feminist, sexual rights	Egalitarian, sexually pluralistic and tolerant
G–Z	?	?	?	?

Source: developed from figures in Giddens (1990) and Hall, Held and McGrew (1992)

ecological despoliation, legitimized by the ideology of consumption-ism. Row C reveals the connection with administration and surveillance, both nationally and internationally; row D that with the military. Row E suggests the increasing role of computers and electronic information and culture – both a cause and an effect of the globalization of capital. Row F argues the crucial role of gender and sexuality, of their commoditization (by capital) and manipulation (by administrators and technical experts, operating via state or inter-state agencies). Row G–Z is left open, to allow for others to argue for additional structures, processes, movements and alternatives. Such a complex model of modernity and globalization is best appreciated in contrast with capital-, imperialism-, state- or modernity-fixated ones. None of these would seem to allow for the variety of movements we find in Column 3 (of which more anon) or, if they do, it would be to rank and prioritize them according to how they confront a prioritized contradiction (or discourse, in the case of some discourse-fixated theorists).

Whilst insisting on the increasing interdependency of the indicated institutions/processes/ideologies, I find it essential to recognize the priority of capital and state. By such priority I mean that I see these as the most dynamic and powerful sources or forces, even if increasingly dependent on the others. Recognizing the *priority* here of (transnational) capitalism and (inter-)statism does not necessarily entail the *primacy* of anti-capitalist, anti-imperialist or anti-statist contradictions or struggles. Capital and state do not necessarily today confront local, national, regional or global communities in such direct and overt ways as in the nineteenth century – with the factory, the prison, the gun, the flag. Studying and engaging in emancipatory global movements will tell us where, when – and for whom – one contradiction has primacy.

The Changing Nature of Globalized Capital

Global capital, in this understanding, thus still confronts labour globally.[5] The rapidity of change in waged work, in its relative growth or decline, in its nature, in its separation by labour market, in the balance and distribution of such nationally, regionally and globally, and in the nature of its products, requires us to radically rethink labour movement strategies, from the local to the global level.

The key to the contemporary transformation of the global capitalist economy and waged work is the leading role played by knowledge and information. In the form of information technology, or computerized equipment (both in production and as product), it is connected with a reduction in the total demand for labour, a shift in control within the labour process from the machine operator to the technician, from economies of scale (mass production) to those of scope (batch production for 'niche' markets), from production to services, with decentralization of production (whilst retaining central managerial or financial control), and with networking relations between such central controllers. Some see this as leading to a new polarization, within national labour forces (skilled, secure, white, male versus unskilled, part-time/temporary, non-white, female), and between an informatized North and an industrial (or at least partly industrial) South. Such an image might suggest the necessity (but not necessarily possibility) for a new kind of *class-like* alliance nationally and internationally. The binary logic here imposed fails to allow for both the divisions within the two opposed categories (e.g. between women and men amongst the casualized) and for the increasing evidence that class or work-situation identity is crossed by others. I would therefore see this process as simultaneously undermining an identity based primarily on (wage) labour and creating the basis for new *cross-class* social movements, questioning the continuing subordination within and enslavement by work, the nature of products, the ethic of competition, consumerism, growth, etc. This suggests the necessity for the existing labour organizations, national and international, to convert themselves into a global social movement around work, but intimately related to those on the new social issues (a matter developed below).

John Allen (1992) raises two additional questions here, one relating to the increasing interpenetration of development and underdevelopment, the other the implications of unevenness in a world in which cities or national economies increasingly become interchangeable sites for production, finance and services:

Alongside the financial and commercial practices of New York and London, for example, we find the sweatshops and outworking practices that are more often associated with Third World economies. Yet they are not opposing developments and nor are they unrelated. There is no simple equation of finance with post-industrialism and the informal practices often undertaken by a migrant workforce with pre-industrialism. On the contrary, they are part and parcel of the same global economic forces which are eroding the identity of the West as the 'Rest', as it were, move to the centres of the modern world. (Ibid.: 202)

And:

> [I]f national economies increasingly become 'sites' across which international
> forces flow, with some parts of a country passed over by the new growth
> dynamics, then the new uneven global order will very likely be characterised
> by more than one line of economic direction[6] within and between countries.
> (Ibid.: 202–3)

The implications of such changes for the labour movement will have to
be considered later.

The Decentring of Capitalist Power

Globalization means that dominating power internationally resides
decreasingly in a unified territorial site (e.g. a state, a bloc), neither
does it rest with a single privileged subject (e.g. the international
bourgeoisie), depend on a primary determinant (e.g. military/
strategic) or lie at a primary level (e.g. the state-national). Far less do we
see these four elements coinciding, as might have been the case during
the Pax Britannica (up to 1914) or Pax Americana (after 1945). During
the war against Iraq we saw the operation of a complex division of
labour:

> The Gulf War coalition pooled different kinds of power possessed by differ-
> ent entities. The United States provided military equipment and trained
> personnel. Some Arab countries provided base areas. The emirs, the Jap-
> anese, and the Germans provided cash. The Security Council, dominated by
> the major powers, provided legitimation for the entire effort. While the war
> drew on nationalist sentiment in the United States and some other countries,
> its coalition model actually reflected the inability of the United States or any
> other single nation to function as a hegemonic power on its own. (Brecher,
> 1993: 5–6)

One could go further, pointing out how the USA provided the (dis)in-
formation, and how ex-Communist and even erstwhile 'non-aligned'
countries of the Third World – oil dependent, with uncertain frontiers
and predatory neighbours – enthusiastically joined the crusade. An
understanding of globalization allows both for attempts to (re)create
hegemonic blocs and for such alliance or networking models for the
preservation of world order. Finally, here, we should remember R.W.
Connell's (1984: 432–3) criticism of World System theory notions of an

international capitalist class. What counts, he suggests, is not the creation of a world ruling class (a socialist fantasy) but keeping in existence the divisions between the world's oppressed and exploited (a continuing reality).

The Changing Interrelationship of Space and Time

Critical globalization theory requires a multidimensional understanding of space; of a simultaneous process of 'space-time scope/stretch' and 'space-time intensity/deepening' (see Giddens, 1990; Harvey, 1989; McGrew, 1992: 68). This passage from Giddens (1990: 19) suggests both aspects:

> In pre-modern societies, space and place largely coincide, since the spatial dimensions of social life are, for most of the population, and in most respects, dominated by 'presence' – localised activities. The advent of modernity increasingly tears space away from place by fostering relations between 'absent' others, locationally distant from any given situation of face-to-face interaction. In conditions of modernity ... locales are thoroughly penetrated by and shaped in terms of social influences quite distant from them.

Social relations in each locale are increasingly (if differentially) impacted by distant processes/events. Differentiation of involvement and impact is also notable between classes, ethnic groups and genders. As Doreen Massey (1991) has pointed out, in the processes of globalization some groups have more initiative, whilst others receive, and yet others are imprisoned by space–time stretching or intensification. There are, she suggests,

1   those who are in charge of time–space compression and able to get most advantage from it – corporate investors, film distributors and currency dealers, the jetsetters and emailers;
2   those who have both contributed in one sense but are imprisoned in another – slum-dwellers of Rio, who may be a source for both global football and global music but may never have been to downtown Rio (or, it occurs to me, to the 1992 UNCED global ecology conference in downtown Rio);
3   a group on the fringe of the first category, including those Western academics and journalists 'who write most about it' (Massey, 1991: 26).

Massey's third category – which needs to include many 'Southern' intellectuals, 'Westernized' or not – is important for three reasons:

1 it enables us to see that theories of space–time compression are not ineffable emanations of social science but reflections/expressions of people occupying specific subject positions;
2 it enables those in such positions (including myself) to relate their experiences/ideas to those of the second category, which is what Massey herself is evidently attempting to do;
3 it helps us to understand how it is that whilst some classes, ethnic/ religious groups, gender/sexual categories, might welcome globalization as liberating, others seek to resist it and yet others to surpass it.

Another crucial new understanding of time has been suggested by Fernando Calderon – as mentioned earlier – when he argues that Latin America is 'living mixed times' (Calderon, 1988, 1994). This notion, which implies the simultaneity within that continent of pre-, present- and post-modern conditions, could, it seems to me, be extended to the whole globalized world. Such a formulation is subversive of the twinned, evolutionary, binary oppositions: tradition/modernity, modernity/post-modernity. This is not just an ontological issue. Recognition of the complex interpenetration and interdependency of past, present and future implies strategies that select critically from all three (since our *present* future is being largely constructed over our heads or behind our backs – and regardless of pre-modern and modern human achievements – by hegemonic forces, their generalist intellectuals and specialist professionals/technicians). An understanding that the whole world is living mixed times enables us, it seems to me, to recognize indigenous peoples not as noble savages, or the last of the Mohicans, but as bearers of pre-capitalist knowledge and experiences essential for a post-capitalist future. It is, surely, in such a manner that it is possible (using different subtitles of Calderon's article) to be simultaneously Bolivian and post-modern, indigenous and post-modern.

The Increasing Irrelevance of Traditional Leftist Strategies
Recognition of the increased scope and intensity of space–time relations, of an increasingly interdependent global sociality, makes, I think, simplistic traditional notions of the social world and its transformation

increasingly archaic. Class, economic and technological determinism, territorial nationalism as primary political identity, political-revolutionism/insurrectionism and global-apocalypticism have been part of the stock in trade of the left. They can possibly even be found combined – if uneasily – in the doctrines of the last Maoist Communist Parties, such as the Communist Party of the Philippines,[7] or Peru's Shining Path. A growing awareness of global complexity and interdependence would allow these notions to be left to reactionary, conservative, authoritarian ideologues. The ASMs, which both continue and break with the classical left, are beginning to point out more complex answers to our growing global concerns.

New Global Social Movements, or Alternative Social Movements as Global

The Rise of Pluralistic Global Movements

Globalization spreads the effects of capitalist development to everywhere and everybody (and every body). It sharpens the combinations, unevenesses, ambiguities and contradictions of high modernity. It gives rise to democratic and pluralistic social movements which point to the possibility of meaningfully postmodern (i.e. post-capitalist, post-militarist, post-patriarchal, etc.) global alternatives beyond.[8] We are now considering Columns 3 and 4 of Table 7.1, once again extending the argument of Giddens (1990). If, previously, ideas of an alternative world order found expression in the writings of individual authors, or of a particular movement, from a particular world area (the West), they are beginning to find collective political expression. Introducing such a collection, which includes writings from a wide range of new and old social movements, ideological traditions and world areas, Jeremy Brecher (1993: 7–8) argues for an ecological world view:

> Such an 'ecological' approach starts from a conception of the individual as a member of many groups – kinship, ethnic, religious, political, etc. – whose boundaries do not generally coincide and no one of which can be regarded as sovereign over the others [...] Such an approach ... recognises the current reality of multiple overlapping transnational power networks. It envisions a multi-level system of regulation cutting across the boundaries of

existing nation-states to control the transnational forces that actually shape today's world.

Previously, emancipatory movements operated with world views in which the enemy was seen (or allied enemies were seen) as homogeneous, or homologous, as omnipresent and as more or less omnipotent.[9] It – or they – also represented evil. The movement represented itself as the naturally, supernaturally or socially and historically ordained alternative, and as virtuous. The new world view offered by Brecher and others is deeply subversive of such a model, but it is consistent with the structure, strategy and activity of the new pluralistic global movements, active at many social levels, in many social spaces, assuming overlapping areas of activity with others, and expecting to be involved in dialogue with them.

In so far as we wish to avoid presenting the new internationalist movements on the model, or self-image, of the old, we need to recognise not only their plurality but their ambiguity. This is suggested in Figure 7.1, concerned to reveal the problematic nature of the global alternative (alternative to globalization), and of its strategy. Figure 7.1a presents three ideal-type responses to globalization and globalism: that of celebration (accepting the role of serialized global consumer, individualized voter); that of rejection (on particularistic, essentialist or fundamentalist grounds); and that of critique/surpassal. The figure also shows, however, that any such alternative (global or not) overlaps with, or is penetrated by, celebratory or rejectionist elements. Figure 7.1b reveals the tensions between engagement and autonomy in alternative social movements/spaces, suggesting the necessity to move or balance between an excess of engagement with capital/state (incorporation) or of autonomy in civil society (self-isolation). Any alternative social movement or related NGO can thus find itself in multiple positions, in local-to-global space, or at particular times.

The Rise of Authoritarian Global Movements

Globalization, as we have seen, does not only provoke democratic, pluralist and forward-looking movements. It also gives rise to authoritarian, militaristic and apocalyptical ones (religious and secular, right and left) attempting to deny, repulse or escape a globalized capitalist modernity (Castells, 1997; Castells, Yazawa and Kiselyova, 1995–6). We

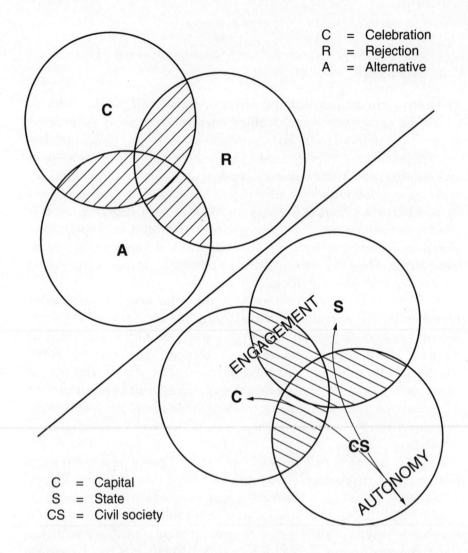

Figure 7.1a (above)   Responses to globalization: local, national, regional, global
Figure 7.1b (below)   Social movement engagement/autonomy: local, national, regional, global

may here again refer to Peru's Shining Path. This movement is (or, hopefully, was) both a result of Peru's peripheralization from the last phases of capitalist globalization and an attempt to isolate it even further. Its contradictory logic, ethical double standards and political hypocrisies are striking. Shining Path assassinates Peruvian proletarians in the name of a proletarian revolution rejected by Peruvian proletarians. It is part of a 'proletarian internationalist' network, of evidently non-proletarian nature. Whilst blowing up the dying body of the feminist leader of a squatter settlement, and denouncing Amnesty International for its bourgeois hypocrisy, Shining Path appeals to world public opinion (actually the more naive, ignorant or romantic part of its socialist and left-liberal middle classes) to defend the human rights of its authoritarian leader (whose sense of infallibility permitted him to fall – without even token resistance – into the hands of the Peruvian authorities). Inhuman, irrational, archaic and grotesque as such movements may seem, they cannot be either dismissed, repressed, or simply named/tamed – as 'fundamentalist', 'fascist', 'racist', 'totalitarian'. Such labels may be necessary to trigger an initial response from the relevant public. But in so far as they seem to be increasingly provoked precisely by our complex, informatized and globalized capitalism, such movements rather require those threatened by them to understand them and take effective action globally against the global conditions that provoke them. And we must not forget, as the last chapter reminds us, that fundamentalism is not only a property of some suitably foreign Other, screaming slogans of hatred, beating a drum, firing a gun, or carrying a burning cross for ease of identification. Fundamentalism is also amongst us and within us, speaking our dialects, dancing our dances.

A Complex Global Order Requires Complex Global Alternatives

The identification above of global problems rather than universal enemies requires us to formulate and develop viable, convincing, attractive and enjoyable global solutions. The word 'enjoyable' is crucial here. In so far as we recognize how globalized capital capitalizes (both literally and figuratively) on enjoyment, those seeking to surpass capitalism must shrug off their fear or hatred of pleasure, sensuality, lust and even of individual consumption (for the last see Ehrenreich, 1990). The notion of a worldwide Maoist Cultural Revolution (actually a top-down political and ideological one imposing a homogenized and impoverished culture) will attract few, especially amongst peoples who have been already subjected to such.

Other leftist traditions, such as the undialectical reform/revolution opposition, must be abandoned. Incremental global reformism from within and radical global 'alternativism' from without imply non-apocalyptical global strategies, and a mutually educative dialectic for civilizing and transforming the world. In so far, indeed, as conservatives and traditionalists may be concerned to preserve the ecology, local cultures and traditional structures from the careless de-structuring/restructuring impact of globalized capitalism – and in so far as they are prepared to have a dialogue with us – we should not set ourselves up in principle against them either.

If we reject (r)evolutionary historical schemas in favour of Calderon's earlier mentioned 'mixed times', we will remember that we live in a historical world and not just a sociological or linguistic universe. Realistic global utopias will then represent not negations of either 'pre-modernity' or 'modernity' but selective rejections and rearticulations – implying the necessary contribution also of those living under, rediscovering, or valuing, pre-capitalist civilizations and cultures. It is, as earlier implied, within such a framework that we can best understand why it is that the 'pre-modern' Yanomami Indians in the Brazilian Amazon speak to 'post-modern' movements in 'modern' North America or Western Europe.

Information Capitalism as an Eminently Disputable Terrain

There is considerable agreement on 'the central importance of knowledge and information' (Allen, 1992: 182) in the current transformation of capitalism globally, even if the question of what the transition is *to* remains unclear or disputed. The growing centrality to social processes of the 'mode of information' – of data, ideas, values, images, theories, cultures – makes it both possible and necessary for life-asserting or emancipatory movements to operate on these terrains. Here they can reveal, as Amnesty International does, what is globally concealed, or suggest, as Friends of the Earth might, new meanings for what is globally revealed (Melucci, 1989: 205–6). A global information capitalism provides far more favourable terrains for emancipatory movements than those of an internationalized industrial capitalism (industry, polity, nation, battlefield). It has proven extremely difficult to radically democratize these old terrains. Typically, in the past, it has been the terrain that has dominated the movement. This has tended to be the case even when it is new alternative social movements that enter the traditional spaces – witness the rise and fall of Green parties in parliamentary elections. As long as these spaces have public legitimacy we cannot ignore them. But the power of the new movements, locally, nationally and internationally, lies rather in their new ideas, values and organizational principles – the latter revealing at least an implicit understanding of the potential of the latest communication technologies.

The new global solidarity movements are, in large part, 'communication internationalisms'. Communication is here increasingly understood not simply as a technical means to be used but as an ethical end to be valued. The slow transformation of one 'organizational internationalism' into such a communication internationalism can be observed in the case of the international labour movement (Waterman, 1992a). Traditionally the labour movement and socialist theorists have tended to see communication instrumentally, as a more or less neutral means to a mobilizing, organizing and controlling end. Socialists have thus also tended to swing between wild optimism and black pessimism, depending on whether the latest means of communication (press, film, radio, video) appeared to favour labour or capital. Most trade unions and socialist parties still overvalue the hierarchical organization. They often seem to rejoice in, rather than recoil from, the 'iron law of oligarchy' – discovered by Michels (1915) precisely on the basis of labour movement practice. The recent development of international labour communication by computer (Lee, 1996) has resulted in large part from enthusiastic and imaginative initiatives by the 'alternative' international labour service centres, and from a slow and cautious response from the traditional international union organizations. As the two forces interact and converge, they reveal problems facing the project as a whole. As with the new internationalisms more generally, it becomes increasingly necessary to research, theorize, strategize – and to have a dialogue with other internationalist communicators – if the new projects are not to reproduce dominant international relations and communications practices. The following will illustrate and specify this matter with particular reference to the women's movement and feminism.

Like the other alternative social movements operating under the conditions of an informatized and globalized capitalism, that of women is, at least implicitly, a communications internationalism. This has several different but interconnected meanings. The first is that it operates on the terrain of ideas, information and images, revealing – as just noted – that which is globally concealed, suggesting new meanings for that which is revealed. The second and consequent meaning is that it is particularly active and effective on the terrain of communication, media, culture. The third is that its basic relational principle is that of the network rather than the organization. The fourth, and consequent, one is that the movement needs to be primarily understood in communicational/cultural rather than in the traditional political/organizational terms. Let us explore these meanings further.

The Global Sphere of Ideas, Information and Images

There is nothing immaterial, superstructural or derivative about this sphere, although in the industrial phase of capitalism it may have appeared as all three. We do not, at the other extreme, need to become discourse-determinists to recognize both the increasing centrality of this sphere and the potential for emancipatory movement and radical democracy it contains. That this sphere is created and dominated by the logic of capital cannot conceal its contradictory nature: capital, capitalists, capitalisms, cannot simply control this sphere in the way they did the factory, the state, the school and the gun. The contradictory nature of even the dominant global media is well expressed by Zillah Eisenstein (1996):

> Feminism, as export, is beamed across the globe. So it exists even where it has no local roots. Anyone can see it if they have a t.v., watch hollywood films, listen to worldwide news, or use e-mail. The feminism they see is affluent and consumerist. But in spite of this capture by the western/global networks, feminism is not entirely contained by its advertisers. Feminism makes women as 'female' visible, even if its partial viewing makes women in 'the' south and east less visible than those in 'the' north and west. [...] Local feminism and women's oppositions can emerge through and in dialogue with this transnational communications network. The telecommunications global web potentially allows communication across the very divides that transnational capital constructs. Women can 'see' themselves, across the globe, in ways that were just not possible before.

The sphere of information, images and ideas is also a non-territorial sphere, meaning one increasingly capable of the expanding growth, flexibility and democratization that the capitalism of industry and the state-nation has promised/denied. It is growth here that will make an ecological steady-state possible globally, without such 'conservatism' implying stagnation or reaction. One problem to be overcome is that of the invisibility of this sphere – that activists literally do not *see* communication as something with its own specific laws. Another, or consequent, problem is that it is handled with concepts and understandings borrowed from, for example, politics, business or management – in terms of a necessary 'aspect', as public relations, promotion or image-projection. The practice of the ASMs, fortunately, is much more advanced than their theory, universalizing subversive/infectious ideas, information and images even through the capitalist CNN and the statist BBC world radio and TV services.

The Global Terrain of Communication, Media, Culture

At national level, or within a nation-state dominated discourse, we can recognize as distinct, overlapping and mutually informing cultural spheres, the Dominant, the Popular and the Alternative. This Alternative sphere evidently overlaps/interacts with the Dominant and Popular ones, on the same model as those in Figure 7.1. But, the Popular (in so far as this implies places actively and intensively lived in and culturally shaped by poorer population sectors) can hardly be said to have a place at global level. The Popular, it seems to me, is here carried, shaped and articulated by either the immensely powerful Dominant global means or the still tiny and marginal Alternative ones – which are in mutual dispute for hegemony over the Popular. The marginality of the Alternative here is less important than recognition of the creative freedom permitted by such marginality, the name and increasing centrality of this terrain, the necessity and possibility of disputing it.

It has been argued, in relation to its democratic potential, that cyberspace is less like a hammer – a means, a tool – than Germany – a place, space, culture (Poster, 1995). It is, actually, simultaneously a hammer *and* Germany *and* utopia ('nowhere', 'a good place', a community yet to be imagined and created). Globally it is a space of increasingly public dispute, as the radical-democratic social movements mobilize for the People's Communication Charter and related political transformations. These, and other such projects, both require and are creating democratic and pluralist global communication networks that are increasingly specialized and professional. The significance of this sphere is now recognized by, for example, feminist internationalists, as here by the Quito-based feminist computer communications specialist, Sally Burch:

> [W]hen it is a matter of demanding rights, or of designing strategies to gain spaces of power, the area of communication is usually forgotten; or, in the better cases, it is considered an area of concern only to the communicators. [. . .] Nonetheless, as an issue that crosses all spheres of action, it ought to concern the movement as a whole. If, additionally, communication today is a space of power contestation, of control, of influence, we women should be present in this contest, with our proposals, our practices, and in defence of our rights; in the absence of this we can surpass our condition of margin-alisation only with difficulty. [. . .] This is one of the great challenges confronting the women's movement at the dawn of the new millennium, since we can anticipate that the right to communicate will be, for the next century, what the right of education was in this century. (ALAI, 1996: ii–iii)

Networking as a Principle of Global Interrelationship

Networking, as has been said earlier in this book, is both the oldest and the most common form of human social relationship. It was only with the development of industrial and state-national capitalism that the formal, hierarchical organization (authoritarian, representative-democratic, participatory-democratic) came to impose itself, to suck power and meaning out of such networks, to concentrate all decision-making power within itself, to project itself as both the real and ideal relational form. The transformation to a globalized and informatized capitalism brings back the networking principle with a vengeance – primarily vengeance against those subaltern strata now locked into and dependent on the traditional hierarchical organization! There is, thus, nothing essentially virtuous about networking either now or in the recent (or, for that matter, pre-capitalist) past.[10]

In talking of networking however, we are considering human inter-relationships, including those within and between organizations, in *communication* terms. In so far as networks are conceived of as hor-izontal, flexible, incorporating participation and feedback, we can also value these over the rigid hierarchical organization, and attempt to thus distinguish 'our' networks from 'their' networks. We have, however, also to recognize that within any particular domain – national, regional, global – networking does not only mean an informal and flexible horizontal relationship between equals and alikes, but also informal horizontal and vertical relationships between unequals/unalikes!

Networks also have different architectures, such as the star, the wheel and the web (including a World Wide Web increasingly used by women's movements and feminist academics) implying differential influence and control. Within the ASMs today network-babble needs to be replaced by network analysis, including consideration of roles within, or in relation to, networks, of the cost of individual/group involvement, of the extent of their connectivity, of their density, and of the role of opinion leaders (who can evidently convert a network into a 'following'). Internationalist feminists are beginning to develop such ideas conceptually so as to analyse, for example, the Latin American/Caribbean preparations for the Beijing conference (Guzman and Mauro, 1996).

All the complexities and qualifications notwithstanding, the idea, value and practice of networking opens wide perspectives to emancipatory global movements, previously (self-)condemned to reproduce the pyramidical and hierarchical structure of the corporation, factory, state, army, prison, church or university. If the extreme form of emancipatory internationalism was at one time represented by the Comintern (combining characteristics of early Islam, the Jesuit Order, the illegal insurrectionary movement, and the police state), the new ideal must be the Italian one of the 'biodegradable organization' – an ideal the new ASMs are more likely to welcome in general theory than in particular effect or as promoted practice.

The Labour Movement in the Era of Globalization

What possibility remains for the old labour movement – locally, nationally, regionally, globally – in a world in which wage labour is being destroyed, de-structured, restructured, imported and exported, and in which any notion of a working-class culture is being undermined not only by repeated changes in the amount, type and site of labour, but also in its consumption patterns and lifestyles? I have elsewhere argued (Waterman, 1993b; forthcoming) for a 'social movement unionism' or a 'new social unionism', in other words for a unionism that not only allies with the ASMs but incorporates their demands, and which responds to their new organizational forms and practices. This proposal recognizes that those who labour for, or under, capitalism do not only exist for and identify with wage labour and as wage labourers. They are also urban residents, women, have ethnic or racial identities, need peace, a healthy environment, etc. In Chapter 3 I proposed a strategy for a 'new labour internationalism' which expressed related principles for international relationships. What is, perhaps, still necessary is a more direct address to wage work, its changing nature, and changing experiences of this.

In so far as we accept the argument of Allen above that the latest phase in capitalist development is significantly different from the Fordist one, then we need a union strategy recognizing this transformation. It would, however, seem to me an error to suggest some kind of post-industrial or post-Fordist strategy for 'New Times' (Hall and Jacques, 1989), based on current changes in and experiences of labour, or – given its current disaggregation – on particular national or international segments/layers thereof. The new model of global capitalism, in any case, does not imply the disappearance of the old one: it can, in a country like India, co-exist with bonded labour. Nor does the new model, obviously, imply the disappearance of domestic labour, carried out overwhelmingly by women. It would seem to me that what is here called for is a new understanding of work under a capitalism that is increasingly informatized and globalized. This means developing a strategy that will not be outdated by the rapidity of movement in the labour process, the product or the site. Nor by the possible appearance of yet newer models, yet more complex syntheses of ancient, old, modern and post-modern. Developing and extending the argument in Chapter 3, I suggest three crucial elements of such a strategy, addressed respectively to

1   hierarchy and authoritarianism within waged work;
2   the nature of work as a multifaceted human activity;
3   space–time compression as it affects the above.[11]

Struggles against Authoritarianism within the Wage-Labour Situation

These struggles are traditional to the labour movement, expressed in terms of 'workers' control', 'workers' self-management' or 'workers' participation'. We need, however, to take these beyond the traditional framework by recognizing the crisis of state-socialist strategies, by taking a truly international comparative perspective, or by making connections between labour demands and those of the ASMs (see Bayat, 1991). Democratization within work is not a project confined to 'advanced' countries or workers. The following possibilities would seem to be open even within the Third World:

1 'natural' workers' control in the small-commodity sector;
2 the democratization of co-operatives;
3 state-sponsored forms resulting from worker pressure;
4 union attempts to influence enterprise management and national development policy;
5 efforts of plant-level unions to counter employers' attacks resulting from changing industrial structures (Bayat, 1991: 172).

Such strategies would allow not only for the revival of the intimate early relationship between the labour and democratic movements, they would also suggest a revived area for international labour/socialist discussion, exchange of experiences and solidarity activity.

Liberation from Work

This is the strategy of Gorz (1989), who seems to believe there can be no such humanization within it as suggested above. Gorz has produced a challenging critique of the ideology of work that dominates the international trade union movement as much as it does the capitalist (or statist) media. This ideology holds that

1 the more each works, the better off all will be;
2 that those who do little or no work are acting against the interests of the community;
3 that those who work hard achieve success and those who don't have only themselves to blame.

He points out that today the connection between *more* and *better* has been broken and that the problem now is one of producing *differently*, producing *other* things, working *less*. Gorz distinguishes between work for economic ends (*the* definition of work under capitalism/statism), domestic labour, work for 'oneself' (primarily the additional task of women), and autonomous activity (artistic, relational, educational, mutual-aid, etc.). He argues for a movement from the first type to the third, and for the second one to be increasingly articulated with the third rather than subordinated to the first.

Gorz points out that, with the new technologies, it will be possible within a few years, in the industrialized capitalist countries, to reduce average working hours from 1,600 to 1,000 a year without a fall in living standards. Under capitalist conditions, of course, what is *likely* to happen is a division of the active population into 25 per cent of skilled, permanent and unionized workers, 25 per cent insecure and unskilled peripheral workers, and 50 per cent semi-unemployed, unemployed or marginalized workers, doing occasional or seasonal work. If the trade unions are not to be reduced to some kind of neo-corporatist mutual protection agency for the skilled and privileged, they will, Gorz argues, have to struggle for liberation from work:

> Such a project is able to give cohesion and a unifying perspective to the different elements that make up the social movement since 1) it is a logical extension of the experience and struggles of workers in the past; 2) it reaches beyond that experience and those struggles towards objectives which correspond to the interests of both workers and non-workers, and is thus able to cement bonds of solidarity and common political will between them; 3) it corresponds to the aspirations of the ever growing proportion of men and women who wish to (re)gain control in and of their own lives. (Gorz, 1989: 224)

This argument reveals no awareness of the existence of a world of labour outside Western Europe. But, in case it should be thought that struggle against wage labour is the privilege only of 'labour aristocrats' in industrialized capitalist welfare states, it should be pointed out that it was with the struggle for the eight-hour working day that the international trade union movement was born in the 1890s, and that similar national or international strategies have been proposed within Latin America (Sulmont, 1988a) and the USA (Brecher and Costello, 1994). The importance of the argument lies precisely in its rooting within international labour movement history and contemporary union concerns, and the explicit connections made with the alternative social movements – or, if you like, with those interests and identities of workers that unions currently ignore, subordinate or repress.

A Labour Strategy on Space–Time Compression

In so far as we recognize space–time compression as a crucial implication of high-capitalist modernity, neither enthusiastic welcome, resigned acceptance nor angry denunciation would seem adequate. What would be needed is appropriate labour movement strategies. Labour has traditionally had explicit strategies on time and implicit ones on space (in that it argued for regional industrialization, housing and urban services or planning, and even for national protectionism). But restrictions of working hours have often been literally traded for cash or other benefits (Brecher and Costello, 1990c), and remaining state-endorsed limitations on capitalist control of these have been seriously undermined by neo-liberalism and globalization. Although there are strategies of dominant forces (military, industrial/ environmental, administrative, as well as capitalist) for particular space–time compressions, there need to be alternatives from labour. Some such issues are implicitly being raised around the USA–Canada– Mexico Free Trade Agreement, a project which proposes a single space for capital and goods but separate ones for people and peoples. Some labour and associated democratic movements have been questioning 'fast-track' decision-taking and the consequent movements of capital, industry and labour (but not of best practice working and environmental conditions). An explicit awareness of time–space compression might, for example, help US carworkers avoid the adoption of strategies which are not only based on a narrow spatial identity (the USA) and therefore possibly hostile to relevant others (Mexico, Canada), but which seem likely to be rapidly circumvented by a capitalism whose timing and freedom of movement have been checked only at one place/time.[12]

It is evident that labour movements and socialist thinkers are today increasingly challenged to move their understandings, forms, allies, strategies, sights (and sites) from those of a nation-state dominated industrial capitalism to those of a complex global information capitalism. This means allying with other forces in radical-democratic struggle globally. There is some evidence of traditional international socialist parties trying to respond to the internationalism of the ASMs (Fourth International, 1990). But, for the major international union centre, the International Confederation of Free Trade Unions, as we have seen, the evidence is more ambiguous. The tendency for even militant and radical forces in the unions to instrumentalize other movements is hard to overcome (DeMartino, 1991). The North American labour movements will need to draw conclusions from the fact that it was the ecological cause rather than theirs that managed, in 1993, to at least temporarily halt NAFTA by a successful court case.

The problems of the old labour movement arise far less for the alternative social movements, born with the crisis of the nation-state and during the transition from industrial to information capitalism. However locally oriented or subject-specific in origin or focus, the ASMs tend to become global, and to operate globally, their efforts being both cause and effect of variegated, democratic and pluralistic global cultures. There is, thus, an international network of indigenous inhabitants of the Polar Circle, this being allied to other international networks of indigenous peoples. The new global cultures of the peace, human rights, ecological and other such movements are themselves in increasing tension with hegemonic movements, globally, nationally, locally. Where states, or blocs of such, publicly fall out at international ecological or human rights conferences, revealing double standards or shabby self-interest, the social movements and non-government organizations are increasingly able to not only demonstrate more co-operative and friendly relationships but to suggest new universal standards. They have increasingly moral authority internationally – something the world trade union movement has yet to regain.

From Cultural Globalization to an Alternative Global Culture

So far we have spoken of culture mostly under the rubric of information and communication. It is also possible and necessary, however, to consider culture more specifically, in terms of a common language, commonly understood symbols and meanings, even shared aesthetic pleasures.

There have been, and are, different ways in which a global culture has been conceived, proposed, or even organized and imposed. At one time, for example, it might have been seen as represented by the single worldwide Catholic faith, Rome, the Pope, by Latin, a shared architecture, symbols, dogma, rituals. In the nineteenth century the *Communist Manifesto* spoke of the disappearance of national narrow-mindedness and the appearance of 'a world literature' from national and local ones (Marx and Engels, 1935: 209). Such a literature, understood in Marxist terms, is, 150 years later, a commonplace. Consider only the way contemporary Chile and China have been brought to English paperback readers by Isabel Allende (1987) and Jung Chang (1991).

But this is culture for the literate, literature-reading public and is brought to them by courtesy of an increasingly globalized capitalist publishing industry. It can hardly be itself isolated from the more general electronic information, media and advertising conglomerates into which publishing is increasingly integrated (see Table 7.1, Row E). World culture, thus, also includes Donald Duck (Dorfman and Mattelart, 1975), MacDonald's and Cable News Network (also known as MacTV). This brave new world of multinationalized culture has therefore often been understood by the Left in terms of North American cultural imperialism, commercializing, homogenizing and destroying local ones (Schiller, 1990).

Conversely, Mike Featherstone (1990) has argued that the existence of a unified global culture (on the nation-state model) is actually impossible, since

> to contemplate this on the global level means imaginatively to construct an 'outside' to the globe, a sphere of global threat captured only in the pages and footage of science fiction accounts of space invaders, inter-planetary and inter-galactic wars. In addition the transnational cosmopolitan intellectuals (serving which masters we might ask?) would have a long way to go to re-discover, formulate and agree upon global equivalents to the *ethnie*. (Ibid.: 11)

There are various ways in which the matter might be reconceived. In the first place one can imagine – indeed describe, as van Steenbergen does below – a culture or sub-cultures which are not primarily territorial, or not necessarily linguistic, in nature (Islamic, socialist, female or feminist). In the second place, one can recognize the 'outside global threat' *intra*-terrestrially, as science fiction increasingly becomes science fact. What of the somewhat pathetic 'transnational cosmopolitan intellectuals', with no master to serve, no *ethnie* for reference? Given the increasing centrality of knowledge and information to a globalized modernity, it is not necessary to assume that its bearers serve masters (or, if feminists, mistresses). Some thinkers even see the knowledge class or elites as themselves the new masters of the universe (Frankel, 1987). I would see Featherstone's category, or something like it, on a cultural avant-garde model (not a political vanguard*ist* one), hypothetically involved in a democratic dialogue or dialectic with mass communities, of territory, interest, affinity, with these, again, hypothetically becoming globally aware.[13]

Do intellectuals, in any case, need an *ethnie* or even a language? Only, perhaps, if one conceives them on the model of Featherstone, as those operating primarily through the written or spoken word. There are other intellectuals, such as those artists whose stock in trade is global synthesis and syncretism, and who are also involved in the complex and contradictory process of creating various kinds of global communities. Their efforts can hardly be understood in terms of 'cultural imperialism'. This is evident in the case of popular music, as when Reebee Garofalo (1992) not only shows rock as a medium for democratic mass movements cross-nationally, from London to Rio and Peking, but as a music of global awareness or protest, from the Band Aid Concert to the Mandela one. The same point is made by Ruben Martinez (1992: 150–65) on Mexican *rocanrol*. Martinez, a Los Angeles-based journalist and poet, experiences a new transnational culture in ways that touch – if tangentially – on religious, liberal or socialist thought and values:

> Weaned on a blend of cultures, languages and ideologies (Anglo/Latino, Spanish/English, individualist/collectivist), I have lived both in the North and the South over my twenty-nine years, trying to be South in the South, North in the North, South in the North and North in the South. Now, I stand at the centre – watching history whirl around me as my own history fissures . . . I cannot tell whether what I see is a beginning or an end. My quest for a true centre, for a cultural, political and romantic home, is stripped of direction. [. . .] One can spy on multilingual store signs in New York or Los Angeles . . . listen to the rhythms of every culture and time on the airwaves, but the fires of nationalism still rage, and in the cities of the United States, blacks and Koreans and Latinos and Anglos live in anything but a multicultural paradise. As for myself, it is all too often that I yearn for the Other even when I am with the Other: nowhere do I feel complete. [. . .] With the walls coming down, it may be possible that I'll be able to see beyond the ruins. Gaze upon the other side and see the others – clearly . . . It has been, it is . . . a search for a one that is much more than two. because, wherever I am now, I must be much more than two. I must be North and South in the North and the South . . . (Martinez, 1992: 3–5)

So, even if we are obliged to recognize that we are still living more in a global theatre than in a global civilization (Anderson, 1990: 232), the issue is not without hope. But can the theatre really become a civilization?

Civilizing Global Society: An Alternative World Order

The Problematic Creation of a Non-Capitalist, Non-Hierarchical Global Order

Globalization implies the growing centrality of the supra- or non-territorial level, of global institutions and instances, and therefore the possibility and necessity for the development of a 'global civil society'. This means a non-capitalist/non-state, or anti-competitive/anti-hierarchical, sphere for democratic efforts, within and without the multiple existing global terrains. There is increasing discussion here, some relating to reform of the UN and other such inter-state instances (Held, 1992), others proposing new standards, such as 'The Right to Communicate' (Bratislava Declaration, 1993), yet others concerned with the structure and functioning of global social movements (Charkiewicz and Nijpels, 1993). There are, finally, increasing efforts to consider the interrelationship between the inter-state organizations, the NGOs modelled on these, and the global movements that go beyond territorially defined constituencies (Brecher, Childs and Cutler, 1993; Galtung, 1980).

Global civil society is no paradise of non-territorial liberty, equality, solidarity, ecological care and pluralistic tolerance. It *may* be the privileged space for the civilizing and surpassing of capitalist, statist, technocratic, etc., structures/processes/ideologies, but it should rather be understood as a habitat to be continuously and jointly constructed than an existing structure even imperfectly represented by international social movement or NGOs. Within this space global movements will inevitably express their external and internal tensions, negotiate their internal and external relations, often revealing or reproducing traits they claim to have surpassed. Increasingly, however, the ambiguity of their own practice is recognized by people in the movements (who thus echo the sentiments of Ruben Martinez):

> We make compromises, we open new processes ... we are facing complexities. We make declarations of interdependence. We take money from the powers that we fight, we try to confuse them and are confused. We go along with the carelessness of using and thoughtlessness of production and

consumption. We try to live with the system and escape it. We are crushed under the bulldozers of capital and technology; we die from hunger and get used to producing statements in the name of the oppressed and the dying; we live within the grids of the Norths and Souths within and against each other. (Charkiewicz and Nijpels, 1993: 18–19)

In so far as civil society depends on, struggles against and is articulated with state and capital, however, the development of a global civil society depends on and stimulates the democratization, deconcentration and decentralization of inter-state organizations, of global capitalist companies and institutions. For car- and other transport-worker unions, consumer and ecological movements, for example, this could mean proposing a worker, democratic and ecologically friendly plan for the world automobile and transport industries.[14]

A New Concept of Global Citizenship

The notion of global citizenship has at least two interrelated problems attached to it. The first is that of the social, territorial inclusion/exclusion anchored historically in the concept of rights/responsibilities within a city (later state-nation). The second is its relationship to a sovereign power, whether aristocratic, monarchical or republican). A global citizenship would be one without outsiders, unless we are thinking of extraterrestrial territories or beings. It would also be one recognizing that, today more than ever, 'sovereign power' at global level is complex and dispersed. Yet, given globalization, some such notion seems not only inescapable but also attractive.

The idea of global citizenship is a logical implication of theoretical and political discussion of multitiered citizenship, itself a result of the creation of such regional polities as the European Union, and of a relativization of state-nation centrality. It is attractive for numerous reasons. One is shown by the way in which women have been able to successfully appeal to the European Court of Justice against the state-nation. Another attraction is that of embodying universal rights and responsibilities in people and peoples rather than the state-nation.

The non-existence of a recognizable global sovereign is less an obstacle than a challenge to emancipatory global movements. That there is no single address for the People's Communication Charter or the Cultural Environment Movement does not prevent them from seeking for and identifying the places where power is concentrated, nor from pressing for citizen-like rights – and responsibilities – in this sphere. In this case, perhaps, global citizens in the making might be also *creating* a global sovereignty (subject to both *perestroika* and *glasnost*) over an increasingly privatized sphere that is monopolistic in tendency, individualizing, intrusive and destructive of human sociality and creativity.

Notions of 'cosmopolitan democracy' (Archibugi and Held, 1995) and extensive related discussion sensitize us to the growing importance of international institutions – and the impact that these have on notions of democracy that assume the sovereign nation-state. They may, however, be based on an overoptimistic projection forward from the 1990s wave of UN activity, and of the NGO/civil society role in global conferences. We do not know, at this uncertain moment, what US or other major state/bloc interest there is in anything more than a slimmed-down set of such institutions, with serious global decision-making confined to smaller and more secretive clubs – with carefully selected, purely decorative, NGO 'consultative committees' as a cheap but decorative fringe.

Discussion around global institutions in terms of democracy has none the less extended the notion of 'double democratization' (Held, 1995) – of both state and civil society – to the global level. If this kind of discussion often makes a simple identification of the latter with the new alternative social movements or NGOs, critical reflection on the latter suggests the necessity for a third democratization – of full citizenship within a sphere that often reproduces the hierarchy, secrecy and competitivity of capital, state, and of those old bureaucratized labour or socialist movements over which superiority is claimed.

The concept of world citizenship appropriate to the era of globalization can no longer be simply that of the religious universalist, the liberal cosmopolitan or the socialist internationalist (for whom see Chapter 3). Bart van Steenbergen has identified as hypothetical global citizens the 'global capitalist', the 'global reformer', the 'environmental manager' and the 'earth citizen'. His 'earth citizen' would seem the relevant successor to past types of international citizen:

> [E]cological citizenship emphasises the importance of the planet as breeding ground, as habitat and as lifeworld. In that sense we could call this type of citizen an *earth citizen* who is aware of his [*sic*] organic process of birth and

growth out of the earth as a living organism. This is based on the notion of care, as distinct from the notion of control. The development of citizenship from the city, via the nation-state and the region to the globe is here not just a matter of an increase in scale. With the notion of the 'earth citizen' a full circle is made. The citizen is back to his roots; the earth as Gaia, as one's habitat. (Steenbergen, 1992: 17)

Global Solidarity: An Internationalism for a World Both Real and Universal

A World Condemned to Choose

Much as nineteenth-century industrial capitalism produced iron and steel, and turned villages and fields into towns and factories, it produced economic and technological determinisms, and tended to reduce Marxism to such determinisms. It likewise exuded the notion of politics as the art of the possible, or as the recognition of necessity. Those who stood in the way of the possible and necessary – the rise and rise of the railway and factory, of capital accumulation, state-building, nationalism, militarism and technocracy – were overridden, incorporated, peripheralized, starved, imprisoned or killed. This was a period and type of capitalism unfriendly to dialectical thinking, to the recognition of complexity, variability, interrelation and internal relations. Social simplification and reductionism, the logic of binary opposition and ethical Manicheanism, spread worldwide.

The move from industrial to information capitalism, the multiple crises of growth, a spreading ecological awareness – all these encourage or provoke dialectical thinking, the recognition of long chains of cause and effect (and the impossibility of separating these), the increasing necessity of choice. It was only in 1968 that 'demand the impossible' became a public slogan. Ours is, thus, a period in which we are increasingly condemned to choose. Such choice is the terrain of ethics, or of an ethically aware, ethically informed politics. This seems to be well understood by Collier (1992: 87):

> The whole planet has become a shared world, even for those who never leave their village. Thus, a tie which is both real and universal has arrived; not yet in the form of a real collectivity embracing humankind, but of real relations of mutual dependence through the sharing of the world; and it is from just such relations ... that values and obligations arise.

Globalization creates a world that can increasingly be experienced, by growing population sectors (although differentially and unevenly), as both real and universal, thus allowing for a universalism that is more than faith or obligation, a global solidarity that is more than a merely imagined community. The new global solidarity projects descend from, selectively rearticulate, allow for, but go beyond, religious, liberal and socialist universalisms; proposing neither a return to an unchanging golden past nor a leap into a perfect future – here or hereafter – they allow for and require a dialogue of civilizations and ages, a solidarity with both past and future.

A Universalism for Plural Worlds

Here, however, one must confront two challenges. The first is that we may produce or reproduce a universalism that is either perverse in intention, particularistic in effect or philosophically illegitimate. The second is that we are producing or reproducing a sentimental humanist universalism, of which the welcoming bark and wagging tail is accompanied by a little bite on our infinitely divided, complex and slippery global reality. Let me deal with the first challenge directly, leaving the second to be met by the rest of the chapter.

The major contemporary philosophical challenge to global solidarity is the widespread current condemnation of 'foundationalism', 'totalization', 'universalism', 'essentialism', 'rationalism', and any 'grand narratives' that offer universal statements of reality, value and obligation, based on initial assumptions or arguments about the universe, nature, man, society, etc. Such grand narratives are those that have descended from Judaism and Christianity, from the European Enlightenment, Liberalism and Socialism – the sources of most internationalist doctrine. They are suspect for presenting their 'story' as truth, and for imposing this truth on others (and an always excluded Other). There are 'right' and 'left' versions of such criticism, sometimes directly targeting globalization theories, humanist universalism or any general international solidarity ethic. I will deal only with the left versions.

There has been much left criticism of Marxism – classical and contemporary – in the above terms. We have noted the deconstruction of traditional internationalist discourse by Fernando Mires (1989, 1991), a man who prefers the cautious language of 'international co-operation' and 'co-ordination' to that of internationalism. We may also note the related plea of the green economist Alain Lipietz (1990) for a 'modest internationalism', a 'minimal universalism'. There is, on the left, evidently an explicit or implicit fear of once again imposing on those from different (and less powerful) worlds the universalizing claims of Western or Westernized intellectuals or movements. Two arguments may be relevant here, an abstract one relating to universalism and civil society, and a concrete one, relating to globalization and universal responsibility.

Following Jeffrey Alexander (1991), we may recognize that cultural universalism has been essential to the development of liberal democracy, its place of residence being civil society. We may further recognize with him how the themes of 'civility, civil society, universalism, and citizenship' (ibid.: 167) have been central to the development of the Western nation-state, as well as in the expansion of concepts of citizenship from the legal to the political and social spheres. We may also, finally, recognize with him the manner in which 'societal community' can expand beyond the nation-state:

> With the construction of a civil society . . . particularistic definitions of membership are broken through; they are replaced by abstract criteria that emphasise simple humanity and participation . . . Citizenship, then, can be understood as a form of social organisation that is anchored in universalistic bonds of community that define every member as equally worthy of respect . . . Members of a civil society can refer to these universalistic values to gain distance from their immediate relationships, in order to change or criticise them. (Ibid.: 168)

Civil society, in other words, implies not the existence of public consensus or consent but the very existence of a public, and therefore the possibility of political scepticism, criticism and moral outrage: global civil society likewise. It seems to me that Alexander's argument provides, in principle, a conceptual basis for notions of global citizenship and civil society. What Alexander does not do is to relate his model to actually existing capitalist society, nationally or globally.

Andrew Collier (1992), as the earlier quote might have already suggested, presents a case for an ethical universalism which is related to capitalism in general and to internationalization processes in particular. Collier recognizes that Marxists have tended to argue for an ethical universalism either *despite* or *as* the self-interest of the working class. He is concerned to escape the horns of this dilemma: that is of appearing either as a 'shamefaced altruist or a shameless collective egoist' (ibid.: 76). He does so on the basis of what he calls a relational ontology. Society, he argues, is not a collection of individuals, a group or organism, it is a network:

> Such a network – 'society' – is not a count-noun. it does not make sense to ask how many societies there are in the world – nor is there only one society. There is society – not societies or a society. Society is an open-textured network, which can be divided in various ways for the purposes of description and analysis, but these divisions are always more or less artificial. (Ibid.: 82)

The ethical implication of this understanding is that it is the lattice of all the relationships within which one is enmeshed that is the source of values and responsibilities. Relating to others is to be understood not so much as something we *do* as what we *are*. This position, again, would seem to allow us to see that in so far as global society exists, it provides a source of values and responsibilities to be weighed against those coming from membership of a nation-state, class, ethnic group, etc. It is the worlds we share with others that provide the social basis for morality. Whereas existence in the world of the market may push us in the direction of individualism and egoism (or to splitting and opposing egoism and altruism), we also exist in other social worlds, which allow us to be moved by the needs of significant others.

Recognizing the Needs and Voices of Others

How are we to avoid foisting another Westocentric universalism on the rest of the world? How are we to recognize the needs and voices of such others? Nancy Fraser (1986) is interested in 'a discourse ethic of solidarity', which she also characterizes as an ethic of discourse for social movements. She points out that means of interpretation and communication (vocabularies for pressing claims, the idioms for communicating needs, the narrative conventions for constructing individual and collective histories, the paradigms of argument considered authoritative for judging competing claims, etc.) cannot be value-neutral. These means of interpretation tend to express the experiences, interests and self-images of dominant social groups. In the case of the West the dominant vocabularies constitute people as rational, self-interested individuals, engaged in exchange with others in utility-maximizing relationships. Such a standpoint is characteristically that of white European male bourgeois property owners.

Fraser argues that this vocabulary can hardly express relationships of ongoing dependency, such as that of mother and child, nor account for such experiences and feelings of connection as exist in 'more extended networks of community and solidarity', as are to be customarily found in the subcultures of the subordinated. The latter are going to be hindered from participating on equal terms with the dominant groups in communicative interaction:

> Unless they were to contest this situation and organise to win a greater measure of collective control over the means of interpretation and communication, it would appear that members of subordinated groups would have only two options: they could either adopt the dominant point of view and see their own experiences repressed and distorted; or they could develop idiolects capable of voicing their experience and see these marginalised, disqualified and excluded from the central discursive institutions and arenas of society. Or they could do both at once. (Fraser, 1986: 426)

Given this situation, and assuming there is a desire to surpass it, what is necessary is the replacement of a 'monological ethic' by a 'discourse or dialogical ethic'. The latter implies: recognition of the unequal relationship to the dominant means of interpretation; making such means themselves a matter of negotiation; and allowing the subordinated to propose alternatives to such. Fraser here provides an effective critique of, and alternative to, precisely the monological universalisms of the past.

Fraser goes further, proposing not only a form of discourse but a content for it – a solidarity ethic – and, whilst she develops her argument in relationship to the women's movement, she herself argues that it is equally appropriate to other social movements of the subordinated or excluded. She also considers it necessary to avoid basing her ethic on either the 'individual' or 'humanity':

> Here one would abstract *both* from unique individuality *and* from universal humanity to focalise the intermediate zone of group identity. The most general ethical force of this orientation would be something like this: we owe each other behaviour such that each is confirmed as a being with specific collective identifications and solidarities. The norms governing these interactions would be ... norms of collective solidarities expressed in shared but non-universal social practices. (Ibid.: 428)

The reference here to group identity and shared practices requires that we address ourselves to – and reflect on – the practices of groups themselves claiming to contribute to global solidarity.

A Complex Solidarity for a Complex Globality

Here I will suggest an understanding of international solidarity that goes beyond both poetic and philosophical discourses, and any attempt at a one-word qualifier ('reciprocal', 'reflexive'), but by building on rather than dismissing such discourses. The understanding offered is a more political and a more complex one. It develops the one offered in Chapter 3. It is also, I think, one that could aid research. Solidarity is here assumed to be:

1 informed by and positively articulated with equality, liberty, peace, tolerance, and more recent emancipatory/life-protective ideals;
2 primarily a relationship between people and peoples, even where mediated by state, market and bureaucratic/hierarchical organizations;
3 an active process of negotiating differences, or creating identity (as distinguished from traditional notions of 'solidarity as community' which may *assume* identity).

International solidarity – old or new, local or global, is here understood in terms of the acronym ISCRAR (an ironic semi-mnemonic: *Iskra* was Lenin's newspaper). This spells out as Identity, Substitution, Complementarity, Reciprocity, Affinity and Restitution.[15] Table 7.2 summarizes and exemplifies the argument, as well as specifying it in relation to the case of international feminism.

Identity or identity creation is what commonly underlies socialist calls for international solidarity, usually in reference to oppressed and divided classes or categories in opposition to powerful and united oppressors (capitalists, imperialists). By itself, however, an Identity Solidarity can be reductionist and self-isolating, excluding unalikes. In so far as the identity is oppositional, it is a negative quality, often determined by the nature and project of the enemy or opponent (as with much traditional socialist internationalism).

Substitution implies standing up, or in, for a weaker or poorer other. This is how international solidarity has been usually understood amongst Development Co-operators and 'First-World Third-Worldists'.

Table 7.2   The meanings of international solidarity

	Definition	General or historical example	Feminist case	Problem, danger or exclusion
Identity	Solidarity of common interest and identity	'Workers of the world unite! You have nothing to lose but your chains. You have a world to win'	'Sisterhood is Global'	Universalistic; exclusion of the non-identical; limitation to the 'politically-conscious'?
Substitution	Standing in for those incapable of standing up for themselves	Charity, development co-operation	Gender and Development programmes	Substitutionism; one-way solidarity, with in-built patron–client relation?
Comple-mentarity	Exchange of different needed/desired goods/qualities	Exchange of different emancipatory experiences, ideas, cultural products	To-and-fro exchanges between movements, feminists on any axis	Decision on needs, desires; value of qualitites, goods exchanged
Reciprocity	Exchange over time of identical goods/qualities	Mutual support between London and Australian dockers, late nineteenth century	Mutual support between differently confronted women's rights activists	Allows for instrumental rationality, empty of emotion/ethics
Affinity	Shared cross-border values, feelings, ideas, identities	Solidarity of pacifists, socialists, ecologists, indigenes	Lesbian, socialist, ecofeminist	Inevitably particular/istic; friendship?
Restitution	Acceptance of responsibility for historical wrong	Swiss compensation for victims of complicity with Nazis	Japanese support for World War II victims of military prostitution	Buying off guilt? Reproduction of guilt/resentment?

By itself, however, a Substitution Solidarity can lead to substitutionism (acting and speaking for the other), and it can permit the reproduction of existing inequalities. This is a criticism of Development Co-operation, which may function to create a single community of guilt and moral superiority within 'donor countries', whilst creating or reproducing further feelings of dependency and/or resentment in countries where social crises have evidently been worsening.

Complementarity suggests the provision of that which is missing, and therefore an exchange of different desired qualities. A Complementary Solidarity would mean that what was moving in each direction could differ but be equally valued by participants in the transaction. In so far as it meant that some kind of physical goods (cash, equipment, political support) were mostly moving in one direction and that some kind of moral or emotional goods (expressions of appreciation and gratitude) were mostly being received, we could be involved in an 'unequal exchange' of a problematic character.

Reciprocity suggests mutual interchange, care, protection and support. It could be taken as *the* definition of the new global solidarity. Global Reciprocity Solidarity, however, could be understood as a principle of equal exchange, in which (as with states) one is exchanging political equivalents, or (as with capitalists) on the basis of calculated economic advantage. It could therefore imply that one would defend the rights of others only in the case of, or in expectation of, reciprocation by the other.

Affinity suggests mutual appreciation or attraction, and therefore a relationship of mutual respect and support, in which what is sought, appreciated or valued by each party is shared. Affinity would seem to have more to do with values, feelings and friendship. An Affinity Solidarity would seem to allow for global linkages within or between ideologies or movements, including between people without contact but acting in the same spirit. In so far as it approximates friendship, it would seem to be inevitably particular, if not particularistic.

Restitution suggests the putting right of a past wrong, the recognition of historical responsibility, a 'solidarity with the past', a solidarity across time rather than space. This comes close to inter-governmental war reparations, with the consequent danger of buying off guilt.

The value of such a general understanding would seem to be the following:

1   that it is multifaceted and complex;
2   that each type holds part of the meaning and that each is only part of the meaning;

3   that it is subversive of simple binary or (r)evolutionary oppositions between bad and good, old and new, material and moral solidarity;
4   that it enables critique of partial or one-sided solidarities;
5   that it could be developed into a research instrument, permitting, for example, surveys of the meaning(s) of solidarity for those involved.

What About the Workers?

Supposing we are agreed that:

1   globalization processes provide the ground for a realistic contemporary universalism;
2   this is understood as related to specific emancipatory projects of a democratic and pluralistic orientation (i.e. neither self-prioritizing nor other-exclusionary);
3   this requires both principles of solidarity and procedures for the development of such.

At least two moves are still necessary. One is to turn these general philosophical principles into political statements. The other is to specify them in a manner relevant to potential collective actors of a quite specific and problematic nature – for example, semi-skilled white male factory workers in industrialized capitalist democracies. Let me try to make these moves simultaneously.

Our previous analysis of globalization enables us to see globalization as a multifaceted, multilevelled and multidirectional process, affecting all people in all parts of the world, although evidently in different ways and with different effects. One crucial aspect is, as we have seen, that of the changing and moving nature of work internationally, this creating highly changeable, differentiated and interdependent working classes. Now, workers in the West are less secure and less homogeneous than they have been for many decades. This can evidently make them more corporatist and racist. But it can also lead them to feel more like workers in other countries, or with other local social identities and concerns. Struggle against the effects of globalization is, as we have seen, something involving women, ethnic minorities, socialists, and people in the South and East as well as the West. In so far as the worker has other identities, interests and aspirations (as s/he always has had) –

as urban resident, as churchgoer, as gay or lesbian, as species being – these are also being challenged by globalization. In other words, the real and inevitably particular worlds of workers are increasingly invaded/interconnected/interdependent.

The need for solidarity in this globalized world does not, furthermore, have to primarily confront the Western worker as a moral responsibility. I mean this in several senses. In the first place, since the worker is no longer conceived of as the privileged revolutionary subject s/he cannot be conceived of as having the primary moral responsibility for internationalism. Recognition of this could reduce the role played by guilt, either as something assumed by workers or imposed on them by socialists (or ecologists, or feminists). In the second place, in so far as interdependency is a global condition, any appeal to such a responsibility must be addressed to workers and labour movements also in the non-West (although the nature of the appeal would have to be relevant to the local experience and possibilities). This can also reduce the moral demands on and expectations of Western workers and movements. In the third place, in so far as we recognize that globalization is equally a condition and a recognition, appeals to workers from above or outside (and these will continue) can be increasingly expressed in terms of stimulating worker self-activity, exploration, imagination and creativity. Global solidarity can thus be seen less as a duty, of ourselves or others, than as an adventure in which all are potentially involved.

Conclusion: A World to Save

Developmentalism (reformist), Third Worldism (radical) and Proletarian Internationalism (revolutionary?) are dependent on old internationalization/internationalism theories, with all the superiority/guilt, dependency/resentment that these imply. A critical and socially committed globalization theory would seem to provide an infinitely richer, more complex and more open view of the world, and one in which superiority and guilt, dependency and resentment can be traded in for recognition, responsibility and reciprocity. The meagre or miserable results of 150 years of communism, 50 or so years of developmentalism and Third Worldism, suggest this may be a more rewarding field to plough – or a more rewarding plough to field.

The year 1998 will be the one hundred and fiftieth anniversary of the

Communist Manifesto, which ended with a rhetorical slogan of biblical grandeur: 'Workers of the world, unite; you have nothing to lose but your chains; you have a world to win!' The slogan echoed, boomed, around the world of industrial capital, disturbing the sleep of crowned and uncrowned heads alike. It inspired massive movements – mostly of decidedly non-proletarian and non-internationalist nature or result. Today the slogan is less likely to frighten crowned heads than frighten off potential supporters.[16] Yet, like Paris in 1968 and the anti-nuclear movement, we too need our slogans, symbols and rituals. But would a simplifying slogan be appropriate to a world of such complexity, to a project so sensitive to ambiguity, to a period in which maximum optimism of the will must be combined with an equal scepticism of the intellect and, if so, what on earth (globe?) could it possibly be?

David Harvey was actually right about modern social movements having their strength in local places rather than globalized spaces, at least up till, say, the 1970s. But his conclusion would be a disastrous guide to the present or future. 'Think globally and act locally'? How the world, and perceptions of it, have changed! We cannot today repeat the slogans of the 1960s, when globalization was a problem without a name and global solidarity was still called internationalism. The revolutionary slogan for the next century has already been invented: 'Think globally, act locally; think locally, act globally'. To which I would like to add: 'Think dialectically: act self-reflexively'. This is then, to repeat, an epoch in which survival demands

1   the replacement of binary by dialectical thinking,
2   a recognition that relating to (distant) others is not what we do but who we are,
3   that, particularly when speaking of the universal, we make ourselves and our 'subject position' visible and ourselves available to the reader, inviting and encouraging her/him to see us as part of an inevitably partial and particular contribution to a new kind of internationalism.

Notes

1.   This argument was first tried out at a seminar at the Institute of Social Studies in The Hague, and a panel involving Anthony Giddens, at a conference of the International Association of Mass Communications

Research, both in June 1993. I am grateful to the two audiences for their critical but friendly response. The same goes for Giddens, to whom my debt is much greater. But here I would also like to draw the attention of readers to two early pioneers, Johan Galtung (1980) and Alan Wolfe (1977), and to one crucial collection (Hall, Held and McGrew 1992).

2.   This is in contradiction with the vision of Vandana Shiva (1993). She presents local/global as a binary and Manichaean division, the first invested with virtue and the second with vice. This reverses rather than surpasses the logic of the globalists she wishes to undermine.

3.   The reference is to John Lennon's song, which tells us both that 'a working-class hero is something to be' and how difficult it is to be one.

4.   The magisterial three volume work on 'the information age' by Manuel Castells (1996, 1997) became available to me only as I was completing this book. It was, regretably, too late for me to absorb the 1000 or so pages so far available and to incorporate his notion of networking into my own understanding of globalization. Castells sees our era in terms of the 'rise of the network society' (title of the first volume), but considers this to be a developmental mode or stage within capitalism. The first volume therefore concentrates on political economy, although one chapter is devoted to electronic communication and 'the culture of real virtuality'. The second volume (1997) is entitled 'the power of identity', ranging over meaning and identity in the network society, social movements (insurrectionary ones of left and right, ecological and women's/sexual rights movements), the crisis of the state and of democracy. The present state, civil societies, political parties and trade unions he sees as increasingly emptied of meaning and capacity for social change. The labour movement and the trade unions seem

> to be historically superseded. Not that it will entirely disappear ... in many instances they are the main, or the only, tools for workers to defend themselves against abuses from capital and the state ... Labour militants will undoubtedly be a part of new, transformative social dynamics. I am less sure that labour unions will. (Castells, 1997: 360)

Hope for the future seems, for Castells, to rest in what he calls 'project identities' (ibid.: 356), of which the significant progressive ones (my term) seem to be primarily the ecological and the women's/sexual rights ones. These are seen as growing out of resistance to the new networked capitalist world order. The power of these movement lies, for Castells, in information and representation, i.e. in people's minds. A major agency of social change is a '*networking, decentred form of organisation and intervention, characteristic of the new social movements*, mirroring, and counteracting, the networking logic of domination in the informational society' (ibid.: 362, original emphasis). I am extremely sympathetic to Castell's general line of argument which I respond to with a mixture of pleasure, regret and relief: pleasure at this powerful support for my own feelings; regret that I have not been able to express them so forcefully and to give them such significance as he does; relief that he does not deal with the NSMs at the global level or in terms of global solidarity! My own ideas on the increasing social centrality of information and networking have been moving in the direction of Castell's argument over a decade or so. The import I give them is revealed in this chapter. I have doubts about his attitude to the old social movements. A full and balanced consideration of Castells's work in the light of my own, or of mine in the light of his, needs more time and another place.

5. I draw on John Allen's (1992) overview of the debate on post-industrialism and post-Fordism. I do this selectively, thus offering a limited image only of the transition, The nature of the transition is, as Allen shows, disputed between theorists and recognized by a number as ambiguous.

6. Is this a misprint for 'division'?

7. The integration of the Philippines into export-oriented industrialization, and the restoration of some kind of liberal democracy (though still with vigilantes), has undermined the basis of this party's Maoism. Its increasingly megalomaniac leader has expelled leading dissidents and, in 1992, for the first time came out openly in identity with the even more megalomaniac Presidente Gonzalo (Abimael Guzman, arrested leader of the Maoist *Sendero Luminoso*) of Peru. The dissidents are attempting to come to terms with actually existing capitalism in the Philippines. Around 1986, during a brief honeymoon period between tendencies of the Filipino Left, I had the privilege of meeting Jose-Maria Sison, founder of the Communist Party of the Philippines and its leading ideologue. Questioning Joma about popular anti-Communism in the Philippines, I received the following response:

> Yes, of course, Peter, we have to recognize this. It is due to the church hierarchy, bureaucratic capitalist control of the media, and the influence of US imperialist culture. But let me assure you, Peter, if we controlled the press for six months, the entire problem would be solved.

Whilst I was merely horrified by this infantile and archaic understanding of media, culture and mass plasticity, members of Joma's entourage were, additionally, mortified.

8. When I say 'meaningfully post-modern' here, I mean it in the same sense as the British postcard that states 'I will be a post-feminist in post-patriarchy'.

9. J.K. Gibson-Graham (1993, 1996: 251–65) considers this an error even in

respect to capitalism. They (because the authors are actually a Gibson and a Graham) claim that Marxists have given 'capitalism' such unity, singularity and totality that it can only be transformed by an apocalyptical revolution in which few Marxists believe any more.

10. I have already mentioned in note 4 above the understanding of globalized capitalism as network, offered by Manuel Castells. This may be compared with the argument of Lipnack and Stamps (1994), who also see ours as 'the age of networking', although without mention of either capitalism or emancipation – though women as managers do get four lines. Lipnack and Stamps (1982) did once toy with networking as something beyond contemporary US reality, and provided me with my first ideas on the subject, but that was under the influence of the alternative 1970s. The more recent work is one evidently addressed, in traditionally US can-do, speedread, self-satisfied, self-promotional, style to Chief Executive Officers with tight schedules and low attention spans. It should not, on these grounds, be ignored, either as a possible illustration of Castells' arguments concerning elite networking, or for more substantial purpose. They argue, thus, that we should recognize four ages of organization in relation to four kinds of society: Small Groups (Nomadic), Hierarchy (Agricultural), Bureaucracy (Industrial) and Networks (Information) (Lipnack and Stamps, 1994: 37). The argument is at the very least thought-provoking and the book deserves much more than this rather dismissive note.

11. The first two arguments below are taken from Waterman, 1993b.

12. The case I have in mind is a successful strike against 'outsourcing' at the Lordstown plant of General Motors in Ohio, USA. As one commentator pointed out: 'For a union to specify which plant will take the brunt of a sales slump is unprecedented and seems likely to accentuate – rather than alleviate – rivalry between competing workforces. It could well put a dent in future efforts at international solidarity' (Slaughter, 1992: 5). This raises a more general theoretical/strategic problem, concerning the understanding of labour impact on space, and of labour strategies for such. These are beginning to be explored at length and depth by Andrew Herod (e.g. 1994, 1997). Herod is critical of those Marxist or other critical social geographers who present labour, if at all, only as 'reacting to' or 'using' the spaces that capital creates. He argues, on the basis of industrial, urban, national and international union activities, that labour has itself shaped space. He himself recognizes the kind of problem Slaughter identifies. In so far as he does not even suggest the strategy options before labour, he would seem to reproduce the reflective but non-engaged posture towards labour of those he himself criticizes. Moreover, he conflates labour with unions, thus obstructing an examination of the tension between these – and a possible force for surpassing the Lordstown Problem. He is,

however, opening up the relationship, under globalization, of unions with space, as another terrain for theoretical/political disputation, and this is promising enough for the time being.

13. On rereading this paragraph I am reminded of Marge Piercy's *He, She and It* (1991). The cover blurb tells us:

> It is the middle of the 21st century, and the world as we know it has been replaced by a vast toxic wasteland dotted with huge, protective domes, surrounded by open areas where most people live. In this cold and poisonous world, information is the most valuable commodity, and Shira Shipman struggles to find her place.

The protected areas are controlled by 'multis', now carrying on the functions of the state in Orwell's *1984*. Living in a small, semi-protected community, existing in a delicately balanced dependence on/autonomy from the multis, Shira is involved in creating a cyborg that will defend it. The novel takes places in the mythical past (of Rabbi Loew creating a community-defending Golem in the ghetto of medieval Prague), in a Jewish free state, where Shira seeks roots and strength, and in a futuristic computerized cyberspace, familiar, perhaps, only to science fiction aficionados and 14-year-old players of computer games. The novel makes a fascinating contrast with Piercy's feminist utopian novel of the 1970s, *Woman on the Edge of Time* (1976). If that one was grounded in the USA, this one, despite its Jewish community, is universal in reference. If the earlier one was an optimistic tragedy, encouraging its readers to realize a plausible utopia, the hope of this one is only human survival in a despoiled world. Despite its grim message, *He, She and It* celebrates human resilience, creativity and love. Piercy's novel is by no means an easy one for those unfamiliar with computers or hostile to technology but, as in many of her novels, she grapples with themes of universal importance.

14. When I proposed this at an international carworkers' consultation, at the Transnationals' Information Exchange, Amsterdam, around 1980, an international officer of the major Dutch trade union confederation, the FNV, confessed total bewilderment. For people like himself, even though supporters of the peace, ecological and human rights movements, such a notion was totally utopian. I would like to hope it will not remain so for another ten or twenty years.

15. All of these terms except the last come from Vos (1976), although he does not address himself explicitly to cross-border solidarity. The last was suggested to me by a South African student, Edgar Pieterse.

16. Such titles today mostly adorn the mastheads of tiny sectarian and self-referential revolutionary socialist papers read by few apart from their editors and their violently competitive opposite numbers (there can, after all, be only one vanguard party of the revolutionary international proletar-

iat). When *A World to Win* survives only as the title of the Maoist Revolutionary International Movement, my inclination to seek a new motto does tend to be reinforced.

POSTSCRIPT: THE NEW GLOBAL SOLIDARITY AS PERSONAL EXPERIENCE

Problematic Pleasure and Pleasurable Problems

In the Introduction to this work I had something to say about the personal, the political and the professional. This was intended to make explicit who I was, my political trajectory and my motivation in writing the book. Many of the papers and articles I have written contain such self-reflective passages, but a major element in the present work has been my shift of attention from proletarian and socialist internationalism to a cross-class and democratic one – and a recognition of the extent to which even nineteenth-century labour internationalism was marked by cross-class and democratic elements. The shift of focus has been accompanied by another recognition: that the active bearers of internationalism have customarily been middle-class cosmopolitan intellectuals. I am obviously aware of belonging to this tradition, as also of the difference in the relationship to mass internationalism of myself and my forebears. I have elsewhere recognized three historical types of left internationalist, the nineteenth-century Agitator, the twentieth-century Agent (overt or covert) and the twenty-first century Networker (Waterman, 1993a). I have played all three roles – although so far only in the twentieth century – and I have proposed this trilogy as a heuristic device for further exploration of the role of the active agents of internationalism.[1]

What I have not yet recorded or reflected on in this work is the experience of being involved in the *new* global solidarity movements. In so far as the book represents some kind of invitation to others to become so involved, it would seem appropriate to reflect on this more recent experience. I will do so by dealing with some of the problems and pleasures of the process (which is not to deny that problems can be pleasurable and pleasures problematic). Along the way I may suggest, at least in parentheses or endnotes, future areas for political or research activity.

The problems, for me, have been primarily those of relating to those I have called the 'new labour internationalists' or the 'new international labour communicators'. I did not originally exclude myself from these categories, but I am here thinking of a post-1968 generation of often full-time organizers, usually working within international labour resource centres or for international labour publications. They would have been, in the 1980s, in their thirties (maybe fifteen to twenty years younger than me), usually with university education or other tertiary-level degrees, often self-trained in journalistic, computer or other relevant skills, nearly always working for low pay, or on short-term contracts, and required to spend much of their time raising money from individual supporters, foundations, development funding agencies, state or inter-state organizations, or even from unions. Such people can be found throughout the Western world, in a number of Third World countries (e.g. South Korea, South Africa, Mexico, Hong Kong), occasionally in Eastern Europe (Poland during the repression of Solidarnosc, Russia since the collapse of communism). Customarily they would be non-partisan socialists, much influenced by the alternative social movements (ASMs), and by ideas coming from feminism, the peace, human rights and ecological movements.

I worked with such people in West Europe and North America in the 1980s, particularly those in or from the UK. 'Working with' included taking part in their seminars and consultations, inviting them to those I organized, providing them with publicity and occasionally with cash, selling their publications, publishing their writings in my *Newsletter of International Labour Studies* (1978–90) and a series of related collections, contributing items to their publications. But I always felt that my prime contribution, as someone with certain research resources and skills, was precisely to reflect on the activity, and thus to stimulate a self-reflexivity in the movement that otherwise seemed largely missing and sorely needed.

During the 1980s, in which new labour internationalisms flourished and spread, rose, fell and rose again elsewhere, there was little serious or sustained discussion or debate (I here exclude occasional brilliant essays and depressing polemic) either amongst the alternative international labour activists, or between them and the institution-alized labour internationals, or between the alternative activists and their university supporters. Nor was there much other self-reflective activity. Some of my attempts to stimulate or provoke such activity are mentioned below.

In 1988 – and under the continuing retreat of labour both in Europe and elsewhere – there took place an implicit re-evaluation of their own efforts by two people closely associated with the new labour internation-alism and communication, the two items being published in the UK-based *International Labour Reports*. These pieces reinforced each other in so far as they represented some kind of reappraisal of over-optimistic expectations amongst the new labour internationalists, a reassertion of 'the valuable activities of official union international bodies' (Humphrey, 1988b: 22–3), a rejection of the notion that it might be possible 'to sidestep the established trade union structures and ideologies' (Spooner, 1988: 27).

I was not happy with the image thereby created of the alternative projects, nor the unproblematized presentation of the traditional trade unions. I argued, in part, as follows:

> We need a realistic recognition of the influence, financial resources and representativity of the traditional trade union internationals. We should . . . dialogue with them . . . But we also need to carefully preserve our own meagre but specific resources: our institutional autonomy, our political integrity and our theoretical/ideological originality. Progressive forces within the traditional trade unions may value these even more than we tend to! (Waterman, 1988: 26)

There was no further response to this comment. I became increasingly concerned not so much about the point at issue as about the continuing absence of discussion on such fundamental matters. I therefore made a number of attempts, both before and after this exchange, either to provoke discussion or to create an electronic space for such. The customary response was a resounding silence.

The one real reply I did receive was to an item on the new labour internationalism I put up on the public Labour Bulletin Board of the Geonet computer network in 1990. This ran as follows:

> Comrade Waterman shouldn't be surprised that no-one has replied to his paper. The people who are actually involved in international solidarity work

have little time for this sort of overblown, academic drivel. One of the first criteria for any labour internationalism should be the ability to write clearly in short sentences with ordinary words. It's not that workers can't understand this sort of overlong, pretentious professorspeak but that they can't be bothered to. Another academic once said that anything worth saying can be said plainly. In the meantime, the development of internationalism between workers will remain the practical task of workers themselves. They are doing it already, and I'm sure PW will be welcomed to the fold when he has something useful to say.

Comrade Waterman was surprised, not to say turned into a block of stone, since he had not been previously flamed in email discourse, and since his argument was fairly underblown, condensed and political. It was a thirteen-point definition of a new labour internationalism, later published without protest or problem by the *South African Labour Bulletin*. But it had obviously gone up an uncomradely nostril. The public rebuke – or sneer – came from an official of one of the International Trade Secretariats.[2] It became clear to me, in succeeding days and months, however, that it represented not simply the hostility of an 'institutional' internationalist. His putdown seemed to be approved of by a couple of the most prominent 'alternative' ones in the UK. One of these friends failed to even inform me of a collection of articles she had edited on the new labour internationalism (a term I may have myself not only conceptualized but even invented). So what seemed to be at issue here was not simply a difference of politics but one of my position/privilege (as an academic overblown driveller) and, possibly, of my personality or style. The latter was evidently coming over to such people as one of a claimed moral or intellectual superiority, as exploitative of the less privileged, irresponsible in the face of their own political efforts or job positions, or lacking respect for those lower down the wealth and security hierarchy.

This dispute, or series thereof, caused me considerable discomfort. I felt this even in respect of the 'institutional' internationalists, since I had always thought that my criticism, although sharp, had been open, above-board, based on evidence and argumentation, and made available – customarily pre-publication – for response. But I obviously felt the discomfort and regret even more towards the alternative activists, since, as far as I was concerned, these were not simply my subject matter but also my *companeros/as* in a joint effort. I have my own ideas about the political part of the conflict. One is well expressed in a critique of the union left in the USA, which identifies a

> bias against abstract theoretical debate on the grounds that it is of little use to the *real* needs of people engaged in practical struggle. Self-critical abstract theory is seen to be counterproductive to the primary task of orga-nising. It is a conceit of ivory-tower intellectuals [...] *This aversion to theory matters and matters deeply*. In the absence of self-critical attention to its own practice, the Left's understanding of trade unionism, of the relationship of unionism to other movements for social change, and consequently, of the Left's role vis-a-vis trade unions, has attained the status of an orthodoxy or a catechism that is beyond debate. Debate is constrained by this orthodoxy. (DeMartino, 1991: 30–1, original emphasis)

The other idea concerns territoriality or property. The professionals of the new internationalism seemed to be reproducing, within their small terrain, the attitude of occupation or ownership expressed by the ITS officer above.[3] I later found feminists (highly sensitive to new feminist values, addressing themselves to civil society and the world) to feel extremely uneasy about my intervention into something they felt was a family affair. I will return to this below. In the meantime, there appears to be no reason to assume that organizations linked with new international social movements have, by this token alone, necessarily escaped from the contradictions and complexes of the old.

Back to the new labour internationalists. I felt justified in resenting a simply negative response to my activities, and the absence of any positive alternative proposal. But, on the level of personal relations, I could not help a feeling of failure and loss. It is one thing to say that international civil society is not a paradise. It is another to feel either excluded or self-excluded from the construction of such. Or that it is the same kind of swamp, or jungle, as everywhere else.

The creation of the new electronic spaces of international solidarity activity are – the earlier mentioned experience notwithstanding – breaking through not only institutional and spatial barriers to a dialogue on internationalism and an internationalist dialectic but also class ones. In the midst of rewriting my book, in The Hague and Lima, 1996, I contributed to an international electronic debate on the role of the International Transportworkers' Federation in a long and bitter dock dispute in Liverpool, in the UK.

Electronic space, it turns out, has strange and promising qualities for constructive international dialogue on internationalism. In the first place, it provides a low-cost and increasingly accessible public platform, thus levelling the playing field with those that may have more expensive or exclusive ones. In the second place, it is a space in which power, privilege and prestige are less visible, audible and enforceable than new information, new ideas and – possibly – new values. In the third place, I was even able to feed bits of this present work into an essentially political discussion – without any complaints. The Liverpool dockers and their marginal electronic friends were carrying out not only low-cost international communication but low-cost, and extremely effective, international mobilization. The Communications Officer of the ITF felt required to enter this arena (at least for a time) and there ensued a novel, if tough, even sometimes bitter, exchange, but with civilities preserved. Not only had the tone of voice changed, however. At the end of 1996 the ITF came out in official support of a unique worldwide industrial action in support of the Liverpool dockers. This was signed by two top ITF officers involved in earlier dismissals of independent dockworker solidarity activity as 'strike tourism'. And the Liverpool dockers (who had expressed their determination to continue the dispute by turning down bribes of £25,000 severance pay) were expressing their gratitude to an ITF they had been bitterly criticizing. There is no guarantee that the international solidarity will continue, that the issue will be won, that the ITF has turned some kind of international corner, but it is reassuring to see internationalist life in the old working class, internationalist potential in the old trade unions.

A Society of Great Friends – on a World Scale

It was actually my interest in the new internationalism that rescued me from a mid-life crisis (personal and professional, if not political). An academic conference invitation in 1984 stimulated me to turn my hobby or hobby-horse – the *Newsletter* – into my paid work. Reflecting on my own current political practice, and that of an increasing number of others, I wrote a paper on the need for a communication model appropriate to the new labour internationalism (Waterman, 1988). Since then almost all my writing has been on the new internationalisms, on alternative international communication, or on the relationship between them. I thus found myself simultaneously involved in two new disciplines, International Relations and International Communications, and helping create two new problem areas or orientations within – or beyond – each of them. I eventually called these 'alternative international relations', and 'a new global solidarity culture'. But, as the 1980s turned into the 1990s, and the centre of the new labour internationalism migrated from Europe to North America, this meant that I also dropped not only my newsletter but also most other directly political activities – with the exception of occasional journalism and conference attendance.

I had been using the word 'networking' to characterize a common form of internationalist activity. I increasingly realized that what we had been doing spontaneously (or as a reaction against the institutionalized left) actually represented the appropriate relational form for a new kind of international solidarity. My own newsletter represented the new principle but used the old technology, being a scissors, paste, print and post job. A decade and more of my life, energy and nerves, *NILS* went to join the Great Alternative International Communication Archive in the Sky, mourned by myself, remembered affectionately by others. As I wept into my soup, however, I was able to welcome the appearance of a number of substantial books with which *NILS* had been associated or to which it in some way contributed.[4] The notion of the 'biodegradable organisation' implies, comfortingly, that *NILS* had not died but was simply in the process of being recycled. And this recycling has been, as I have suggested, not so much a matter of new organizations or publications as in the movement from geographical into electronic space (Lee, 1996).

The political value of my academic work, moreover, seemed to be receiving more recognition, at least outside North-Western Europe. Thus I have had, since around 1991, increasing numbers of items requested or accepted by national or international labour, socialist or left publishers or magazines, in Spain, Peru, Venezuela, South Africa, India and the USA. I have also received invitations to labour movement conferences on internationalism, or communication for such, from Australia, the USA and the ex-USSR. I have had a seminar with radical trade unionists in Bogota and spoken to a rally of striking dockers in Durban. Academic recognition of my (political?) work also seems to have been increasing to some extent, with guest or exchange posts in the USA and South Africa. The political recognition provides considerable compensation and comfort in the face of the occasional boycotts or snubs. The academic recognition is immensely gratifying after many years in the wilderness, wondering whether my hobby and hobby-horse were anything more than these. I would, of course, continue without such recognition, since there are clearly other pleasures in being – in the words of my most intimate friend – an *internacionalista de mierda*. (I prefer to translate this as 'an obsessive internationalist'.) There also appears, at last, to be a new generation of left academics, particularly in North America, interested in labour and other internationalisms (see, for example, Borgers, 1996; DeMartino, forthcoming; Drainville, 1995a, 1995b; Gabriel and MacDonald, 1994; Herod, 1995; Kidder and McGinn, 1995; MacDonald 1995; Wills, 1997).

Since settling in the Netherlands in 1972, I have moved nowhere else, but I have been able to travel for my work to West, East and North Africa, to India, to Peru and other parts of Latin America, to much of West and part of East Europe, to North America, and to East and South-East Asia. I also had six months in South Africa, just after the first liberal-democratic election in 1994. Here it was extremely gratifying to find that my name and work were known widely by both labour and feminist sociologists (the latter customarily being ex-labour sociologists). Labour and feminist communicators, preoccupied with finding their feet in a dramatically changed situation, none the less provided generous assistance to my research.

My professional, political, personal and intimate friends are scattered thinly over a world that can be reached rapidly and effectively by mail, modem, phone and fax. They can also be occasionally met, usually in the course of my work or theirs. This partly invisible community surrounds me with its own particular compensations, stimuli and comforts. In so far as these friends are feminists, ecologists, or involved in human rights or alternative communications movements, they have implicitly or explicitly reminded me of these other global communities of solidarity.

I know – or do I mean I care to know? – few people who are not cosmopolitans and/or internationalists, involved in increasingly international dialogue, concerned with at least such global issues as human rights, ecology, peace. On the other hand, I must admit, I have difficulty with even this exclusive band unless they have warm hearts, a sense of humour and the capacity to mock themselves (a survival mechanism in a world with so little respect for our philosophies, and that changes more rapidly than we can hope to). The new internationalism is evidently in large part reliant on the creation of an international 'society of great friends'.[5]

I never joined another political party after dropping out of the Communist Party of Great Britain (CPGB) around 1970. I discovered it was not Communist political meetings (national and international) I could not tolerate, just meetings. I retain, from my international Communist days, however, an obsession with preserving and spreading a message, being unable to prevent myself from collecting documents, creating bibliographies, with copying, faxing and emailing. And also feeling the necessity, privilege and pleasure of showing personal solidarity, supporting a campaign, or occasionally initiating one.[6]

I recognized some years ago that I was not, and could not be, an Organic Intellectual of a non-existent internationalist class (I never was convinced by Gramsci's biological metaphor anyway). I have come out of the closet as a rootless petty-bourgeois cosmopolitan internationalist. I am a member of a growing and increasingly self-conscious international category of progressive, democratic, socialist and cosmopolitan intellectuals. But I don't speak for them either. I speak as *one* of them and, as such, I certainly try to speak to and with other social movement specialists, activists and leaders nationally and internationally.

It is certainly easier to relate to the metropolitan middle class than the provincial proletariat. But my specific interest in and address to workers and the labour movement prevents, I like to think, my notions of internationalist communication or global solidarity from floating above my head like two brightly-coloured gas-filled balloons, ready to be brought down by the first critical sling or arrow. Trying to translate my writings into a form that makes them suitable for political and labour publications likewise prevents my work from being the self-referential and self-satisfied activity of the academy.[7] I also recognize my good luck. Like John Berger's country doctor, I am a fortunate man. I must be one of the few people in the world who is actually paid to reflect on and promote a new kind of global solidarity. This should be reworded: I am one of the few people in the world who both reflects on and tries to promote global solidarity, and who gets well paid whilst doing so. This is a unique privilege, given that my institute is one of Third World development rather than international emancipation studies.[8] What we are involved in is, as I may have already suggested, is not so much 'globalization from below' (Brecher and Costello, 1994: 7–8, 78–80) but 'globalization from the middle'. I am thus acutely aware of the necessity to communicate internationalism both outwards and downwards, and to involve those at the famous shop-floor, grass-roots and community level in the creation of the new internationalism. We have 'beginners guides' to everything from nuclear power to feminism. We need one for internationalism.

Peru in a World both Broad and Alien

Readers of this book may become aware of more references to Peru than are warranted by its size (I mean that of Peru), its role in globalization or its involvement in global solidarity movements. Poor Peru, so close to God, so far from the USA![9] Here, I have experienced most dramatically the complex intertwining of personal, political and professional relationships in the period of globalization and the new global solidarity. It was due to a coincidence of personal affection, political commitment and professional concern that I first found myself in Peru in 1986. This visit seems to have led to a continuing involvement with Peru and Peruvians. I had intended, on my first visit, to carry out a little exploratory study on international labour communication (which succeeded) and to set up a more ambitious collaboratory project (which failed). My exploratory study seemed to stun the labour support centre in Lima that had so much encouraged and supported it. My friends appeared shocked to discover that the Peruvian labour press had been so much more internationalist in the 1920s than 60 years later. Yet they also seemed to be so overwhelmed by the growing crisis of Peruvian state and society, so much incorporated into the radical-nationalist discourse and practices of the left in Peru,[10] as to be unable or unwilling to respond to a project proposal on international labour communication that they in principle agreed with.

Ten years later the situation seemed not to have changed significantly. Globalization is still widely understood by the local left as a threat to be resisted or an inevitability to be adjusted to. Peru's little nineteenth century territorial-cum-resource war with Ecuador (both sides employing indigenous inhabitants of the Amazonian forest zone they are destroying) was the object of no discernible left opposition or even discussion.[11] International solidarity still does not seem to be something many progressive Peruvians are publicly discussing, even where they are involved in it. Is this the invisible price paid for left dependence on development funding? In other words, does heavy involvement in the discourse and practices of 'development co-operation' both insulate and isolate the left from the much richer practices of both traditional and new internationalisms? Or is it Peru's twenty-year long national calvary that does this? Whatever the case, for progressive Peruvians the world is still broad and alien.[12]

The problems, privileges and pleasures of my Peruvian connection continue, however. I have been able to host a whole number of Peruvian feminists, including several smart, warm-hearted, independent and resilient women from the squatter settlements of Lima, to meet a number of its leftist academics and politicians. I have witnessed the martyrdom of Peru, crushed by global financial capital (the World Bank and International Monetary Fund). I have seen how the left-wing, militarist and populist authoritarianism of its would-be President Gonzalo led to its opposite in the right-wing, militarist, populist author-itarianism of would-be President-for-Life Fujimori. I became involved in international activity against the international supporters of President Gonzalo's *Sendero Luminoso* (Shining Path). And one of the campaigns I felt I had to play an active part in was the protest following the 1992 assassination by Shining Path of Maria Elena Moyano, a popular elected feminist and socialist leader of Peru's largest squatter settlement. Here I seem to have been involved in the one-way, North to South, interna-tionalism of an earlier period or an earlier type. But I did suggest that an international human rights conference held in The Hague imme-diately after her death be dedicated to her name – a suggestion that was welcomed and endorsed. In 1996 I was finally able to visit Maria Elena's pathetic cement tomb (itself damaged in a Sendero attack) in the sandy cemetery of Villa El Salvador – a city of cement and sand – where she lived too intensely and died too young. I still respond to the image or name of Maria Elena as if she, too, had been one of the Peruvian women I had hosted in The Hague.

In 1996 I was also to observe a discussion, between my Peruvian feminist and internationalist *companera* and a human rights one, on how the life and death of Maria Elena could – five years later – become internationally known and useful. But for Peru more generally, it seemed, Maria Elena was part of a historical period of violence they would rather forget. In late 1996 the chickens of this forgotten violence were coming home, less to roost than to crow. The left-militarist Movimiento Revolucionario Tupac Amaru (MRTA) was holding some 100 or more prominent people in a Japanese embassy building they had occupied in a brilliantly organized coup. Reproducing vanguardist and left-terrorist strategies, slogans and symbols from the 1970s, they seemed to belong to an earlier era than the Zapatistas in Mexico. And President Fujimori seemed to be torn between national-authoritarian-populist *raison d'etat*, and the new global wave of liberal-democratic, human rights and pacifist sentiment. This wave had certainly swept over Peruvian TV companies, which demonstrated their role as a major new political and civil actor. It had also borne with it the Peruvian middle classes, which turned out in their tens of thousands, in religious and civic events, calling for peace, liberation and negotiation. Amongst those on the biggest demonstration were smaller contingents of what one Lima mayor called 'the humble people' (shorter, darker and shabbier), 50–100 'Women for Peace', left politicians and NGO activists, and me. In Lima squatter settlements and provincial cities other services or demonstrations took place.[13]

Messages from Mariategui

There was no visible labour presence on the biggest march. Yet the old red internationalism of Peru *could* still inspire and inform a new multicoloured and global one. In 1986, in the house of an acquaintance in Lima, I found a set of the writings of the Peruvian revolutionary, Jose Carlos Mariategui, the 'Peruvian Gramsci', internationally little known, but widely respected where he is known. Flipping through one volume I found an essay on 'internationalism and nationalism', which I later translated and published in my newsletter. Mariategui was himself both an ardent nationalist and internationalist, and his is a quite remarkable little essay, combining in equal proportion classical Marxist proletarian utopian internationalism with a cosmopolitan modernist one. So, while I was researching international labour communication in Peru, I found what may be the only classical Marxist statement on the relationship between communication and internationalism! Writing in 1923, this Marxist, nationalist, cosmopolitan and modernist says that

> Communications are the nervous system of . . . internationalism and human solidarity. One of the characteristics of our epoch is the rapidity, the velocity,

with which ideas spread, with which currents of thought and culture are transmitted. A new idea that blossoms in Britain is not a British idea except for the time that it takes for it to be printed. Once launched into space by the press, this idea, if it expresses some universal truth, can also be instantaneously transformed into an internationalist idea. (Mariategui, 1973: 164–5; 1986: 7)

I have discussed this passage, and argued with the paper from which it comes. I have been able to tell South African and Korean labour activists about Mariategui and, simultaneously, have been able to use a South African labour magazine to launch my British-cum-internationalist ideas back to a Europe which, otherwise, would consider them of no account, or not know of them at all. If I think of an international rainbow coalition, it is one that stretches across time as well as space.

Living Adventurously, Living Ambiguously

In June 1997, I was revising this work for publication and worrying away again at whether I had got all the balances right. Taking a one-day break in Amsterdam, I met striking dockers from Liverpool. I think of these as the Zapatistas of Western Europe, deeply rooted in their local community whilst reaching out with the latest technologies – and not a few new strategies and attitudes. They were taking part in what may well have been the largest and most European march-cum-demonstration-cum-conference yet held on the continent. It was an Alternative Europe event of a most heterogenous nature, boycotted by the national and international unions, virtually ignored by the press – except for its noisy, extremist, neo-anarchist contingent. (In a pedestrian street parallel to that on which the march was taking place, a more significant part of the Dutch public was involved in a more traditional demonstration of globalization: how to shop until you drop.) One of the dockers had a t-shirt, bearing on its front this strange device: '500 SACKED LIVERPOOL DOCKERS WORLD TOUR'. On the back were printed the fifteen countries visited in 1995–6. More recently these have included – amazingly – India, and an Indian Ocean labour solidarity event. He traded his well-travelled t-shirt with me for another, more recent but less internationalist one. Were we here witnessing a desperate and romantic expression of the old internationalism, from the Last of the

Proletarians, or the beginning of a new, pluralistic and radical-democratic one? Or both? Balanced, at this moment, on the cusp of the impossible past and a possible future, I simultaneously involve myself and doubt – or doubt and yet involve myself.

Being at the same time balanced between a quarter-century of waged employment at my institute and a Third Age of retirement (to academic work? organizational work? communications activity?) only increases my sense of uncertainty. The privilege of working on global solidarity within an institute of development studies continues to have its price. Thus, in 1997, the Institute was planning to mark a particular anniversary with a conference on 'Global Futures'. The institute is itself, it seems to me, balanced between development and globalization discourses (or developmentalism and globalism?). It is also balanced, in its internal structures and procedures, between a past of *laissez-faire*, or participatory democracy, and a future inspired (if anything, and if 'inspiration' is the appropriate word for something so dispirited) by a shame-faced neo-liberal managerialism. The conference preparations were marked by these ambiguities. The theoretical, political and ethical orientation of the event revealed an eclectic mix of neo-liberal, neo-Keynesian, managerial and radical-democratic elements, of Euro-centric particularist with new universal and emancipatory ones – and all this without any recognition of the tensions or options between them. The organization of the event was centralized, personalized and top-down, expressing a bureaucratic rather than an academic logic. Given the option between subordinate collaboration with, and independent criticism of, the event I chose for ... both. This, it seems to me, is good neither for the institute, for an emancipatory notion of our global future, or for me. Retirement provides the possibility of attaching myself, or creating, an institution or network more compatible with the project I am attempting to promote.

I have, in my sixties, thus, little feeling of self-satisfaction. But I also have little taste for self-condemnation. The most I can do is to reflect on the ambiguities I have lived or am living. Even though it is more than a quarter-century since I was a communist, I recognize a responsibility for the crimes committed by communists or in the name of international Communism, both before and after my association.[14] I still seek to decipher the age-old and deeply felt human dream of international community and to relate it to today's quite particular possibilities and needs.

The current quest, it seems to me, is no longer led by a self-elected Vanguard, by a Chosen People, by the Civilized West, by a priesthood of Social Scientists, by elderly male European Revolutionaries with long white beards (or even short grey ones). It will have to be made this time in an egalitarian and pluralist spirit, by many of us, or it will be made by none at all. Today's internationalists may be both middle class and cosmopolitan but they are less likely to be rootless. The skills necessary for networking are far more widely spread, as are knowledge of languages (imperial English and the military-academic internet alone will get you quite far), access to international information and foreign cultures. To be an effective internationalist today does not require the dedication, the obsession, the clandestinity, the constant travel of the nineteenth or twentieth centuries. Identifying with Daniel Cohn-Bendit in 1968, the student movement in Paris declared, 'We Are All German Jews!'. Today, in some sense, progressive people are all internationalists. In so far as this is so, or comes to be so, it might make it easier for us to communicate with those more rooted in a particular class, national, religious or other ground.

In Chapter 2 I mentioned how – writing midway between the international Communist crises of 1956–7 and 1989–90 – Edward Thompson (1978) felt obliged to talk of his continuing commitment to an international of the imagination. But the world is different today. The socialist division between means and ends, between the national and international 'stages' and 'levels', is being overcome – at least in the imagination. It is not that things are inevitably becoming better: they are often getting worse. It is that the options are becoming more and more crucial. Ethnic and national self-identity and territory itself – in Iraq, Ireland, Central America, the Levant, the Amazon or the Balkans – is increasingly recognized to require democratic and pluralist form, and to depend on the support of civil society globally. The alternative today is for peoples to do to their own territory what the Yugoslavs did – to destroy it in order to cleanse it.

Internationalism today is, then, both means and end: communication for global solidarity and global solidarity as communication. Being involved in the search for a useful, meaningful and enjoyable global community is also, surely, one of the great personal, political and professional adventures of our time.

Notes

1. I am thinking of following up the present work, at some time, with one on 'the internationalists', or 'the red internationalists', using biographies and autobiographies of those who have played this role, interviews with living ones, and possibly feeding in my own experience also. Such a work would communicate the argument to far more people than the present one. Social science is, by and large, read by social scientists. History and (auto)biography are read by far more than historians and (auto)biographers. I have, thus, had far more – and far more enthusiastic – response to my autobiographical essay than to anything else I have ever written. This response was not just from family, friends and the cast of characters involved: it came also from social scientists who, it surprisingly appears, also like to read a good yarn with psychological and ethical undertones.

2. It is amazing, and revealing, that the unions have made do for 100 years with a name that conjures up trade rather than unions. As for this particular ITS officer, he finally made a conciliatory gesture at a public event. This was after I had myself made an effort to: 1. contribute to the ITS history project under discussion and 2. refrain from proposing any role for myself in its realization!

3. In the case of some of the new labour internationalists, this went to an extreme degree. Even after their own publication had joined my newsletter in the great beyond, they obstructed access to its archives. I was left with the strong impression that they would rather these were lost than that I would get hold of them. All this is in striking contrast to, for example, the Barcelona dockworkers whose international communications I was researching at this time. They left me their office key over a weekend, providing me access to their files and copying machine. Opening one box file, I found it was stuffed full of bank notes – which I stuffed back and said nothing about.

4. Ronaldo Munck's 'book of the newsletter', *The New International Labour Studies* (1988), Roger Southall's collection, *Trade Unions and the New Industrialisation of the Third World* (1988), Robin Cohen's work on international labour migration, *The New Helots* (1987), Assef Bayat's on workers' control and self-management internationally, *Work, Politics and Power* (1991). Whilst writing this present work I had the opportunity of discussing with Ronaldo the success or failure of 'the new international labour studies'. Given the disappearance of *NILS* and the difficulties Zed Press was having in selling sufficient copies of some of the above titles, he felt it had failed. So why were we not as depressed as we should have been? Perhaps we are incorrigible optimists. Perhaps we are unable to recognize – or to accept – neo-liberal realities. Perhaps we were too busy with a

succeeding project (Munck and Waterman, forthcoming).

5. This was the unkind cut delivered by a Comintern leader to the British Communist Party in 1928 before it had been more or less successfully Bolshevized. The leader was Stalin's faithful servant, Dimitri Manuilsky (1883–1959), who also complained of the CPGB that it had not yet learned that in a revolution it was necessary to carry out purges and cut off heads (Samuel, 1985: 34). Manuilsky was then talking figuratively, but discourse is intertwined with desire and action. In the late 1930s Manuilsky was responsible within the Comintern for purging the Polish party and executing its leadership (Trepper, 1977: 314). Raph Samuel implies that it was a sense of personal friendship that kept the British Communist Party together despite the slings and arrows of Comintern fortune. It is clear to me that no meaningful internationalism can exist without such personal friendships – another issue requiring exploration.

6. As Alberto Melucci puts it in an interview with John Keane and Paul Mier (1989: 206):

    Within the new movements there is a more balanced sense of the proper relationship between the latent and visible dimensions of action. Involvement in public-political action is perceived as only a temporary necessity. One does not live to be a militant. Instead, one lives, and that is why from time to time one can be a public militant.

7. I do not, incidentally, consider myself a particularly good academic, any more than I think I was a particularly good journalist – or a particularly Good Soldier Waterman in the army of international communism. Jorge Semprun, speaking to his underground alter ego, expresses the last matter more elegantly:

    it cannot be said, in all truth, that you were an exemplary militant. You have always been bored by the nostalgic, victory-shall-be-ours platitudes . . . ; the beatific murmurs of meetings completely out of touch with any sort of social reality; the manipulation of a ritualistic Marxist language, as though the essential task were to keep a prayer wheel turning. When all is said and done, the day-to-day aspect of politics has always bored you; politics has interested you only as risk and as total commitment. In other words, admit it once and for all and be damned: you have never been a proper militant. (Semprun, 1979: 7)

    The only thing I would like to add from my own experience is that beatific murmurs, manipulation of language and day-to-dayism are no monopoly of communism. Which is one reason (amongst one or two others, of course) why I, unlike Semprun, never became the Minister of Culture of a Social Democratic government.

8. The implications of this for my own work are contradictory. On the one hand I have been marginal within the institute, on the other my work has been tolerated, financially supported and even, in some ways, recognized.

Marginalization has its privileges as well as its price. I was neither invited nor even informed when colleagues carried out a major evaluation of Dutch trade union development projects in the early 1990s. I heard about it, by chance, in the corridors after it had been under way for a year or more. Given that I was the only person in the institute who had researched and published on union relations North–South (including development co-operation projects), and who had extensive archives and computerized bibliography on the subject, I was initially stunned by this exclusion. On reflection, however, I realized such marginalization left me free to evaluate both their nature and their subject matter, politically and theoretically. My analysis of one outcome of this particular project was incorporated into a book review on international labour studies (Waterman, 1996b).

9. I am here playing with the saying about Mexico attributed to one-time President Porfirio Diaz. Mexico's closeness to the USA and incorporation into the latest phase of capitalist globalization seem to be making possible a surpassing of its traditional isolationism. Peru's closeness to God is suggested by it being a birthplace of Liberation Theology. Peru's relative distance from globalization implies a continuing isolation or self-isolation. More on this below.

10. For a critique of the Peruvian left from a feminist position, see Vargas (1992b). Vargas sees the problem as being due to a traditional leftism rather than radical nationalism. The two are evidently intertwined, making it difficult for Peruvian leftists to come to terms with their own fundamentalists, with liberal democracy, women, feminism, globalization and the new global solidarity.

11. The only peace efforts I noted in the Peruvian media during a three-month period, in late 1996, were the following: a meeting of Peruvian and Ecuadorian academics (liberal?); a joint declaration of biblical opposition to war by Peruvian and Ecuadorian evangelicals; an appeal, by a left intellectual, to terrorists holding a leading Peruvian negotiator hostage, to release him for current Peru-Ecuador negotiations – on grounds of their respect for the 'national interest'; and the chanting of 'Viva la Paz', by the Ecuadorian audience when a Peruvian singer was awarded a second prize during a pop music contest! Of course, we do not know what they would have chanted if she had won first prize. But they did so chant, in public, and the Peruvian left has not.

12. Title of classical novel of the isolation, alienation and destruction of the indigenous rural world in Peru by Ciro Alegria (1942). At that time, and for these people, it was the world of Peru that was broad and alien.

13. As TV news viewers all over the world know, the siege ended in 1997 with Fujimori having the last triumphant crow over the bodies of the pathetic insurgents. The national–authoritarian–populist tradition still rules in

Peru, as in so many other countries.

14. I am not sure whether Liberals, Christians, Muslims and Social Democrats have yet begun to make peace with their own troubled international traditions. I look forward to them so doing and thus making their own contributions to a new kind of internationalism.

REFERENCES

Adkin, L. (forthcoming) 'Ecology and Labour: Towards a New Societal Paradigm', in Munck, R. and Waterman, P. (eds), *Labour Worldwide in the Era of Globalisation: Alternative Union Models in the New World Order*. London: Macmillan.

ALAI (1996) 'Comunicacion de genero para el tercer milenio' [Gender communication for the third millennium], *ALAI Servicio Informativo* (Supplement), no. 240, 11 October, pp. i–viii.

Alcocer, M. (1990) 'Superbarrio: Un superheroe de la lucha urbana popular' [Superbarrio: a superhero in the popular urban struggle], *Dialogos*, no. 26, pp. 66–70.

Alegria, C. (1942) *Broad and Alien Is the World*. London: Nicholson and Watson.

Alexander, J. (1991) 'Bringing Democracy Back in: Universalistic Solidarity and the Civil Sphere', in Lemert, C. (ed.), *International and Politics: Social Theory in a Changing World*. London: Sage, pp. 157–76.

Allen, J. (1992) 'Post-Industrialism and Post-Fordism', in Hall, S., Held, D. and McGrew, T. (eds), *Modernity and Its Futures*. Cambridge: Polity, pp. 169–204.

Allen, M. (1991) 'New Internationalism ... or Old Rhetoric?', *South African Labour Bulletin*, vol. 16, no. 2, pp. 61–9.

Allende, I. (1987) *Of Love and Shadows*. London: Black Swan.

Alvarez, S. (1997) 'Latin American Feminisms "Go Global": Trends of the 1990s and Challenges for the New Millennium', in Alvarez, S., Dagnino, E. and Escobar, A. (eds), *Cultures of Politics/Politics of Cultures: Revisioning Latin American Social Movements*. Boulder: Westview.

Anderson, W.T. (1990) *Reality Isn't What It Used to Be: Theatrical Politics, Ready-to-Wear Religion, Global Myths, Primitive Chic and Other Wonders of the Postmodern World*. San Francisco: Harper.

Anon. (1991) 'South Asian Feminist Declaration' in Bhasin, K. (ed.), *Pressing Against the Boundaries: Report of an FAO/FFHC/AD South Asian Workshop on Women and Development*. New Delhi: FAO–FFHC/AD, pp. 8–11.

Anon. (1993) 'Estrategias para conformar redes informativas' [Strategies for the formation of information networks], in ALER-ALAI-CERIGUA, *Rompiendo el silencio: Encuentro Latinoamericano de medios de comunicacion alternativa y popular – Quito, 19 al 23 de abril de 1993.* Quito: Agencia Latinoamericana de Informacion, pp. 12–13.

Archibugi, D. and Held, D. (eds) (1995) *Cosmopolitan Democracy: An Agenda for a New World Order.* Cambridge: Polity Press.

Aronowitz, S. (1988) 'Postmodernism and Politics', in Ross, A. (ed.), *Universal Abandon? The Politics of Postmodernism.* Edinburgh: Edinburgh University Press, pp. 46–62.

Arrighi, G. (1990) 'Marxist Century, American Century: The Making and Remaking of the World Labour Movement', *New Left Review*, no. 179, pp. 29–63.

Arrighi, G., Hopkins, T. and Wallerstein, I. (1989) *Antisystemic Movements.* London: Verso.

Arthur, C.H. (ed.) (1970) *Karl Marx and Frederick Engels: The German Ideology.* London: Lawrence and Wishart.

Ashworth, G. (ed.) (1996) *What the Platform for Action Means to You ... : Conference Report.* London: Change.

Asia Labour Monitor (1988) *Min-Ju No-Jo: South Korea's New Trade Unions.* Hong Kong: Asia Monitor Resource Centre.

Asian Labour Update (1996) 'The Informal Sector: The Hidden Workforce', *Asian Labour Update* (Special Section), no. 24, April–June, pp. 1–28.

Aubry, B. and Vermote, M. (1983) 'Een Zomer van agitatie aan de Antwerpse dokken in het teken van de internationale solidariteit: Juni–September 1896' [A summer of agitation in the Antwerp docks under the sign of international solidarity: June–September 1896], *AMSAB Tijdingen*, vol. 2, no. 1–2, pp. 77–104.

Autonomous Feminists (1996) 'Taller de profundizacion del feminismo autonomo' [Workshop on the deepening of autonomous feminism]. Document presented to the Plenary of the Seventh Feminist Encounter, Cartagena, Chile.

Bahro, R. (1978) *The Alternative in Eastern Europe.* London: New Left Books.

Baldwin, N. (1985) *The International Transport Workers' Federation Archive.* Coventry: University of Warwick Library.

Banas, J. (1979) *The Scapegoats: The Exodus of the Remnants of Polish Jewry.* London: Weidenfeld and Nicolson.

Bandarage, A. (1987) 'Towards an International Feminism', *Outwrite: Women's Newspaper*, pp. 1, 12–13.

Bandarage, A. (1991) 'In Search of a New World Order', *Women's Studies International Forum*, vol. 12, no. 4, pp. 345–55.

Barchiesi, F. (1996) 'South Africa in Transition: Scenarios Facing Organized Labor', *Critical Sociology* (Special Issue: Social Change in South Africa), vol. 22, no. 3, pp. 79–112.

Bauer, O. (1978) 'The Concept of the Nation, and Socialism and the Principle of Nationality', in Bottomore, T. and Goode, P. (eds), *Austro-Marxism*. Oxford: Clarendon Press, pp. 106–17.

Bauman, Z. (1986) 'The Left as the Counter-Culture of Modernity', *Telos*, no. 70, pp. 81–93.

Bayat, A. (1991) *Work, Politics and Power: An International Perspective on Workers' Control and Self-Management*. London: Zed Press.

Beck, U. (1992) *Risk Society: Towards a New Modernity*. London: Sage.

Belgrade Praxis Group (1978) 'The Meaning of the Struggle for Civil and Human Rights', *Telos*, no. 35, pp. 185–92.

Berger, J. and Mohr, J. (1975) *A Seventh Man: The Story of a Migrant Worker in Europe*. Harmondsworth: Penguin.

Bergh, G. v. B. v.d. (1986) 'Cosmopolitanism', in Pauling, L., Laszlo, E. and Yoo, J. Y. (eds), *World Encyclopedia of Peace*. Oxford: Pergamon Press, pp. 203–5.

Berman, M. (1983) *All That Is Solid Melts into Air: The Experience of Modernity*. London: Verso.

Bernard, J. (1987) *The Female World from a Global Perspective*. Bloomington: Indiana University Press.

Billington, J. (1980) *Fire in the Minds of Men: Origins of the Revolutionary Faith*. New York: Basic Books.

Borgers, F. (1996) 'Globalization and US Labor', *Critical Sociology*, vol. 22, no. 2, pp. 67–88.

Boulding, E. (1975) 'Female Alternatives to Hierarchical Systems, Past and Present', *International Associations*, vol. 27, no. 6–7, pp. 340–5.

Bouvier, B. (1988) 'Die Marseillaise in der deutschen Arbeiterbewegung vor 1914' [The Marseillaise in the German labour movement before 1914], in Holthoon, F. van and Linden, M. van der (eds), *Internationalism in the Labour Movement 1830–1940*. Leiden: Brill, pp. 137–62.

Brandt, W. and Manley, M. (1985) *Global Challenge*. London: Pan.

Bratislava Declaration (1993) 'The Bratislava Declaration of the Expert Seminar on the Right to Communicate in the Post Cold War Period'. Part of the NGO Forum on Human Rights of the World Conference on Human Rights, Vienna, 10–11 June.

Braunthal, J. (1980) *History of the International. vol. 3: 1943–1968*. London: Nelson.

Brecher, J. (1987) 'The "National Question" Reconsidered: An Ecological Perspective', *New Politics*, vol. 1, no. 3 (New Series), pp. 95–111.

Brecher, J. (1993) 'The Hierarchs' New World Order – and Ours', in Brecher, J., Childs, J. B. and Cutler, J. (eds), *Global Visions: Beyond the New World Order*. Boston: South End Press, pp. 3–12.

Brecher, J., Childs, J. B. and Cutler, J. (eds) (1993) *Global Visions: Beyond the New World Order*. Boston: South End Press.

Brecher, J. and Costello, T. (1990a) 'The Great Time Squeeze', *Z Magazine* (Boston), October, pp. 102–7.

Brecher, J. and Costello, T. (1990b) 'A Worldwide Social Charter?', *Z Magazine* (Boston), January, pp. 122–6.

Brecher, J. and Costello, T. (eds) (1990c) *Building Bridges: The Emerging Grass-roots Coalition of Labor and Community.* New York: Monthly Review Press.

Brecher, J. and Costello, T. (1991) *Global Village vs. Global Pillage: A One-World Strategy for Labor.* Washington: International Labor Rights Education and Research Fund.

Brecher, J. and Costello, T. (1994) *Global Village or Global Pillage: Economic Reconstruction from the Bottom Up.* Boston: South End Press.

Bueso, D. (1996) 'Nicaragua: La mujer hacia su autonomia' [Nicaragua: woman moving towards her autonomy]. *El Viejo Topo* (Barcelona), no. 99, September, pp. 12–13.

Buketov, K. (forthcoming) 'Russian Trade Unions: From Chaos to a New Paradigm', in Munck, R. and Waterman, P. (eds), *Labour Worldwide in the Era of Globalization: Alternative Union Models in the New World Order.* London: Macmillan.

Bunch, C. (1987a) 'International Feminism: "A Passionate Politcs"', *Woman of Power: A Magazine of Feminism, Spirituality and Politics* (Interview by Connie Griffin and Linda Roach), no. 7, pp. 6–9, 76–9.

Bunch, C. (1987b) 'Global Feminism', in Bunch, C., *Passionate Politics.* New York: St Martin's Press, pp. 267–352.

Burawoy, M. (1990) 'Marxism Is Dead, Long Live Marxism!', in Tabb, W. (ed.), *The Future of Socialism: Perspectives from the Left.* New York: Monthly Review Press, pp. 159–72.

Burbach, R. and Nunez, O. (1987a) *Fire in the Americas: Forging a Revolutionary Agenda.* London: Verso.

Burbach, R. and Nunez, O. (1987b) 'The Internationalisation of Struggle in the Americas', in Burbach, R. and Nunez, O., *Fire in the Americas: Forging a Revolutionary Agenda.* New York: Verso, pp. 81–94.

Calderon, F. (1988) 'America Latina, identidad y tiempos mixtos: O como pensar la modernidad sin dejar de ser Boliviano' [Latin America, identity and mixed times: or how to think about modernity without ceasing to be Bolivian], in CLACSO (ed.), *Imagenes desconocidas: La modernidad en la encrucijada postmoderna.* Buenos Aires: Ediciones CLACSO, pp. 225–9.

Calderon, F. (1994) 'America Latina: Identidad y tiempos mixtos: O como tratar de pensar la modernidad si dejar de ser indios' [Latin America: identity and mixed times – or how to think about modernity without ceasing to be Indians], in Calderon, F. (ed.), *Cultura, estetica y politica en America Latina.* Caracas: CENDES, pp. 89–98.

Cantor, D. and Schor, J. (1987) *Tunnel Vision: Labour, the World Economy and Central America.* Boston: South End Press.

Cardoso, F. H. (1996) 'La globalizacion y el nuevo orden mundial' [Globalization and the new world order], *Boletin Editorial de el Colegio de Mexico*, no. 68, July–August, pp. 3–12.

Castells, M. (1979) 'Immigrant Workers and Class Struggles in Advanced Capitalism: The West European Experience', in Cohen, R., Gutkind, P. and Brazier, P. (eds), *Peasants and Proletarians: The Struggles of Third World Workers*. London: Hutchinson.

Castells, M. (1996) *The Information Age: Economy, Society and Culture. Vol. 1: The Rise of the Network Society*. Oxford: Blackwell.

Castells, M. (1997) *The Information Age: Economy, Society and Culture. Vol. 2: The Power of Identity*. Oxford: Blackwell.

Castells, M., Yazawa, S. and Kiselyova, E. (1995–6) 'Insurgents Against the New Global Order: A Comparative Analysis of Zapatistas in Mexico, the American Militia and Japan's Aum Shinrikyo', *Berkeley Journal of Sociology*, vol. 40, pp. 21–61.

Cavanagh, J., Gershman, J., Baker, K. and Helmke, G. (eds) (1992) *Trading Freedom: How Free Trade Affects Our Lives, Work and Environment*. San Francisco: Institute for Food and Development Policy.

Chang, J. (1991) *Wild Swans: Three Daughters of China*. London: Flamingo.

Chapkis, W. (1987) *Beauty Secrets: Women and the Politics of Appearance*. Boston: South End Press.

Charkiewicz, E. and Nijpels, M. (1993) 'Reflection', *Balancing the Future: NGO Conference on Environment and Development* (World Information Service on Energy, Amsterdam), vol. 2, no. 3, July, p. 3.

Chhachhi, A. (1996) 'Weaving a New Tapestry of Peace: Indian and Pakistani Women Connect Across Borders', *Communalism Combat* (Mumbai, India), August, pp. 22–3.

Chhachhi, A. and Pittin, R. (1996a) 'Multiple Identities, Multiple Strategies', in Chhachhi, A. and Pittin, R. (eds), *Confronting State, Capital and Patriarchy: Women Organising in the Process of Industrialisation*. London: Macmillan, pp. 93–130.

Chhachhi, A. and Pittin, R. (eds) (1996b) *Confronting State, Capital and Patriarchy: Women Organising the Process of Industrialisation*. London: Macmillan.

Chuan R. (1995) 'Thoughts on the World Conference on Women: A Chinese Woman Speaks', *Women in Action*, no. 3, pp. 36–9.

CLADEM (ed.) (1996) *La muralla e el laberinto: Huellas de las mujeres en la conferencia de Beijing* [The wall and the labyrinth: footsteps of women in the Beijing conference]. Lima: Comite de America Latina y el Caribe para la Defensa de les Derechos de la Mujer.

Claeys, G. (1988) 'Reciprocal Dependence, Virtue and Progress: Some Sources of Early Socialist Cosmopolitanism and Internationalism in Britain, 1790–1860', in Holthoon, F. van and Linden, M. van der (eds), *Internationalism in the Labour Movement 1830–1940*. Leiden: Brill, pp. 235–58.

Claudin, F. (1970) *The Communist Movement: From Comintern to Cominform*. London: Penguin.

Cleaver, H. (1989) 'Close the IMF, Abolish Debt and End Development: A

Class Analysis of the International Debt Crisis', *Capital and Class,* no. 39, pp. 17–50.

Cohen, R. (1987) *The New Helots: Migrants in the International Division of Labour.* Aldershot: Avebury.

Colas, A. (1994) 'Putting Cosmopolitanism into Practice: the Case of Socialist Internationalism', *Millennium,* vol. 23, no. 3, pp. 513–34.

Collier, A. (1992) 'Marxism and Universalism: Group Interests or a Shared World?', in Attfied, R. and Wilkins, B. (eds), *International Justice and the Third World.* London: Routledge, pp. 77–92.

Collins, H. and Abramsky, C. (1965) *Karl Marx and the British Labour Movement: Years of the First International.* London: Macmillan.

Confederation of Japanese Autoworkers' Unions (1992) *Japanese Automobile Industry in the Future: Toward Coexistence with the World, Consumers and Employees.* Tokyo: Confederation of Japanese Autoworkers' Unions.

Confederation of Trade Unions of Yugoslavia (1986) *International Trade Union Meeting South–South: Belgrade, June 1 and 2, 1986.* Belgrade: Confederation of Trade Unions of Yugoslavia.

Congress of South African Trade Unions (1989) *Resolution on International Policy Passed at the Third National Congress.* Johannesburg: Congress of South African Trade Unions.

Connell, R.W. (1984) 'Class Formation on a World Scale', *Review,* vol. 7, no. 3, pp. 407–40.

Coordinadora (1988) *Estrategia capitalista y resistencia obrera en los puertos del Mediterraneo Occidental – 1* [Capitalist strategy and worker resistance in the ports of the western Mediterranean – 1]. Barcelona: Centro de Estudios de Coordinadora.

Coordinadora (1989) *Estrategia capitalista y resistencia obrera en los puertos del Mediterraneo Occidental – 2* [Capitalist strategy and worker resistance in the ports of the western Mediterranean – 2]. Barcelona: Centro de Estudios de Coordinadora.

COSATU (1989) Conference document of the Congress of South African Trade Unions.

Cotidiano Mujer (1996a), *Cotidiano Mujer* (Special Beijing Issue), no. 21, pp. 1–22.

Cotidiano Mujer (1996b) 'Se busca un encuentro, se busca, se busca ...' [Searching for an encounter, searching, searching ...]. *Cotidiano Mujer* (Special Section), no. 22, May, pp. 1–7.

Court, T. de la (1990) *Beyond Brundtland: Green Development in the 1990s.* London: Zed Press.

Cox, R. W. (1981) 'Social Forces, States and World Orders: Beyond International Relations Theory', *Millennium: Journal of International Studies,* vol. 10, no. 2, pp. 126–55.

Debate Feminista (1995) 'Feminismo: Movimiento y pensiamiento' [Feminism: movement and thought], *Debate Feminista* (Special [Beijing] Issue), no. 12, October, pp. ix–xii, 16–84.

Degregori, C. I. (1991) 'How Difficult It Is to Be God: Ideology and Political Violence in Sendero Luminoso', *Critique of Anthropology*, vol. 11, no. 3, pp. 233–50.

DeMartino, G. (1991) 'Trade Union Isolation and the Catechism of the Left', *Rethinking Marxism*, vol. 4, no. 3, pp. 29–51.

DeMartino, G. (forthcoming) 'Speculations on the Future of the US Labor Movement in an Era of Global Economic Transformation', in Munck, R. and Waterman, P. (eds), *Labour Worldwide in the Era of Globalisation: Alternative Union Models in the New World Order*. London: Macmillan.

Devreese, D. E. (1988) 'An Inquiry into the Causes and Nature of Organisation: Action, Organisation, Ideology and Perspective of the Future: Some Observations on the International Working Men's Association – 1864–1872/76)', in Holthoon, F. van and Linden, M. van der (eds), *Internationalism in the Labour Movement 1830–1940*. Leiden: Brill, pp. 283–304.

Dienstbier, J. (1988) 'A Strategy for Europe – Through Central European Eyes', *Bulletin of the European Network for East–West Dialogue*, no. 1–2, pp. 45–57.

Dorfman, A. and Mattelart, A. (1975) *How to Read Donald Duck: Imperialist Ideology in the Disney Comic*. New York: International General.

Downing, J. (1989) 'Computers for Political Change: Peacenet and Public Data Access', *Journal of Communication*, vol. 39, no. 3, pp. 154–62.

Drainville, A. (1995a) 'Of Social Spaces, Citizenship, and the Nature of Power in the World Economy', *Alternatives*, vol. 20, no. 1, January–March, pp. 51–79.

Drainville, A. (1995b) 'Left Internationalism and the Politics of Resistance in the New World Order', in Smith, D. and Borocz, J. (eds), *A New World Order: Global Transformation in the Latin 19th Century*. Westport: Praeger, pp. 217–37.

Dunn, J. (1985) 'Unimagined Community: the Deceptions of Socialist Internationalism', in Dunn, J., *Rethinking Modern Political Theory*. Cambridge: Cambridge University Press, pp. 103–18.

Dutt, R. P. (1964) *The Internationale*. London: Lawrence and Wishart.

Ehrenreich, B. (1990) 'Laden with Lard', *Z Magazine* (Boston), July–August, pp. 46–7.

Eide, A. (1986) 'The Human Rights Movement and the Transformation of the International Order', *Alternatives*, vol. 11, no. 3, pp. 367–402.

Eisenstein, Z. (1996) 'Women's Publics and the Search for New Democracracies'. Paper to Conference on Women, Citizenship and Difference, University of Greenwich, London, 16–18 July.

El Pais (1988) *Annuario El Pais* [El Pais annual]. Madrid: El Pais.

Elson, D. (1983) 'The Brandt Report: A Programme for Survival?', *Capital and Class*, no. 16, pp. 110–27.

Elson, D. (1986) 'Workers in the New International Division of Labour', *Newsletter of International Labour Studies*, no. 30–31, pp. 8–13.

Eltit, D. and Nelly, R. (1996) 'Gladys Marin, un retrato' [Gladys Marin, a portrait], *Revista de Critica Cultural* (Santiago), no. 13, November pp. 28–33.

Engels, F. (1953) 'The Condition of the Working Class in England in 1844', in Marx, K. and Engels, F., *Marx and Engels on Britain.* London: Lawrence and Wishart.

Eppink, D. J. and Straaten, F. van (1991a) 'Ongecontroleerd hobbyisme kenmerkt ontwikkelingshulp: Ontwikkelingswerkers krijgen het geld niet op' [Uncontrolled amateurism hallmarks development aid: aid workers cannot use up cash], *NRC Handelsblad*, 16 November.

Eppink, D. J. and Straaten, F. van (1991b) '"Autonomie" vrouwen derde wereld omstreden' ['Autonomy' of Third World women disputed]. *NRC Handelsblad*, 16 November.

Escobar, A. and Alvarez, S. (1992) *The Making of Social Movements in Latin America: Identity, Strategy and Democracy.* Boulder: Westview.

Ettinger, E. (1987) *Rosa Luxemburg: A Life.* London: Harrap.

Evers, T. (1982) 'European Social Democracy in Latin American: The Case of West Germany', in Pearce, J. (ed.), *The European Challenge: Europe's New Role in Latin America.* London: Latin America Bureau, pp. 80–129.

Evert V. S. (1985) *North–South – Who Makes What Where . . . : Industrialisation and People in the Third World.* Amsterdam: Evert Vermeer Stichting.

Featherstone, M. (1990) 'The Global Culture: An Introduction', in Featherstone, M. (ed.), *Global Culture: Nationalism, Globalisation and Modernity.* London: Sage, pp. 1–14.

Feher, F. and Heller, A. (1987) 'Introduction', in Feher, F. and Heller, A., *Eastern Left, Western Left: Totalitarianism, Freedom and Democracy.* Cambridge: Polity Press.

Feminist (1980) 'Feminist International no. 2: Asian Women '80', *The Feminist* (Tokyo), pp. 125.

Filipijnen Groep Nederland (1989) *De Filipijnen: Infomap arbeiders* [The Philippines: worker information folder]. Utrecht: Filipijnen Groep Nederland.

Fine, A. (1992) 'Democratic Socialism or Social Democracy?', *South African Labour Bulletin*, vol. 16, no. 3, pp. 82–5.

FINRRAGE-UBINIG International Conference 1989 (1989) 'Declaration of Comilla', in UBINIG, *Declaration of Comilla.* Dhaka: UBINIG, p. xii.

First Women's Conference on Security and Co-operation in Europe (1990) 'Draft of Proclamation'. Berlin.

Fischer, A. (1994) 'Feministas Latinoamericanas, las brujas y sus aquelarres'. [Latin American feminists: the witches and their covens]. Unpublished.

Fitz, D. (1988) 'La Coordinadora: A Union without Bureaucrats', *Workers' Democracy*, no. 27, pp. 12–21.

Foner, P. (1986) *Mayday: A Short History of the International Workers' Holiday, 1886–1986.* New York: International Publishers.

Forbes, J. (1993) 'Cross-Boundary Sub-States', in Brecher, J., Childs, J. B. and

Cutler, J. (eds), *Global Vision: Beyond the New World Order*, Boston: South End Press, pp. 233–8.

Ford-Smith, H. (1990) 'Women and Funding', *Women in Action*, no. 3–4, pp. 36–42.

Forum '95 (1996) *Forum '95: The Independent Daily of the NGO Forum on Women, Beijing '95.* New York: Facilitating Committee, NGO Forum on Women, Beijing '95.

Foster, C. (1989) *Women for All Seasons: The Story of the Women's League for Peace and Freedom.* Athens: University of Georgia Press.

Fourth International (1991) *For a Revival of Internationalism! An Appeal of the Fourth International.* Montreuil: Inprecor/International Viewpoint.

Frank, A. G. and Fuentes, M. (1987) 'Nine Theses on Social Movements Internationally', *Newsletter of International Labour Studies*, no. 34, pp. 1–19.

Frank, A. G. and Fuentes, M. (1990) 'Civil Democracy: Social Movements in Recent World History', in Amin, S., Arrighi, G., Frank, A. G. and Wallerstein, I., *Transforming the Revolution: Social Movements and the World System.* New York : Monthly Review Press, pp. 139–80.

Frank, P. (1979a) *The Fourth International: The Long March of the Trotskyists.* London: Ink Links.

Frank, P. (1979b) *Histoire de l'Internationale Communiste, 1919–43* [History of the Communist International, 1919–43]. Paris: La Breche.

Frankel, B. (1987) *The Post-Industrial Utopians.* Oxford: Polity Press.

Fraser, N. (1986) 'Towards a Discourse Theory of Solidarity', *Praxis*, vol. 5, no. 4, pp. 425–9.

Friedemann, P. and Holscher, L. (1982) 'Internationale, International, Internationalismus' [Internationals, international, internationalism], in Brunner, O., Conze, W. and Koselleck, R. (eds), *Geschichtliche Grundbegriffen: Historisches Lexikon zur politisch-sozialen Sprache in Deutschland.* Stuttgart: Ernst Klett.

Friedlander, E. (ed.) (1996) *Miremos al mundo a traves de los ojos de las mujeres: Discursos pronunciados en sesion plenaria ante el foro de ONG sobre la mujer, Beijing 1995* [Looking at the world through the eyes of women: speeches pronounced at the plenary session of the NGO Forum on Women, Beijing 1995]. New York: NGO Forum on Women.

Frundt, H. (1987) *Refreshing Pauses: Coca-Cola and Human Rights in Guatemala.* New York: Praeger.

Gabriel, C. and Macdonald, L. (1994) 'NAFTA, Women and Organising in Canada and Mexico: Forging a "Feminist Internationality" ', *Millennium*, vol. 23, no. 3, pp. 535–62.

Gallin, D. (1994) *Drawing the Battle Lines Inside the New World Orders.* Geneva: International Union of Food and Allied Workers.

Galtung, J. (1980) 'The Non-Territorial System', in Galtung, J., *The True Worlds: A Transnational Perspective.* New York: Free Press. pp. 305–40.

Gandhi, N. and Shah, N. (1991) *The Issues at Stake: Theory and Practice in the*

Contemporary Women's Movements in India. New Delhi: Kali for Women.

Gargallo, F. (1993) *Feminismo con/en los NNUU.*

Garofalo, R. (1992) *Rockin' the Boat: Mass Music and Mass Movements.* Boston: South End Press. 333 pp.

Garrido, L. (1996) 'Entrevista a Margarita Pisano: "Mas claro, echale agua"' [Interview with Margarita Pisano]. *Cotidiano Mujer* (Montevideo), no. 22, May, pp. 4–6.

Gatehouse, M. and Reyes, M. A. (1987) *Soft Drink: Hard Labour: Guatemalan Workers Take on Coca-Cola.* London: Latin America Bureau.

Geoghegan, V. (1987) *Utopianism and Marxism.* London: Methuen.

George, S. (1992) *The Debt Boomerang: How Third World Debt Harms Us All.* London: Pluto.

Gibson-Graham, J. K. (1993) 'Waiting for the Revolution: Or How to Smash Capitalism While Working at Home in Your Spare Time', *Rethinking Marxism,* vol. 6, no. 2, pp. 10–24.

Gibson-Graham, J. K. (1996) *The End of Capitalism (as We Knew It): A Feminist Critique of Political Economy.* Oxford: Blackwell.

Giddens, A. (1990) *The Consequences of Modernity.* Cambridge: Polity.

Giguere, J. and Sulmont, D. (1984) *Construir la solidaridad sindical internacional: Documento de trabajo para el primer encuentro de coordinacion minero metalurgico de Bolivia, Chile y Peru* [Construct international trade union solidarity: Working paper for the first encounter of the Mining and Metal Coordination of Bolivia, Chile and Peru]. Lima: Associacion Trabajo y Cultura.

Giguere, J. and Sulmont, D. (1988) 'Outline for a Strategy of International Trade-Union Solidarity in Latin America', in Waterman, P. (ed.), *The Old Internationalism and the New: A Reader on Labour, New Social Movements and Internationalism.* The Hague: ILERI Foundation, pp. 44–9.

Gobbi, C. (1996) 'VII Encuentro feminista Latinoamericano y del Caribe: El encuentro que no fue?' [Seventh Latin American and Caribbean feminist encounter: the encounter that wasn't?]. *Mujer/Fempress,* no. 183, pp. 8–9.

Golding, K. A. (1964) 'Transport Workers International: The History of the International Transport Workers' Federation. Part I: 1896–1916'. Unpublished proofs of proposed book. MSS 159/4/526. Coventry: University of Warwick Library.

Goldman, E. (1977) [1931] *Living My Life.* New York: Meridian.

Gordon, P. and Reilly, D. (1986) 'Guestworkers of the Sea: Racism in British Shipping', *Race and Class,* vol. 28, no. 2, pp. 73–80.

Gorz, A. (1989) 'Summary for Trade Unionists and Other Left Activists', in Gorz, A., *Critique of Economic Reason.* London: Verso, pp. 219–42.

Greer, G. (1986) 'World Conference, United Nations' International Women's Year, Mexico City, June 1975', in Greer, G., *The Madwoman's Underclothes: Essays and Occasional Writings.* New York: Atlantic Monthly Press, pp. 198–203.

Grewal, I. and Kaplan, K. (eds) (1994) *Scattered Hegemonies: Postmodernity and*

Transnational Feminist Practices. Minneapolis: University of Minnesota Press.

Guerena, J. L. (1988) 'De l'Anti Deux Mai au premier mai: Aspects de l'internationalisme dans le mouvement ouvrier espagnol' [From anti May the second to the first of May: aspects of internationalism in the Spanish labour movement], in Holthoon, F. van and Linden, M. van der (eds), *Internationalism in the Labour Movement 1830–1940.* Leiden: Brill, pp. 173–87.

Gurney, P. (1988) '"A Higher State of Civilisation and Happiness": Internationalism and the British Cooperative Movement between c.1869–1918', in Holthoon, F. van and Linden, M. van der (eds), *Internationalism in the Labour Movement 1830–1940.* Leiden: Brill, pp. 543–64.

Guzman, V. (1996) *Beijing – las agendas: Global y regionales* [Beijing – The agendas: global and regional]. Santiago: Centro de Estudios de la Mujer.

Guzman, V. and Mauro, A. (1996) 'Redes sociales y participacion ciudadana' [Social networks and citizen participation]. Paper to Seminar 'Mujeres, cultura civica y democracia', 8–12 July, Mexico D.F.

Hall, S. (1992) 'The Question of Cultural Identity', in Hall, S., Held, D. and McGrew, T. (eds), *Modernity and Its Futures.* Cambridge: Polity, pp. 273–326.

Hall, S., Held, D., and McGrew, T. (eds) (1992) *Modernity and Its Futures.* Cambridge: Polity Press.

Hall, S. and Jacques, M. (1986) 'People Aid: A New Politics Sweeps the Land', *Marxism Today,* July, pp. 10–14.

Hall, S. and Jacques, M. (eds) (1989) *New Times: The Changing Face of Politics in the 1990s.* London: Lawrence and Wishart.

Hamon, H. and Rotman, P. (1981) *Les Porteurs de valises: La Resistance francaise a la guerre d'Algerie* [The suitcase carriers: French resistance to the Algerian war]. Paris: Albin Michel.

Hancock, G. (1989) *Lords of Poverty: The Freewheeling Lifestyles, Power, Prestige and Corruption of the Multibillion Dollar Aid Business.* London: Mandarin.

Harding, S. (1987) 'Introduction', in Harding, S. (ed.), *Feminism and Methodology: Social Science Issues.* Bloomington: Indiana University Press, pp. 1–14.

Harrison, R. (1957) 'British Labour and the Confederacy', *International Review of Social History,* vol. 2, no. 1, pp. 78–105.

Harrison, R. (1965) 'British Labour and American Slavery', in Harrison, R., *Before the Socialists: Studies in Labour and Politics, 1861–81.* London: Routledge and Kegan Paul, pp. 40–72.

Hart, A. (1987) 'Consuming Compassion: The Live Aid Phenomenon', *Links: Quarterly Publication of Third World First,* no. 28, pp. 15–17.

Hartmann, H., Bravo, E., Bunch, C., Hartstock, N., Spalter-Roth, R. Williams, L. and Blanco, M. (1996) 'Bringing Together Feminist Theory and Practice: A Collective Interview: Heidi Hartmann, Ellen Bravo, Charlotte Bunch, Nancy Hartsock, Roberta Spalter-Roth, Lindia Williams, and Maria Blanco', *Signs,* vol. 21, no. 41, pp. 917–51.

Harvey, D. (1989) *The Condition of Postmodernity.* Oxford: Basil Blackwell.

Haupt, G. (1986) 'International Leading Groups in the Working-Class Movement', in Haupt, G., *Aspects of International Socialism, 1871–1914.* Cambridge: Cambridge University Press, pp. 81–100.

Haworth, N. and Ramsay, H. (1984) 'Grasping the Nettle: Problems with the Theory of International Trade Union Solidarity', in Waterman, P. (ed.), *For a New Labour Internationalism.* The Hague: ILERI Foundation, pp. 60–87.

Hedevary, C. de (1985) 'The United Nations: "Good Grief, There Are Women Here"', in Morgan, R. (ed.), *Sisterhood Is Global.* Harmondsworth: Penguin, pp. 695–8.

Held, D. (1992) 'Democracy: From the City State to the Cosmopolitan Order', *Political Studies,* vol. 40, pp. 10–39.

Held, D. (1995) 'Cosmopolitan Democracy and the Global Order: Reflections on the 200th Anniversay of Kant's "Perpetual Peace"', *Alternatives,* vol. 20, no. 4, pp. 415–30.

Helie-Lucas, M.-A. (1991) *The Original Sin and Internationalism.* Combaillaux, France: Women Living under Muslim Laws.

Helie-Lucas, M. (1996) 'La solidaridad de las redes de mujeres' [The women's networks], in CLADEM (ed.) *La muralla e el laberinto: huellas de las mujeres en la conferencia de Beijing.* Lima: Comite American Latina y el Caribe para la Defensa de los Derechos de la Mujeres [The Solidarity of Women's Networks], pp. 12–14.

Heller, A. and Feher, F. (1989) 'Does Socialism Have a Future? Thoughts About Crisis and Regeneration', *Dissent,* Summer, pp. 371–5.

Hernandez, R. (1989) 'Superbarrio: We Didn't Make the Border, We Don't Want the Border', *The Other Side of Mexico,* no. 9, pp. 1–2.

Herod, A. (1994) 'On Workers' Theoretical (In)visibility in the Writing of Critical Urban Geography: A Comradely Critique', *Urban Geography,* vol. 15, no. 7, pp. 681–93.

Herod, A. (1995) 'The Practice of International Labor Solidarity and the Geography of the Global Economy', *Economic Geography,* vol. 71, no. 4, pp. 341–63.

Herod, A. (1997) 'Of Blocs, Flows and Networks: The End of the Cold War, Cyberspace and the Geo-economics of Labor at the "Fin de millenaire"', in Herod, A., Roberts, S. and Tuathail, G. (eds), *An Unruly World: Globalisation, Governance and Geography.* London: Routledge.

Herrmann, K. G. (1988) 'Der britische Bergarbeiterkampf 1926 und die internationale Gewerkschaftsbewegung: Schwierigkeiten eines "Kampferischen" Internationalismus' [The British coalminers' strike of 1926 and the international trade union movement: difficulties of 'militant' internationalism], in Holthoon, F. van and Linden, M. van der (eds), *Internationalism in the Labour Movement 1830–1940.* Leiden: Brill, pp. 489–517.

Himmelstrand, K. (1990) 'Can an Aid Bureaucracy Empower Women?', in Staudt, K. (ed.), *Women, International Development and Politics: The Bureaucratic Mire.* Philadelphia: Temple University Press, pp. 101–13.

Hobsbawm, E. (1984) 'What Is the Workers' Country?', in Hobsbawm, E., *Worlds of Labour*. London: Weidenfeld and Nicolson, pp. 49–65.

Hobsbawm, E. (1988) 'Opening Address: Working-Class Internationalism', in Holthoon, F. van and Linden, M. van der (ed.), *Internationalism in the Labour Movement 1830–1940*. Leiden: Brill, pp. 1–18.

Holdt, K. van (1993a) 'A New Labour Internationalism?', *South African Labour Bulletin*, vol. 17, no. 2, pp. 76–81.

Holdt, K. van (1993b) 'The New World Economy – Challenge by Labour', *South African Labour Bulletin*, vol. 17, no. 5, pp. 72–9.

Holdt, K. van and Zikala, S. (1993) 'The ICFTU in South Africa', *South Africa Labour Bulletin*, vol. 17, no. 1, pp. 67–71.

Holland, D. (1990) 'Solidarity with Whom?', *International Labour Reports*, no. 37, pp. 12–14.

Holthoon, F. van and Linden, M. van der (eds) (1988) *Internationalism in the Labour Movement 1830–1940*. Leiden: Brill.

Horne, D. (1986) *The Public Culture: The Triumph of Industrialism*. London: Pluto.

Howells, K. (1986) 'Losing Old Allies', *International Labour Reports*, no. 13, pp. 14–15.

Humphrey, J. (1988a) 'If the Bosses Are International . . .', *International Labour Reports*, no. 27–8, pp. 24–5.

Humphrey, J. (1988b) 'Back to Base', *International Labour Reports*, no. 29, pp. 22–3.

Indian Journal of Gender Studies (1996) 'Beijing 1995', *Indian Journal of Gender Studies* (Special Section), vol. 3, no. 4, pp. 81–132.

Institut fur Marxismus-Leninismus (1986) *Geschichte der internationalen Arbeiterbewegung in Daten* [History of the international working class movement in dates]. Berlin: Dietz Verlag.

Institut Socialiste d'Etudes et de Recherches (1983) *Emancipations nationales et nouvel internationalisme* [National liberations and a new internationalism]. Paris: Club Socialiste du Livre.

International Confederation of Free Trade Unions (1988a) *Report of the ICFTU/APRO Mission to the Republic of Korea. International Confederation of Free Trade Unions Executive Board, Madrid, 14–16 December 1988*. Brussels: ICFTU.

International Confederation of Free Trade Unions (1988b) 'Agenda Item *(d) (ii): Report of the ICFTU/APRO Mission to the Republic of Korea'. Unpublished ICFTU Executive Board Meeting, Madrid, 14–16 December. Brussels: International Confederation of Free Trade Unions.

International Confederation of Free Trade Unions (1995) *Changing the World Through Equality: The Trade Union Vision Document*. Brussels: International Confederation of Free Trade Unions.

International Conference on Korean Workers (1988) 'The Need and Reality of International Solidarity in the Labour Movement'. Unpublished paper to the International Conference for the Korean Workers' Union Movement, Seoul).

International Labour Reports (1989) 'Philippines: Retraction', *International Labour Reports*, no. 34–5.

International Longshoremen's and Warehousemen's Union (1949) *Report from Europe by the Rank and File Delegation* . . . . San Francisco: International Longshoremen's and Warehousemen's Union.

International Longshoremen's and Warehousemen's Union (1963a) *Report on the Third All Pacific and Asian Dockworkers Conference, October 4–9, 1963, Djakarta, Indonesia.* San Francisco: International Longshoremen's and Warehousemen's Union.

International Longshoremen's and Warehousemen's Union (1963b) *The ILWU Story: Three Decades of Militant Unionism.* San Francisco: International Longshoremen's and Warehousemen's Union.

International Women's Tribune Centre (1994) 'Get Ready! Connecting Beijing to Action at Home', *The Tribune: A Women and Development Quarterly* (Beijing 1995, Special Issue no. 1), no. 52, November, pp. 2–48.

International Women's Tribune Centre (1995a) 'Get Set! NGOs Worldwide Prepare for Beijing', *The Tribune: A Women and Development Quarterly* (Beijing 1995, Special Issue no. 2), no. 53, July, p. 31.

International Women's Tribune Centre (1995b) 'Go! Beijing 1995 Special Issue no. 3', *The Tribune: A Women and Development Quarterly*, no. 54, August.

IZ Bulletin (1995) 'De FNV als bedrijf' [The FNV as a business], *IZ Bulletin* (Amsterdam, Federatie Nederlandse Vakbonden).

Jenkins, B. and Minnerup, G. (1984) *Citizens and Comrades: Socialism in a World of Nation States.* London: Pluto.

Jensen, K. (1990) 'Getting to the Third World: Agencies as Gatekeepers', in Staudt, K. (ed.), *Women, International Development and Politics: The Bureaucratic Mire.* Philadelphia: Temple University Press, pp. 247–64.

John, J. and Chenoy, A. (eds) (1996) *Labour, Environment and Globalisation: Social Clause in Multilateral Trade Agreements: A Southern Response.* New Delhi: Centre for Education and Communication.

Johnson, R. (1979) '"Really Useful Knowledge": Radical Education and Working-Class Culture, 1790–1848', in Clarke, J., Critcher, C. and Johnson, R. (eds), *Working-Class Culture: Studies in History and Theory.* London: Hutchinson, pp. 75–102.

Jones, S. (1988) *Sport, Politics and the Working Class: A Study of Organised Labour and Sport in Inter-War Britain.* Manchester: Manchester University Press.

Kaarsholm, P. (1988) 'The South African War and the Response of the International Socialist Community to Imperialism Between 1896 and 1908', in Holthoon, F. van and Linden, M. van der (eds), *Internationalism in the Labour Movement, 1830–1940.* Leiden: Brill, pp. 42–67.

Karat, P. (1984) 'Action Groups/Voluntary Organisations: A Factor in Imperialist Strategy', *The Marxist*, vol. 2, no. 2, pp. 21–53.

Kardam, N. (1990) 'The Adaptability of International Development Agencies: The Response of the World Bank to Women in Development', in Staudt, K. (ed.), *Women, International Development and Politics: The Bureaucratic Mire.* Philadelphia: Temple University Press, pp. 114–28.

Katsiafikas, G. (1987) *The Imagination of the New Left: A Global Analysis of 1968.* Boston: South End Press.

Keane, J. and Mier, P. (1989) 'New Perspectives on Social Movements: An Interview with Alberto Melucci', in Melucci, A., *Nomads of the Present: Social Movements and Individual Needs in Contemporary Society.* London: Hutchinson Radius, pp. 180–234.

Keysers, L. (1996) 'Is Gendering Population and Development Negotiations a Paradigm Shift?'. Paper for Conference on 'A World in Transition: Feminist Perspectives on International Relations', Lund University, Sweden, 14–16 June.

Keysers, L. and Smyth, I. (1991) 'Reflections on Global Solidarity for Women's Health and Reproductive Rights', *VENA Newsletter*, pp. 26–31.

Kidder, T. and McGinn, M. (1995) 'In the Wake of NAFTA: Transnational Workers Networks', *Social Policy*, vol. 25, no. 4, Summer, pp. 14–21.

Kilminster, A. (1990) 'Courting Western Capital', *International Labour Reports*, no. 37, pp. 15.

Kilusang Mayo Uno (1989a) *Press Statement, June 11, 1989.* Manila: Kilusang Mayo Uno.

Kilusang Mayo Uno (1989b) *Clarification of the KMU Position on the Beijing Incident.* Manila: Kilusang Mayo Uno.

Kilusang Mayo Uno (1990) *Draft Document – KMU-COSATU-CUT Trilateral Conference.* Manila: Kilusang Mayo Uno.

Knudsen, K. (1988) 'The Strike History of the First International', in Holthoon, F. van and Linden, M. van der (eds), *Internationalism in the Labour Movement 1830–1940.* Leiden: Brill, pp. 304–22.

Koch-Baumgarten, S. (1988) 'Die Internationale Transportarbeiter-Foderation 1945 bis 1985 – Grenzen und Moglichkeiten internationaler Gewerkschaftspolitik' [The International Transportworkers' Federation 1945 to 1985 – Limits and possibilities of international trade union policy]. Unpublished PhD thesis, Free University, Berlin.

Kramer, D. (1988) 'Internationalismus in den deutschen Arbeiterkultur-Organisationen: Eine Problemskizze' [Internationalism in the German worker culture organizations: an outline], in Holthoon, F. van and Linden, M. van der (eds), *Internationalism in the Labour Movement 1830–1940.* Leiden: Brill, pp. 217–34.

Kubalkova, V. and Cruickshank, A. (1980) *Marxism-Leninism and the Theory of International Relations.* London: Routledge and Kegan Paul.

Kubalkova, V. and Cruickshank, A. (1989) *Marxism and International Relations.* Oxford: Oxford University Press.

Labour File (1996) 'The Unique Struggle of the Fishworkers', *Labour File* (Special Issue), vol. 2, no. 7–8, p. 44.

Laclau, E. and Mouffe, C. (1981) 'Socialist Strategy: Where Next?', *Marxism Today*, vol. 25, no. 1, pp. 17–22.

Lambert, R. (1992) 'Constructing the New Internationalism: Australian Trade Unions and the Indian Ocean Regional Initiative', *South African Labour Bulletin*, vol. 16, no. 5, pp. 66–73.

Lambert, R. (1996) 'Regional Solidarity and Union Rights: Asia/Pacific Region-Western Australia', *International Union Rights*, vol. 3, no. 2, pp. 6–7.

Lattek, C. (1988) 'The Beginnings of Socialist Internationalism in the 1840s: The "Democratic Friends of all Nations" in London', in Holthoon, F. van and Linden, M. van der (eds), *Internationalism in the Labour Movement 1830–1940*. Leiden: Brill, pp. 392–409.

Lavalette, M. and Kennedy, J. (1996) *Solidarity on the Waterfront: The Liverpool Lock Out of 1995/96*. Liverpool: Liver Press.

Lee, E. (1996) *Labour and the Internet: The New Internationalism*. London: Pluto.

Lenin, V. I. (1952) 'What Is to Be Done? Burning Questions of Our Movement', in Lenin, V. I., *Selected Works in Two Volumes*. Vol. 1, Part 1, Moscow: Foreign Languages Publishing House, pp. 203–409.

Leon, I. (1996) 'VII Encuentro feminista de America Latina y el Caribe: Por la autonomia y la construccion de movimiento'. Unpublished (Area Mujeres – Agencia Latinoamericana de Informacion, Quito).

Linden, M. van der (1988a) 'The Rise and Fall of the First International: An Interpretation', in Holthoon, F. van and Linden M. van der (eds), *Internationalism in the Labour Movement 1830–1940*. Leiden: Brill, pp. 323–35.

Linden, M. van der (1988b) 'The First, Second and Third Internationals: A Note on Their Historiography', in Waterman, P. (ed.), *The Old Internationalism and the New*. The Hague: ILERI Foundation, pp. 6–13.

Linden, M. van der (1988c) 'Internationalism in the Labour Movement, 1830–1940: Fragments of a Bibliography', in Holthoon, F. van and Linden, M. van der (eds), *Internationalism in the Labour Movement 1830–1940*. Leiden: Brill, pp. 624–54.

Lipietz, A. (1990) 'Pour un internationalisme modeste' [For a modest internationalism], in Mappa, S. (ed.), *Ambitions et illusions de la cooperation nord-sud: Lome IV*. Paris: Harmattan.

Lipietz, A. (1992) *Berlin, Bagdad, Rio: La XXe Siecle est commence* [Berlin, Baghdad, Rio: The 20th century has already begun]. Paris: Quai Voltaire.

Lipnack, J. and Stamps, J. (1982) *Networking: The First Report and Directory*. Garden City: Doubleday.

Lipnack, J. and Stamps, J. (1994) *The Age of the Network: Organising Principles for the 21st Century*. New York: Wiley.

Logue, J. (1980) *Toward a Theory of Trade Union Internationalism*. Kent: Kent Popular Press.

Logue, J. and Callesen, G. (1979) *'Social Demokraten' and Internationalism: The Copenhagen Social Democratic Newspaper's Coverage of International Labour Affairs, 1871–1958*. Kent: Kent Popular Press.

Lokayan Bulletin (1995) 'Women towards Beijing: Voices from India', *Lokayan Bulletin* (Special Isue), vol. 12, no. 1–2, July–October, pp. 1–186.

Longmore, C. (1985) *The IWA Today: A Short Account of the International Workers' Association and Its Sections*. London: South London Direct Action Movement/International Workers' Association.

Lova (1986) 'International Feminism: Critical Issues', *LOVA Nieuwsbrief*, vol. 7, no. 3 (special issue).

Lovell, D. (1988) *Marx's Proletariat: The Making of a Myth*. London: Routledge.

Lovell, J. (1969) *Stevedores and Dockers: A Study of Trade Unionism in the Port of London 1870–1914*. London: Macmillan.

Lowy, M. (1988) 'Internationalism Today', *International Marxist Review*, vol. 3, no. 2, pp. 129–34.

Lumis, D. (1991a) 'Development Against Democracy', *Alternatives*, vol. 16, no. 1, pp. 31–66.

Lumis, D. (1991b) 'The Great Aid Swindle: A Review of "Lords of Poverty"', *AMPO Japan-Asian Quarterly Review*, vol. 22, no. 2–3, pp. 103–5.

Macdonald, L. (1995) 'A Mixed Blessing: The NGO Boom in Latin America', *NACLA Report on the Americas*, vol. 28, no. 5, March/April, pp. 30–5.

McGrew, T. (1992) 'A Global Society', in Hall, S., Held, D. and McGrew, T., *Modernity and its Futures*. Cambridge: Polity Press, pp. 61–116.

MacShane, D. (1992a) 'Welcome to the Working Class! The Significance of the New East-European and Third-World Unionism for the Labour Movement'. Unpublished (Social Movement Studies Seminar, Institute of Social Studies, The Hague).

MacShane, D. (1992b) 'The New International Working Class and Its Organizations', *New Politics*, vol. 4, no. 1, pp. 134–49.

MacShane, D. (1992c) 'Asia: The Next Frontier for Trade Unions', *Pacific Review*, vol. 5, no. 1, pp. 1–12.

MacShane, D. (1994) 'The Changing Contours of Trade Unionism in Eastern Europe and the CIS', in Hyman, R. and Ferner, A. (eds), *Changing Frontiers in European Industrial Relations*. Oxford: Blackwell, pp. 337–67.

Mamdani, M. (1989) 'How Not to Intervene in Internal Conflicts', *Bulletin of Peace Proposals*, vol. 20, no. 4, pp. 437–40.

Mann, M. (1983) 'Nationalism and Internationalism', in Griffith, J. (ed.), *Socialism in a Cold Climate*. London: Allen and Unwin.

Mann, M. (1987) 'The Roots and Contradictions of Modern Militarism', *New Left Review*, no. 162, pp. 35–50.

Mariategui, J. C. (1973) 'Internacionalismo y nacionalismo' [Internationalism and nationalism], in Mariategui, J. C., *Historia de la crisis mundial: Conferencias anos 1923 y 1924*. Lima: Amauta, pp. 156–65.

Mariategui, J. C. (1986) 'Internationalism and Nationalism', *Newsletter of International Labour Studies*, no. 30–1, pp. 3–8.

Martinez, R. (1992) *The Other Side: Notes from the New L.A, Mexico City, and Beyond.* New York: Vintage.

Marx, K. (1904) *A Contribution to the Critique of Political Economy.* Chicago: Charles Kerr.

Marx, K. (1935) *Karl Marx: Selected Works: Vol. 1.* Moscow: Cooperative Publishing Society of Foreign Workers in the USSR.

Marx, K. and Engels, F. (1935) 'The Manifesto of the Communist Party', in Marx, K., *Selected Works.* Moscow: Cooperative Publishing House of Foreign Workers in the USSR.

Marx, K. and Engels, F. (1953) *Marx and Engels on Britain.* London: Lawrence and Wishart.

Massey, D. (1991) 'A Global Sense of Place', *Marxism Today,* June, pp. 24–9.

Mattelart, A. and Siegelaub, S. (ed.). (1983) *Communication and Class Struggle. Vol. 2: Liberation, Socialism.* New York: International General.

Meecham, R. *et al.* (1993) 'COSATU, the ICTFU, and Dictatorship in Asia', *South African Labour Bulletin*, vol. 17, no. 3, pp. 78–81.

Melchiori, P. (1996) 'Messages from Huariou: For a Redefinition of the Spaces of Politics'. Unpublished (Course on NGOs and Social Movements, El Taller, Hammamet, Tunisia, 20 May–13 July 1996).

Mellor, M. (1992) *Breaking the Boundaries: Towards a Feminist Green Socialism.* London: Virago.

Melucci, A. (1989) *Nomads of the Present: Social Movements and Individual Needs in Contemporary Society.* London: Hutchinson.

Mendes, C. (1989) *Fight for the Forest: Chico Mendes in His Own Words.* London: Latin American Bureau.

Mendes, C. (1992) 'Peasants Speak: Chico Mendes – The Defence of Life', *Journal of Peasant Studies*, vol. 20, no. 1, pp. 160–76.

Mergner, G. (1988) 'Solidaritat mit den "Wilden"? Das Verhaltnis der deutschen Sozialdemokratie zu den afrikanischen Widerstandskampfen in den ehemaligen deutschen Kolonien um die Jahrhundertwende' [Solidarity with the 'savages'? The relationship of the German Social Democrats to resistance in the former German colonies around the turn of the century], in Holthoon, F. van and Linden, M. van der (eds), *Internationalism in the Labour Movement 1830–1940.* Leiden: Brill, pp. 68–86.

Meszaros, I. (1989) 'The Constitution of Solidarity', in Meszaros, I., *The Power of Ideology.* London: Harvester Wheatsheaf, pp. 288–380.

Michanek, E. (1985) 'Democracy as a Force for Development and the Role of Swedish Assistance', *Development Dialogue*, no. 1, pp. 56–84.

Michel, J. (1988) 'Corporatisme et internationalisme chez les mineurs europeens avant 1914' [Corporatism and internationalism amongst European miners before 1914], in Holthoon, F. van and Linden, M. van der

(eds), *Internationalism in the Labour Movement 1830–1940*. Leiden: Brill, pp. 440–58.

Michels, R. (1915) *Political Parties*. London: Jarrold and Sons.

Mies, M. (1983) 'Marxist Socialism and Women's Emancipation: The Proletarian Women's Movement in Germany', in Mies, M. and Jayawardena, K. (eds), *Feminism in Europe: Liberal and Socialist Strategies 1789–1919*. The Hague: Institute of Social Studies, pp. 111–56.

Mies, M. (1986) *Patriarchy and Accumulation on a World Scale: Women in the International Division of Labour*. London: Zed Press.

Mies, M. (1992) 'The Global is in the Local', in Corral, T. and Darcy de Oliveira, R. (eds), *Terra Femina*. Rio de Janeiro: pp. 54–67.

Miles, A. (1996) *Integrative Feminisms: Building Global Visions 1960s–1990s*. London: Routledge.

Miliband, R., Panitch, L. and Saville, J. (eds) (1990) *Socialist Register 1990: The Retreat of the Intellectuals*. London: Merlin Press.

Miller, F. (1990) 'Latin American Feminism and the Transnational Arena', in Seminar on Feminism and Culture in Latin America (ed.), *Women, Culture, and Politics in Latin America*. University of California Press: Berkeley, pp. 10–26.

Miller, F. (1992a) *Latin American Women and the Search for Social Justice*. Hanover: University Press of New England.

Miller, F. (1992b) 'National Liberation, Redemocratisation, and International Feminism, 1974–1990', in Miller, F., *Latin American Women and the Search for Social Justice*. Hanover: University Press of New England, pp. 187–237.

Mires, F. (1989) 'La crisis del internacionalismo' [The crisis of internationalism], *Servicio Mensual de Informacion y Documentacion ALAI*, Quito, no. 113, pp. 17–20.

Mires, F. (1991) *The Crisis of Internationalism*. The Hague: ILERI Foundation.

Mitter, S. (1986) *Common Fate, Common Bond: Women in the Global Economy*. London: Pluto.

Mitter, S. and Rowbotham, S. (eds) (1996) *Women Encounter Technology: Changing Patterns of Employment in the Third World*. London: Routledge.

Mohanty, C. T. (1992) 'Feminist Encounters: Locating the Politics of Experience', in Barrett, M. and Phillips, A. (eds), *Destabilising Theory: Contemporary Feminist Debates*. Cambridge: Polity Press. pp. 74–92.

Moody, K. and McGinn, M. (1992) *Unions and Free Trade: Solidarity vs. Competition*. Detroit: Labor Notes.

Morgan, R. (ed.) (1984a) *Sisterhood Is Global: The International Women's Movement Anthology*. London: Penguin.

Moser, C. (1991) 'Gender Planning in the Third World: Meeting Practical and Strategic Needs', in Grant, R. and Newland, K. (eds), *Gender and International Relations*. Milton Keynes: Open University Press, pp. 83–121.

Mujer/Fempress (1991) 'V Encuentro feminista Latinoamericano y del Caribe' [Fifth Latin American and Caribbean feminist encounter], *Mujer/Fempress*, no. 111, pp. 1–8.

Munck, R. (1986) *The Difficult Dialogue: Marxism and Nationalism.* London: Zed Press.

Munck, R. (1988) *The New International Labour Studies: An Introduction.* London: Zed Press.

Munck, R. and Waterman, P. (eds) (forthcoming) *Labour Worldwide in the Era of Globalisation: Alternative Union Models in the New World Order.* London: Macmillan.

Muto, I. (1983) 'Keynote Report: Ideology of Aid and People's Solidarity', *AMPO: Japan-Asia Quarterly Review*, vol. 15, no. 3–4, pp. 14–24.

Nairn, T. (1975) 'The Modern Janus', *New Left Review*, no. 94, pp. 3–29.

Nairn, T. (1979) 'Das Elend des Internationalismus' [The poverty of internationalism], *Kursbuch*, no. 57, pp. 137–64.

Nairn, T. (1980) 'Internationalism: A Critique', *Bulletin of Scottish Politics*, no. 1, pp. 101–25.

Naves, J. (1988) 'Balance y futuro del movimiento obrero' [Balance and future of the Labour movement], *Todos a Una*, no. 13, pp. 15–17.

Nerfin, M. (1986) 'Neither Prince nor Merchant: Citizen – An Introduction to the Third System', *IFDA Dossier*, no. 56, pp. 3–29.

Neruda, P. (1977) *Memoirs.* London: Souvenir.

Newsletter of International Labour Studies (1989) 'USA: Beyond Trade Union Imperialism', *Newsletter of International Labour Studies* Special Double Issue, no. 40–1, January–April, p. 52.

NGO Forum on Women Secretariat (1996) *Foro de ONG sobre la mujer, Beijing '95* [NGO forum on women, Beijing '95]. New York: NGO Forum on Women Secretariat.

Niemeijer, M. (1996) 'Grassroots Labour Internationalism: The Transnationals Information Exchange'. Unpublished draft MA thesis, International Relations, University of Amsterdam.

Northrop, H. and Rowan, R. (1983) *The International Transportworkers Federation and Flag of Convenience Shipping.* Philadelphia: University of Philadelphia Press.

Papandreou, M. C. (1988) 'Global Feminism for the Year 2000', in Gioseffi, D., *Women on War: Essential Voices for the Nuclear Age.* New York: Simon and Schuster, pp. 309–14.

Parodi, J. (1986) '*Ser obrero es algo relativo . . .*': *Obreros, clasismo y política* ['Being a worker is something relative . . .': workers, classism and politics]. Lima: Instituto de Estudios Peruanos.

Peijnenburg, J. and Ridgers, B. (1987) *Protectionism and Internationalism: An International Programme for Trade Unionists from the Auto Industry.* Amsterdam: Transnationals' Information Exchange.

Perrault, G. (1987) *A Man Apart: The Life of Henri Curiel (Part I).* London: Zed Press.

Peterson, L. (1988) 'Internationalism and the British Coal Miners' Strike of 1926: The Solidarity Campaign of the KPD among Ruhr Coal Miners', in

Holthoon, F. van and Linden, M. van der (eds), *Internationalism in the Labour Movement 1830–1940*. Leiden: Brill, pp. 459–88.

Peterson, V. S. and Runyan, A. S. (1993a) *Global Gender Issues*. Boulder: Westview.

Petras, J. (1990) 'Retreat of the Intellectuals', *Economic and Political Weekly*, vol. 35, no. 38, pp. 2143–56.

Pettman, J. J. (1996) *Worlding Women: A Feminist International Politics*. London: Routledge.

Pfeil, F. (1994) 'No basta teorizar: In-Difference to Solidarity in Contemporary Fiction, Theory, and Practice', in Grewal, I. and Kaplan, C. (eds), *Scattered Hegemonies: Postmodernity and Transnational Feminist Practices*. Minneapolis: University of Minnesota Press, pp. 197–230.

Picciotto, S. (1984) 'The Battles at Talbot-Poissy: Workers' Divisions and Capital Restructuring', *Capital and Class*, no. 23, pp. 5–18.

Piercy, M. (1976) *Woman on the Edge of Time*. New York: Knopf.

Piercy, M. (1991) *He, She and It*. New York: Fawcett.

Pieterse, J. N. (1990) 'Enlightenment and Emancipation', in Pieterse, J. N., *Empire and Emancipation: Power and Liberation on a World Scale*. London: Pluto, pp. 47–71.

Pieterse, J. N. (1991) 'Dilemmas of Development Discourse: The Crisis of Developmentalism and the Comparative Method', *Development and Change*, vol. 22, pp. 5–29.

Pinto-Duschinsky, M. (1991) 'Foreign Political Aid: The German Political Foundations and their US Counterparts', *International Affairs*, vol. 67, no. 1, pp. 33–63.

Pisano, M. (1993) 'Hace Beijing – De dinero y decisiones: Carta al movimiento' [Towards Beijing – of money and decisions: Letter to the movement]. Unpublished, 'Feminist Encounter', Costa de Sol, El Salvador.

Poster, M. (1984) *Foucault, Marxism and History: Mode of Production Versus Mode of Information*. Cambridge: Polity Press.

Poster, M. (1990) *The Mode of Information: Poststructuralism and Social Context*. Cambridge: Polity Press.

Poster, M. (1995) 'Cyberdemocracy: Internet and the Public Sphere'. Unpublished (email received 27 August 1996).

Prugl, E. (1996) 'Gender in International Organization and Global Governance: A Critical Review of the Literature', *International Studies Notes*, vol. 21, no. 1, Winter, pp. 15–24.

Purtill, G. (1980) 'The International Transport Workers' Federation 1896–1920: A View of International Trade Unionism with Special Reference to Britain and Australia'. MA dissertation, University of Warwick, Coventry, England.

Quest (1978) 'A Feminist International', *Quest: A Feminist Quarterly* (Special Issue), vol. 4, no. 2, pp. 51–4.

Radcliffe, S. and Westwood, S. (ed.) (1993) *'Viva': Women and Popular Protest in Latin America.* London: Routledge.

Rahman, R. (1988) 'Third World Solidarity Movement'. Paper to Society for International Development Conference, New Delhi.

Reinalda, B. and Verhaaren, N. (1989) *Vrouwenbeweging en internationale organisaties 1868–1986* [The women's movement and international organizations 1868–1986]. Nijmegen: Ariadne.

Resnick, S., Sinisi, J. and Wolff, R. (1985) 'Class Analysis of International Relations', in Hollist, W. L. and Tullis, J. I. (eds), *An International Political Economy.* Boulder: Westview, pp. 87–123.

Rivero, M. (1996) 'La Globalizacion de la vida de cada dia' [The globalization of everday life], *Cotidiano Mujer* (Special Beijing Issue), no. 21, pp. 18–20.

Rjazanov, D. (1928) 'Zur Geschichte der Ersten Internationale: 1) Die Entstehung der Internationaler Arbeiterassoziation' [On the history of the First International: 1) The creation of the International Workingmen's Association]. *Marx-Engels Archiv,* vol. 1, pp. 119–204.

Rowbotham, S. and Mitter, S. (eds) (1994) *Dignity and Daily Bread: New Forms of Economic Organising Among Poor Women in the Third World and the First.* London: Routledge.

Safa, H. I. (1990) 'Women's Social Movements in Latin America', *Gender and Society,* vol. 4, no. 3, pp. 354–69.

Samuel, R. (1985) 'The Lost World of British Communism', *New Left Review,* no. 154, pp. 3–54.

Samuel, R., MacColl, E. and Cosgrove, S. (eds) (1985) *Theatres of the Left 1880–1935: Workers' Theatre Movements in Britain and America.* London: Routledge.

Saunders, J. (1989) *Across Frontiers: International Support for the Miners' Strike 1984–85.* London: Canary Press.

Saville, J. (1988) 'Britain: Internationalism and the Labour Movement between the Wars', in Holthoon, F. van and Linden, M. van der (eds), *Internationalism in the Labour Movement 1830–1940.* Leiden: Brill, pp. 565–82.

Schiller, H. (1990) 'The Global Commercialisation of Culture', *Directions,* vol. 4, no. 1, pp. 1–4.

Scipes, K. (1985) 'San Francisco Longshoremen: "When that Ship Came in, We Were Ready"', *International Labour Reports,* no. 9, May–June, pp. 12–13.

Scipes, K. (1996) *KMU: Building Genuine Trade Unionism in the Philippines, 1980–1994.* Quezon City: New Day Publishers.

Seddon, D. (1986) 'A Socialist Strategy of Cooperation and Development for Britain'. Unpublished paper. Development Studies, University of East Anglia, Norwich.

Semprun, J. (1979) *Communism in Spain in the Franco Era: The Autobiography of Federico Sanchez.* Brighton: Harvester.

Shaw, M. (1994) 'Civil Society and Global Politics: Beyond a Social Movements Approach', *Millennium,* vol. 23, no. 3, pp. 647–67.

Shiach, M. (1989) 'A History of Changing Definitions of "The Popular"', in Shiach, M., *Discourse on Popular Culture: Class, Gender and History in Cultural Analysis, 1730 to the Present.* Cambridge: Polity, pp. 19–34.

Shiva, V. (1993) 'The Greening of the Global Reach', in Brecher, J., Childs, J. B. and Cutler, J. (eds), *Global Visions: Beyond the New World Order.* Boston: South End Press, pp. 53–60.

Shiva, V. (1996) 'Social and Environmental Clauses: A Political Diversion', in John, J. and Chenoy, A. (eds), *Labour, Environment and Globalisation: Social Clause in Multilateral Trade Agreements: A Southern Response.* New Delhi: Centre for Education and Communication, pp. 101–12.

Sim, F. G. (1991) *IOCU on Record: A Documentary History of the International Organization of Consumers' Unions 1960–1990.* Yonkers: Consumers' Union.

Simon, H. (1983) 'Organised Labour Against National Socialism: A Case Study of the International Transport Workers' Federation'. PhD thesis, University of Warwick, Coventry, UK.

Simpson, A. (1985) 'Developing the Developers', *Links*, no. 21, pp. 20–8.

Sims, B. (1992) *Workers of the World Undermined: American Labor's Role in U.S. Foreign Policy.* Boston: South End Press.

Sklair, L. (1991) *Sociology of the Global System.* Hemel Hempstead: Harvester Wheatsheaf.

Slaughter, J. (1992) 'Auto Union Wins Outsourcing Protection After Nine-Day Strike: Agreement Could Dent International Solidarity', *Labor Notes*, no. 163, pp. 5–6.

Smith, M. (1989) 'Ports Strike Leader Who Is Unmoved by Legal Threats: Michael Smith Listens to Jimmy Nolan's Views', *Financial Times*, 13 June.

Sogge, D. (ed.) (1996) *Compassion and Calculation: The Business of Private Foreign Aid.* London: Pluto.

Sousa Santos, B. de (1995) *Toward a New Common Sense: Law, Science and Politics in the Paradigmatic Transition*, New York: Routledge.

South African Labour Bulletin (1991a) 'Towards a New Worker Internationalism?', *South African Labour Bulletin* (Special Section), vol. 15, no. 7, pp. 12–43.

South African Labour Bulletin (1991b) 'ICFTU Debate', *South African Labour Bulletin* (Special Section), vol. 16, no. 2, pp. 61–75.

South African Labour Bulletin (1993) 'Debate: The ICFTU and SA', *South African Labour Bulletin* (Special Section), vol. 17, no. 3, pp. 76–84.

Southall, R. (ed.) (1988) *Trade Unions and the New Industrialisation of the Third World.* London: Zed Press.

Southall, R. (1995) *Imperialism or Solidarity? International Labour and South African Trade Unions.* Cape Town: University of Cape Town.

Spooner, D. (1988) 'Labour Goes On-Line', *International Labour Reports*, no. 27–8, pp. 26–7.

Spooner, D. (1989) *Partners or Predators: International Trade Unionism and Asia.* Hong Kong: Asia Monitor Resource Centre.

Spyropoulos, G. (1991) *Sindicalismo y sociedad: Problemas actuales del sindicalismo en el mundo* [Trade unionism and society: contemporary problems of unionism internationally]. Buenos Aires: Humanitas.

Staudt, K. (1985) *Women, Foreign Assistance, and Advocacy Administration.* New York: Praeger.

Staudt, K. (1987) 'Programming Women's Empowerment: A Case from Northern Mexico', in Ruiz, V. and Tiano, S. (eds), *Women on the US–Mexico Border: Responses to Change.* Boston: Allen and Unwin, pp. 155–76.

Staudt, K. (ed.) (1990) *Women, International Development and Politics: The Bureaucratic Mire.* Philadelphia: Temple University Press.

Steenbergen, B. van (1992) 'Towards a Global Ecological Citizen: Citizenship and Nature, a Pair Apart?'. Paper to Symposium on Current Developments in Environmental Sociology, Woudschoten, Utrecht, 17–21 July.

Stefanik, N. (1993) 'Sustainable Dialogue/Sustainable Development', in Brecher, J., Childs, J. B. and Cutler, J. (eds), *Global Visions: Beyond the New World Order.* Boston: South End Press, pp. 263–72.

Steinberg, H.-J. (1988) 'Der Internationalismus in der deutschen sozialistischen Lyrik vor 1914' [Internationalism in German socialist lyrics before 1914], in Holthoon, F. van and Linden, M. van der (eds), *Internationalism in the Labour Movement 1830–1940.* Leiden: Brill, pp. 163–72.

Sternbach, N. S., Navarro-Araguren, M., Chuchryk, P. and Alvarez, S. (1992) 'Feminisms in Latin America: From Bogota to San Bernardo', *Signs,* vol. 17, no. 2, pp. 393–434.

Sulmont, D. (1988a) 'Nuevos pistas para el viejo internacionalismo proletario' [New avenues for the old proletarian internationalism], *Quadernos Laborales,* no. 45, pp. 28.

Sulmont, D. (1988b) *Deuda y trabajadores: Un reto para la solidaridad* [Debt and workers: a challenge to solidarity]. Lima: ADEC/ATC.

The Other Side of Mexico (1987) 'Superbarrio: Bane of the Landlords, Defender of Poor Tenants (An Interview with the Hero and His Shadow)', *The Other Side of Mexico,* no. 3, pp. 3–5.

Thomas, H. (ed.) (1995) *Globalisation and Third World Unions: The Challenge of Rapid Economic Change.* London: Zed Press.

Thompson, E. (1978) *The Poverty of Theory and Other Essays.* London: Merlin.

Thompson, E. (1988) 'Eurocentrism, Indocentrism and Internationalism', *END: Journal of European Disarmament,* no. 31, pp. 22–5.

Thompson, E. (1990) 'Comment: The Ends of the Cold War', *New Left Review,* no. 182, pp. 139–46.

Thorpe, V. (1994) 'Globalisation, New Production Plans, Regional Changes: Do Trade Unions Need a New Internationalism?'. Brussels Workshop on European and International Aspects ... and the Reform of the DGB, 24–25 May.

Thorpe, W. (1990) 'Syndicalist Internationalism Before World War II', in

Linden, M. van der and Thorpe, W. (eds), *Revolutionary Syndicalism: An International Prospective*. Aldershot: Scolar.

Tichelman, H. (1988) 'Socialist "Internationalism"' and the Colonial World: Practical Colonial Policies of Social Democracy in Western Europe before 1940', in Holthoon, F. van and Linden, M. van der (eds), *Internationalism in the Labour Movement 1830–1940*. Leiden: Brill.

Torr, D. (1956) *Tom Mann and His Times. Volume 1: 1856–1890*. London: Lawrence and Wishart.

Torres, L. (1994) 'To Socialism via Social Democracy?', *South African Labour Bulletin*, vol. 18, no. 2, pp. 63–7.

Trade Union Committee, Philippine Support Group (1989) *Criticism of the June 11th KMU Statement on Events in China*. London: Philippine Support Group.

Transnationals' Information Exchange (1989a) *Herstructurering en vakbondsmacht in de havens* [Restructuring and union power in the ports]. Amsterdam: Transnationals' Information Exchange.

Transnationals' Information Exchange (1989b) *The Global Chocolate Factory*. Amsterdam: Transnationals' Information Exchange.

Transnationals' Information Exchange (1989c) *Fourth Conference of Auto Workers*. Amsterdam: Transnationals' Information Exchange.

Trepper, L. (1977) *The Great Game: Memoirs of a Master Spy*. London: Joseph.

Trinational Women's Conference (1992) 'La memoria informal: Trinational Women's Conference on Free Trade and Economic Integration'. Mexico City: Mujer a Mujer.

Truong, T.-D. (1991) *Sex, Money and Morality: Prostitution and Tourism in South East Asia*. London: Zed Press.

Truong, T.-D. (1996) 'Social Reproduction, Migrant Women and the State: Experiences from East and South East Asia'. State/Society Relations Research Seminar, Institute of Social Studies, The Hague, March 12.

UBINIG (1989) *Declaration of Comilla*. Dhaka: UBINIG.

Valle, N., Hiriart, B. and Amado, A. M. (1996) *El ABC de un periodismo no sexista: Espacio para la igualdad* [The ABC of non-sexist journalism: space for equality]. Santiago: Fempress/ILET.

Vanderveken, J. (1990) 'The Pressing Need for a Social Dimension', *Free Labour World*, no. 14, pp. 1, 4.

Vargas, V. (1991) 'The Women's Movement in Peru: Streams, Spaces and Knots', *European Review of Latin American Studies*, no. 50, June, pp. 7–50.

Vargas, V. (1992a) 'The Feminist Movement in Latin America: Between Hope and Disenchantment', in Pieterse, J. N., *Emancipations, Modern and Postmodern*. London: Sage, pp. 195–214.

Vargas, V. (1992b) 'Women: Tragic Encounters with the Left', *Report on the Americas*, vol. 25, no. 5, pp. 30–4.

Vargas, V. (1992c) 'International Solidarity in the Latin American Feminist Movement: Notes for the Debate'. Unpublished Paper to Workshop on

Feminism and Internationalism, Institute of Social Studies, The Hague, April 1992.

Vargas, V. (1996a) '1996: Odisea feminista' [1996: feminist odyssey], *Cotidiano Mujer* (Special Issue: Seventh Latin American and Caribbean Feminist Encounter), no. 23, November 1996–March 1997, pp. 2–6, 8.

Vargas, V. (1996b) *International Feminist Networking and Solidarity*. Combaillaux, France: Women Living Under Muslim Laws.

Vargas, V. *et al.* (1991) 'El feminismo de los 90: Desafios y propuestas' [The feminism of the 90s: challenges and proposals]. *Mujer/Fempress*, no. 111, pp. 4–6.

Vervoersbond F. N. V. (1989) *Betreft: Vergadering Britse havenstaking* [Concerning the British port strike meeting]. Utrecht: Vervoersbond FNV, Bedrijfsgroep Havens.

Visvanathan, S. and Kothari, R. (1985) 'Bhopal: The Imagination of a Disaster', *Lokayan*, vol. 3, no. 4–5, pp. 48–76.

Vogler, C. (1985) *The Nation State: The Neglected Dimension of Class*. London: Gower.

Vos, H. (1976) *Solidariteit: Elementen, complicaties, perspectieven* [Solidarity: elements, complications, perspectives]. Baarn: Amboboeken.

Walker, R. B. (1981) 'Media and Money: The London Dock Strike of 1889 and the Australian Maritime Strike of 1890', *Labour History* (Canberra), no. 41, pp. 41–56.

Wapner, P. (1995) 'In Defense of Banner Hangers: The Dark Green Politics of Greenpeace', in Taylor, B. R. (ed.), *Ecological Resistance Movements: The Global Emergence of Radical and Popular Environmentalism*. Albany: SUNY Press. pp. 300–14.

Waterman, P. (1980) 'The Foreign Impact on Lagos Dockworker Unionism', *South African Labour Bulletin*, vol. 5, no. 8, pp. 17–54.

Waterman, P. (1983) 'Aristocrats and Plebeians in African Unions? Lagos Port and Dock Worker Organisation and Struggle'. Unpublished PhD Thesis, Nijmegen: University of Nijmegen.

Waterman, P. (1986) 'Some Reflections and Propositions on Labour Internationalism', *Newsletter of International Labour Studies*, no. 30–1, pp. 13–26.

Waterman, P. (1987) 'Internationale solidariteit via het onderwijs: Mondiale vorming, open-projectonderwijs en de wereld' [International solidarity through education: global education, open project education and the world], *Vernieuwing*, vol. 46, no. 9, pp. 5–8.

Waterman, P. (1988) 'Needed: A New Communications Model for a New Working-Class Internationalism', in Southall, R. (ed.), *Trade Unions and the New Industrialisation of the Third World*. London: Zed Press. pp. 351–78.

Waterman, P. (1989a) 'For the Liberation of Internationalism: A Long March Through the Literatures', *Alternatives*, vol. 14, no. 1, pp. 5–47.

Waterman, P. (1989b) 'International Dockworker Networking: Fragmentation

or Revival? Reflections on an Amsterdam Consultation'. Unpublished paper. The Hague: Institute of Social Studies.

Waterman, P. (1990a) 'One, Two, Three, Many New Internationalisms! On a New Third World Labour Internationalism and its Relationship to Those of the West and the East', *Working Paper*, no. 76. The Hague: Institute of Social Studies.

Waterman, P. (1990b) 'The New Labour Internationalism: The Case of the Network of European Dockworkers in the 1980s', *Workers' Democracy* (St Louis), no. 34, pp. 1, 11–20.

Waterman, P. (1990c) 'International Communication and International Solidarity: The Experience of the Coordinadora of Spanish Dockworkers'. Unpublished research report, Institute of Social Studies, The Hague.

Waterman, P. (1991) 'A New Worker-Controlled Internationalism: What Content and What Form?', *South African Labour Bulletin*, vol. 16, no. 2, pp. 69–75.

Waterman, P. (1992a) 'International Labour Communication by Computer: The Fifth International?', *Working Paper* no. 129, Institute of Social Studies, The Hague, p. 80.

Waterman, P. (1992b) 'The Transmission and Reception of International Labour Information in Peru', in Wasko, J. and Mosco, V. (eds), *Democratic Communications in the Information Age*. Toronto: Garamond, pp. 224–47.

Waterman, P. (1993a) 'Hopeful Traveller: The Itinerary of an Internationalist', *History Workshop*, no. 35, Spring, pp. 165–84.

Waterman, P. (1993b) 'Social Movement Unionism: A New Model for a New World Order', *Review*, vol. 16, no. 3, Summer, pp. 245–78.

Waterman, P. (1993c) 'The ICFTU in South Africa: Admissions, Revelations, Silences', *South African Labour Bulletin*, vol. 17, no. 3, pp. 76–81.

Waterman, P. (1993d) 'Hidden from Herstory: Women, Feminism and New Global Solidarity', *Economic and Political Weekly* (Bombay), vol. 28, no. 44, October 30, pp. WS83–100.

Waterman, P. (1995) 'Holding Mirrors out of Windows: A Labour Bulletin, a Feminist Agenda, and the Creation of a Global Solidarity Culture in the New South Africa', *Working Papers*, no. 188, Institute of Social Studies, The Hague, March.

Waterman, P. (1996a) 'Review Article: Beyond Globalism and Developmentalism: Other Voices in World Politics', *Development and Change*, vol. 27, no. 1, pp. 167–82.

Waterman, P. (1996b) 'The Newest International Labour Studies: Fit for the New World Order?', *Working Papers*, no. 217. Institute of Social Studies, The Hague, April.

Waterman, P. (1996c) 'Review Article: A New Global Solidarity Praxis for a World in Which "The Future Is Not What It Used to Be"', *Transnational Associations*, no. 3, pp. 163–80.

Waterman, P. (forthcoming) 'The New Social Unionism: A New Union Model

for a New World Order', in Munck, R. and Waterman, P. (eds), *Labour Worldwide in the Era of Globalisation: Alternative Union Models in the New World Order.* London: Macmillan.

Waterman, P. and Arellano, N. (1986) 'The Nervous System of Internationalism and Solidarity: Transmission and Reception of International Labour Information in Peru', *Working Paper*, no. 32. Institute of Social Studies, The Hague, p. 58.

Webster, E. (1984) 'The International Metalworkers' Federation in South Africa (1974–80)', *South African Labour Bulletin*, vol. 9, no. 6, pp. 72–94.

White, A. (1990) 'Glasnost Breaks the Ice: The Revolution that Is Shaking European Journalism', *Free Labour World*, no. 290.

Wieringa, S. (1990) 'Open Letter to Mr Jan Pronk, Minister of Development Cooperation in the Netherlands', *Institute of Social Studies Bulletin*, no. 35, pp. 5–8.

Wilczyniski, J. (1981) *An Encyclopaedic Dictionary of Marxism, Socialism and Communism.* London: Macmillan.

Willets, P. (ed.) (1982) *Pressure Groups in the Global System: The Transnational Relations of Issue-Orientated Non-Governmental Organisations.* London: Frances Pinter.

Williams, R. (1983) *Keywords: A Vocabulary of Culture and Society.* London: Flamingo.

Williamson, H. (1993) 'Letting People Know, It's a Workers' World: Report on the IRENE/ILR Seminar on Workers' Information Internationally', *News From IRENE*, no. 18–19, pp. 5–17.

Williamson, H. (1994) *Coping with the Miracle: Japan's Unions Explore New International Relations.* London: Pluto.

Wills, J. (1997) 'Taking on the CosmoCorps? Experiments in Trans-National Labour Organisation', *Rescaling Workplace Solidarity.* Working Paper. no. 1, University of Southampton, Southampton, p. 32.

Wolfe, A. (1977) 'Globalising Contradictions', in Wolfe, A., *The Limits of Legitimacy.* New York: Free Press, pp. 214–44.

Woman of Power (1987) 'International Feminism', *Woman of Power: A Magazine of Feminism, Spirituality and Politics* (Special Issue), no. 7, pp. 6–79.

Women and Development Project (1994a) *New Trade Union Perspectives: Organising Women Workers in the Agricultural Sector, Export Processing Zones, Informal Economy – Discussion Paper.* Amsterdam: CNV/FNV.

Women and Development Project (1994b) *New Trade Union Perspectives: Organising Women Workers in the Agricultural Sector, Export Process Zones, Informal Economy.* Amsterdam/Utrecht: FNV/CNV.

Women's Studies International Forum (1991) 'Reaching for Global Feminism: Approaches to Curriculum Change in the Southwestern United States', *Women's Studies International Forum*, vol. 14, no. 4.

Wright, M. (1990) 'Longshore Union Head Stood up to Redbaiting', *Guardian*, 18 April, p. 9.

Yanz, L. (1992) 'Women Examine Integration', *Canadian Tribune*, vol. 70, no. 2773, 24 February, pp. 1, 8.

Young, N. (1986) 'The Peace Movement: A Comparative and Analytical Survey', *Alternatives*, vol. 11, pp. 185–217.

Yudelman, S. (1990) 'The Inter-American Foundation and Gender Issues: A Feminist View', in Staudt, K. (ed.), *Women, International Development and Politics: The Bureaucratic Mire*. Philadelphia: Temple University Press, pp. 129–44.

Yuval-Davis, N. (1995) 'The Cairo Conference, Women and Transversal Politics', *Women Against Fundamentalism Journal*, no. 6, February, pp. 19–21.

INDEX

DATE DUE
